CARLING

PRESENTS

THE GUIDE TO THE FA CARLING PREMIERSHIP

UMBRO
AUTOGLA
BURTO

CARLING

PRESENTS

THE GUIDE TO THE FA CARLING PREMIERSHIP

EDITED BY CHRIS DIGHTON AND FRANK NICKLIN

WITH AN INTRODUCTION BY PETER LEAVER

31
Fox Leisure
31
Fox Leisure

List of Contents

THE F.A.
CARLING
PREMIERSHIP
CARLING

Foreword *by Seamus McBride, Marketing Director, Bass Brewers*

No Ordinary Lager . . . No Ordinary League . . . No Ordinary Guide!

On behalf of Carling I welcome you to 'The Guide To The FA Carling Premiership 1997'. If it's an in-depth look at the Carling Premiership you are after, this guide is hard to beat.

Covering every aspect of the Carling Premiership from detailed facts and figures on all twenty teams, to articles on the flamboyant crowd-pleasers that light up the game – it's got the lot.

A look at the chapter about last season's classic games, 'Great Eight', highlights why the Carling Premiership is seen as the world's most exciting club competition. Who could have predicted Southampton's 6-3 drubbing of Manchester United? Liverpool's last-gasp winner at Anfield after Newcastle's dramatic fight back from 3-0 down? Or Coventry overcoming Tottenham on the last day of the season to escape the drop?

The start of the 1997-98 season marks the beginning of Carling's new four-year, £36 million deal as sponsors of the Carling Premiership. What a season we have to look forward to! England's young stars, such as Beckham, Campbell and Scholes, showed at Le Tournoi they have the ability to succeed on the world stage. And major stars, like Overmars, Riedle, Poyet and Eranio, continue to be attracted to the Premiership. Not to mention the return of Paul 'The Guvnor' Ince!

It's not only the players in the Carling Premiership that are first-class. Take a look at the stadia. In the last few years a large number of teams have invested vast sums in redeveloping their grounds, while the fans of Derby County and Bolton Wanderers can look forward to watching their teams in multi-million pound stadia this season.

We've got the players and the grounds but the Carling Premiership would not be as successful without one other vital ingredient – English football fans. It is they who provide the passion and create the electric atmosphere that makes attending a football match so exciting.

Interest in the Carling Premiership is at an all-time high. Attendance figures continue to soar every year. Last season the total attendance at the 380 games was 10,882,453, an average of 28,638 per game. That is 5,598 more per game than when we began the sponsorship in 1993. It isn't just the high-profile clubs that are benefiting. Newly promoted Barnsley sold every available ticket for every home game in a matter of weeks.

The England football team, like the Carling Premiership, is in excellent condition. Following the victory at Le Tournoi, England moved up the FIFA world rankings to number seven, its highest position since 1991. Let's hope the England lads can join the numerous Carling Premiership players who will be starring in the 1998 World Cup finals. I'm certainly looking forward to joining the hordes of England fans on their way to France next June.

Enjoy the season!

Seamus McBride

Seamus McBride
Marketing Director, Bass Brewers

Seamus McBride

United and Fergie . . . again!

TELFER
12

We're the success story of European football

says Peter Leaver, Chief Executive of the Premier League

The ever-changing world of the Premier League has welcomed a new man to the helm. Peter Leaver QC, a former director of Tottenham Hotspur, was appointed Chief Executive of the Premier League in April 1997 and has had his hands full ever since. However, it is a job that many would kill for and he is revelling in the challenge.

"I'm enjoying it very much. My only complaint about it is that there's far too much law involved and that is what I thought I was getting away from," says Mr Leaver with a wry smile.

English football seems to have a smile on its face at the moment and this is felt too in the corridors of power. "There's certainly a buzz about English football at the moment," he says, "but there is a general acceptance that while we're doing well off the field, we're not doing as well on the field as we might be, although the success of the England team in Le Tournoi has been a tremendous boost.

"A successful England team assists the whole of football. It makes everybody feel good and people want to come to a place where there is success. English football is seen to be successful at the moment. The next stage, though, has to be European success for the clubs, World Cup success for the England team and, in three years' time, European success for the England team.

"I think that the Premier League can take some credit for the success because it has encouraged – largely because of the money involved – a number of foreign players to come here and they have assisted the development of English players.

"The Premiership is perceived to be the success story of European football – it's what people are trying to copy. So I think we will see more foreign players come into the Premiership, although we must not take our eyes off the ball in terms of developing our own young players. That's why I'm so keen on the success of Howard Wilkinson's Charter for Quality – that's the future."

The future, according to Mr Leaver, may also mean a change to the structure of the professional game in this country.

"One of the things we may have to look at is whether it is possible to support 92 professional clubs or whether we might have to remodel ourselves into a smaller professional league. I know that remodelling would be a bitter pill for a lot of smaller clubs to swallow. There's a lot of local pride invested in these clubs and I understand that. But we are going to have to look at things again.

"There has been much talk about feeder clubs or nursery clubs and it's something we're discussing. We've had a look at how temporary transfers can be made longer and allowing clubs to use them more frequently. The thing about feeder clubs is that you have to protect the integrity of the competition. If you end up playing against your feeder club in a cup or because they have been promoted, or you have been relegated, that doesn't seem to me to be very desirable. One way round that is not to have your feeder club in the same country. There is a lot to be said for that."

Peter Leaver

Opposite: Dion Dublin of Coventry celebrates the first hat-trick of the 1997-98 season

England coach Glenn Hoddle

The Bosman ruling concerning the transfer of players whose contracts have ended has already made an impact and further waves will soon be felt.

"We have been in discussion with the Football League, the PFA and the FA about how to proceed over the Bosman ruling and hope that decisions can be made in the not too distant future," says Mr Leaver. "But the future is in education and training. I think that the Premier League is doing its bit by making money available for the training and education of players at lower league clubs and also the improvement of their stadia."

One of the proposals made by Howard Wilkinson, the FA's technical director, is that of Football Academies run by the clubs, institutions which are already starting to take shape in many parts of the country. Mr Leaver is also happy to consider the merits of residential academies.

"Provided that the educational and pastoral needs of the child as well as the football needs are taken care of, it doesn't seem to me outlandish or outrageous that a football club might want to start a school – even a school with boarding facilities. Obviously it has to be closely monitored and that's exactly what the Premier League, which has the responsibility for licensing the Football Academies, will do. If the Charter for Quality goes through, we will build up our youth and education department so that it can work closely with the technical department of the FA.

"I hope we can make a start on organising Football Academies within the year but it will take some time to get the expertise together to ensure that the academies are properly funded and properly run. It's intended to be a requirement of every Premiership club that they have an academy, but we must make sure the balance is right between education – primary, secondary and tertiary – and football. We must offer them all the educational opportunities that their abilities require. For example, if we discover that a kid of 16 is good at languages, the academies have to be able to provide education in those languages. We must ensure that there are opportunities for kids to go to university while continuing their football."

Academies may appear to be the beginning of a young player's career but, in fact, their footballing passions will have been aroused many years earlier, either by attending games live or watching on television. Since the Premier League's birth, both grounds and television coverage have changed considerably and further change may be on the way. Pay-per-view are words that can cause an immediate argument in pubs and club boardrooms alike.

"I don't know how pay-per-view will develop nor digital broadcasting either," admits Mr Leaver. "I have to say, I'm a bit of an agnostic about pay-per-view. I think the organisation of it has to be very carefully worked out if it is going to be remunerative to the clubs. The experience abroad hasn't proved to be that beneficial. If each club is to organise its own matches, then it's going to be faced by the opposing club saying it wants half of the money. If it doesn't agree to that, then it may find itself in a difficult position.

"Alternatively, if a club wanted to provide a pay-per-view service for its away matches, it might find itself being held to ransom when it plays away. It has to be very carefully worked out and then you have to think about the effect on attendances. If you sell a season ticket to all your matches, come a wet, cold Saturday in February, there must be a tremendous incentive to sit at home and watch the game live on television.

"We are at the start of another four-year agreement with BSkyB and also with the BBC. There are 380 matches in the Premier League each season. Sky show 60 live matches and the BBC show 68 matches in highlight form. Allowing for a degree of overlap, you're getting something like one third of the matches being shown on television together with goals from all of the matches.

It doesn't seem to me to be a bad way of organising the televising of matches but plainly there are going to be developments in the future.

"What we can do with television is make the Premier League visible all over the world. One thing we are trying to do when we renegotiate our overseas TV deal is to ensure that overseas players are seen in their own country. So we don't have Juninho, for example, saying one of the reasons he wants to play in Spain is because Spanish football is shown in Brazil and that's how he can impress his national team manager. I think there is a great deal of scope for development in that area. The effect of that may be that the Premier League becomes even more attractive to overseas players, but we must take care to ensure that our domestic talent is given a fair chance to develop and flourish."

Many supporters have complained about the change in atmosphere within the grounds since all-seaters have become commonplace. The Premier League is trying to address that.

"We've had a number of meetings of our supporters' panels," says Mr Leaver, "and a number of ideas have been raised. We've done a survey of what goes on in Italian grounds and we think there are things that could be used in our grounds. So we're going to put our toe in the water in 1997 to feel the temperature. It will be interesting to see how things develop. Anything we can do to make football more of an enjoyable family occasion the better.

"In Italy, they allow people to take large banners and flags into the grounds and microphone systems to cheerlead the chants and the songs. The organisers in that section have to surrender their season tickets when they go in and they are only returned if they have behaved themselves properly and the game has gone off without a problem. The chanting and singing is a part of a football match and, of course, there is a lot that goes on in our grounds. But sometimes in the lead up to a match, you can do more to enhance the atmosphere. There's Tangoman at Sheffield Wednesday and that's the sort of entertainment we might want during the match. Certainly, Sheffield Wednesday supporters have been doing their bit for entertainment during matches – even though one's ear drums suffer!

"People tend to shy away from the idea of orchestrating chanting or singing but we're living in a different age. It may be something we have to investigate. The vast majority of noise at football matches is still made spontaneously but there may be some matches which need a kick-start.

"In the 1997-98 season, we're starting our anti-abusive language campaign, trying to cut out the use of persistently abusive language. You'll never be able to stop people swearing but a persistent torrent of abuse can be offensive to many people. The campaign itself was suggested by our supporters' panel and we are pleased to have support from the FA, the Football League and the PFA as well. Although the genesis of it was in our supporters' panels, the whole of football is saying 'let's clean up our language'.

"There will be a poster campaign at grounds right the way through the season reminding people we don't like abusive language at grounds. Hopefully, the stewards and spectators themselves will be alert and make sure the people who persistently use abusive language will be kicked out."

The Premier League is already considered innovative in many ways and the reception for its ideas in Europe has thus far been positive. Certainly, the commercial success of the Premier League has had the federations of Europe scampering to find out the secrets of Lancaster Gate.

Mr Leaver, though, in his first full season as Chief Executive, wants more. "There's a great desire to copy what we do off the field from Italy, Holland and, to some extent, France and Spain," he says. "But the day they decide to copy what we do on the field will be the day I will consider that the Premier League has been truly successful."

Unmistakable – Eric Cantona

*** Peter Leaver was talking to John Stern.**

JVC

England – The Great Stage for The Best in The World

by Chris Dighton

Even in cosmopolitan England of the late 1990s the names conjure up images of the exotic: Ravanelli, Asprilla, Bergkamp, Zola and Gullit – five world-class footballers who have brought glamour and excitement to the Carling Premiership. They are at the forefront of a revolution that has swept England since the USA World Cup in 1994 and sparked a mass migration that has produced more winners than losers.

Why England? Why now? And why at a growing pace?

The Premiership has always had a fearsome reputation and been regarded universally as 'the toughest in the world' – more perhaps for the endurance qualities needed to win it than for the finesse of the football.

The stars of Serie A in Italy would claim they had the upper hand because they play cultured, artistic football as opposed by the more prosaic version of English Saturday afternoons but such a comparison is akin to that of the Grand National to the Derby. Or at least it used to be. The times are a-changin' in the Premiership.

No longer is it all about big-hearted, iron-lunged grafters lasting the distance. This season, like last, it is about craftsmen, players capable of carving openings and fashioning glorious victories. Even much-maligned Wimbledon have been winning plaudits in this direction! Backed by an influx of Sky television money and continental players wanting the English challenge, the game has moved forward into a brave new world without denying its history.

And the importance of that in selling England cannot be over-estimated. When Jurgen Klinsmann, the World Cup winning German striker, played for Tottenham Hotspur in the 1994-95 season, he dreamed of playing at Wembley in an FA Cup Final. His dream died with a semi-final defeat by Everton but it is that vision which inspires players the world over, regardless of what they have achieved for club and country. Klinsmann left but Wembley beckoned in 1997 for Gianfranco Zola, for Frank Leboeuf, for Gianluca Vialli of Chelsea, while the Middlesbrough foreign legion of Juninho, Emerson and Fabrizio Ravanelli twice took the bus to the Venue of Legends.

To do that, these imports had proved they could survive in football's hardest school, that they could still use their silky skills despite the tight marking and the raw pace of the game.

Consider this. At the end of the 1995-96 campaign Ravanelli won the European Cup with Juventus, the very pinnacle for a club player, yet almost before the prize had been put in the Italian club's boardroom cabinet, he had signed for Middlesbrough – a team based in the unfashionable north-east of England and with not a trophy of note to their name from a history that stretches back more than 120 years. Why? Because Boro, led by chairman Steve Gibson and under manager Bryan Robson, had a footballing vision and the money to make it possible. That, and the test of the football along with the fevered passion

Juninho of the Boro Legion

Derby's import Igor Stimac

generated by the club's followers, created an intoxicating atmosphere and made it difficult for Ravanelli to say 'No'.

"I knew all about Bryan Robson and I wanted to join him," he said. "I love the club's ambition, but I also love the challenge. It is something that teams like Manchester United and Liverpool would not have given me."

A dream start from Ravanelli vindicated Robson's daring in signing him. Three times on his Premiership debut, Ravanelli reached for his shirt to pull it over his head to celebrate a goal as Liverpool found the man dubbed 'The White Feather' floated like a butterfly and stung like a bee. Of course such a spectacular start – a 3-3 draw – could not be maintained but irrespective of the trials and tribulations that Middlesbrough endured during their doomed Premiership survival campaign, two Cup Finals in a season is not bad going. The Ravanelli verdict after a testing first season in England: "All the top teams are really comfortable on the ball and perhaps Serie A is still the best, but very soon I can see the Premiership catching up and even taking over."

Andrei Kanchelskis was an early invader

Ravanelli in scoring mood at The Riverside

This was a good endorsement and another shove to help the continental domino-effect gather pace. Where once just the lone intrepid Johnnie Foreigner made the trip, now dozens stand wanting the same experience. Supply and demand for once are in harmony, and the number of clubs queuing up to tap in to the source is still growing by the day and down the leagues, so that there are now over 100 in the Premiership alone and with Arsenal's summer signings of 1997, including Marc Overmars, the brilliant Dutch striker, the Gunners reached the stage where they and Chelsea could play one another and not field a home-grown player.

Sometimes the appeal of the foreigner is all about glamour and a world class reputation, sometimes for the cost-effectiveness of an unknown player brought in from abroad, and sometimes just because the local rivals have started to load their squad with players carrying unpronounceable names. Football clubs want to keep up with the Joneses as much as they do with the Manchester Uniteds of this world.

And talking of United, they have played the football business game more cannily than most. Andrei Kanchelskis, the Ukrainian, was one of their first modern-day imports. He was followed by Eric Cantona, even if he did arrive from France via Leeds United. Since then the gates have opened wider. Ole Gunnar Solskjaer, Jordi Cruyff, Karel Poborsky and Ronny Johnsen all played first-team games during 1996-97 with varying degrees of success.

Yet the story does not end there. Alex Ferguson, the United manager, has from the very outset of his triumphant reign at Old Trafford put an emphasis on youth development, setting up a system and being actively involved with it. The sense of satisfaction when one of your own boys becomes a man in the first team is huge; after all the home-grown tomato always tastes better than the one bought in the supermarket. By blending the foreigners with the youngsters as Ferguson has done, everyone benefits and especially Manchester United.

It is impossible fully to quantify the effect Cantona has had on the likes of

Above: **Boro's No 2 South American, Emerson the £4 million capture from Porto**
Left: **From Parma for £6.7 million, Faustino Asprilla the canny Colombian**

David Beckham but you cannot argue with four out of five Premiership titles; now, just the European Cup remains as the ultimate sanction of Ferguson's policy and an absolute endorsement that Premiership is best.

The continental drift in England has been enthusiastically embraced by all but particularly by the visionary overseas manager. Arsene Wenger, at Arsenal, has reshaped his team around the impressive French youngster Patrick Vieira, while upfront Dennis Bergkamp continues to be good value. London rivals Chelsea have followed the same path and Gianfranco Zola, Gianluca Vialli, Roberto Di Matteo, Dan Petrescu, Frode Grodas and Gullit himself have all been effective in a team that, when on song, has been thrilling to watch.

Alan Shearer, made England captain by Glenn Hoddle, admitted as much when he revealed he had voted for Zola as the Premiership player of the season. "He's come in from abroad, which is never easy with the language and culture changes, yet he has taken everything in his stride," said Shearer. "He is a tremendous player, great with both feet and very strong. He was certainly my player of the Premiership season even if he did hurt England with that goal at Wembley for Italy in the World Cup qualifier." Zola was pipped by Shearer for the 'Players' Player of the Year' title but picked up the football writers' award – proof, if ever it was needed, of his impact on the English game.

And there are more stars still to come. Gullit, well before the 1997 FA Cup Final, was already looking ahead by signing Celestine Babayaro, the Nigerian defender from Anderlecht, and then set his sights on Gustavo Poyet, from Real Zaragoza. In fact it reached a stage where you could throw in a hat the names of any named football star in the world, pull them out and take your pick of Premiership clubs chasing them.

A glance through the professional playing lists of all the Premiership clubs revealed more than a smattering of exotic world players. There was Benito Carbone at Sheffield Wednesday, having arrived there from Inter Milan, and Dejan Stefanovic from Red Star Belgrade. West Ham played Danish international Marc Reiper, had Slaven Bilic, a qualified lawyer from Croatia, and Florin

Patrick Vieira . . . leader of the French invasion of Highbury

Gianfranco Zola . . . as always a marked man

Raducioiu, the Romanian signed from Espanol for £2.4 million, on their books.

At Spurs, Steffen Iversen, signed from Rosenborg in Norway, helped to fill a void in attack caused by a long-term injury to Chris Armstong, while Southampton fought their battle against relegation with their own Graeme Souness-assembled foreign legion of Egil Ostenstadt, from Viking Stavanger, Eyal Berkovic, an Israeli from Maccabi Haifa, and Ulrich Van Gobbel, a Dutch international from Galatasaray. Meanwhile Derby County, predicted by many as certainties for relegation, survived in relative comfort and were bolstered by the likes of Jacob Laursen, a Danish international, and Croatians Igor Stimac, a rock-solid defender, and Aljosa Asanovic, an experienced midfielder.

The trade has been made easier by the Bosman ruling, which has allowed players out of contract to go where they choose without being restricted by their club demanding a high transfer fee. This new freedom goes hand-in-hand with a cash bonanza in the Premiership, underpinned by Sky TV money and assisted by booming interest that has seen season tickets sell like never before, replica kit sales shoot through the roof and clubs' commercial activities thrive on the back of footballing success.

The fiscal balance has tilted away from huge transfer payments upfront to larger week-by-week salaries. Ravanelli, Bergkamp and Asprilla apart, clubs have discovered you can get more for your money by casting your net wide. Bilic cost £1.65 million, Stefanovic £2.7 million, Ostenstadt £900,000 from Viking Stavanger, and Berkovic £1 milllion from Maccabi Haifa. Their home-grown equivalents would be Harrods price-range.

"Our football suffered from the island mentality for many years," said Jon Smith, the agent who handles Zola. "The influx of foreign players has sparked life into our game but the boom won't last forever."

Eyal Berkovic, a happy scorer for the Saints before joining West Ham

The Premiership has now become the place for watching world stars. No longer do viewers around the world tune in with that slightly supercilious 'mad dogs and Englishmen' attitude; they turn on to see real talent at work, faces for now and for tomorrow. Of course, there is always an element of risk buying a new player, be he from home or away, be he an established pro with a fabulous track record or a new arrival with huge potential. Success is down to the chemistry of the team, an enthusiasm to work and, in the case of the foreigner, a willingness to integrate with a new culture.

In the case of the South Americans, time in the Premiership is time well spent, especially with a World Cup in Europe coming up. Acclimatisation has always been a concern but the likes of Brazil's Juninho can only be better prepared for it by his ultimately torrid Middlesbrough experience – stronger, too, in terms of raw fitness. The Premiership is the ultimate testing ground and it is fitting that the country which gave the world this priceless gift, the game of football, should be the stage for the best players – a place for the masters of this global language truly to express themselves.

The Great Eight *by Chris Dighton*

Robbie Fowler gets in first as Albert closes in

Liverpool: James, Kvarme, Wright, Matteo, McAteer, Redknapp, Barnes, Bjornebye, McManaman, Berger, Fowler.
Newcastle: Hislop, Watson, Peacock, Albert, Elliott, Gillespie, Barton, Batty, Clark (Ginola 45min), Beardsley (Ferdinand 45min, Crawford 55min), Asprilla.
Referee: D Elleray.
Attendance: 40,751.
Goals: McManaman (29min) **1-0**, Berger (30min) **2-0**, Fowler (42min) **3-0**, Gillespie (71min) **3-1**, Asprilla (87min) **3-2**, Barton (88min) **3-3**, Fowler (90 min) **4-3**.

Monday March 10, 1997

Liverpool 4 Newcastle United 3

There was a sense of deja vu about the events at Anfield on this March night as Liverpool and Newcastle met again with minds very much tuned to the battle for the Premiership title and the chase of Manchester United. It was ever thus.

A year earlier, Newcastle's title hopes were all but destroyed when they lost 4-3 against Liverpool – and here they were again, going down by the same scoreline.

This time, however, instead of leading for most of the way only to be pipped at the post, Newcastle were doing all the chasing as Liverpool constructed what looked, by half-time, to be an unassailable lead.

Two goals in the space of a minute set Liverpool on their way. Steve McManaman started it off with a curling shot from the edge of the penalty area to beat Shaka Hislop and he then set up the second, via Robbie Fowler, following a determined charge that saw him dispossess David Batty. Fowler's shot came off the post but the alert Patrik Berger was on hand to tuck the ball into the goal.

Three minutes before half-time and Fowler got it right as he scored after latching on to a pass from Jamie Redknapp. The 3-0 lead left the Liverpool fans looking forward to the second half expecting more of the same. Game, set and match to Liverpool? Not a bit of it.

Far from accepting that Newcastle were chasing a lost cause, manager Kenny Dalglish reorganised with Les Ferdinand and David Ginola coming on in place of Peter Beardsley and Lee Clark respectively and the new Tyneside alchemy worked wonders, even though Ferdinand lasted just ten minutes.

First Keith Gillespie discovered the truth of that first rule of shooting at goal – hit the target. The shot was innocuous enough but David James in the Liverpool goal got it all wrong and, in the split second of blundering, savaged his self-confidence and dented the spirit of his defence.

Now it was Newcastle's turn to score two in a minute. First Ginola lofted a gorgeous through ball down the centre of the pitch. The Colombian Faustino Asprilla was on it in a flash and lobbed the advancing James. Asprilla then taunted and teased the Liverpool goalkeeper to set up the equaliser for Warren Barton.

The clock ticked down but, as they say, the fat lady was not singing yet. Stig Inge Bjornebye swung over a cross from the left and there was Fowler rising to head the ball home and make it 4-3.

We thought after the football extravaganza these two produced in the 1995-96 season it couldn't happen again – but it did. What price now on a repeat thriller? Liverpool v Newcastle is one of the most eagerly awaited fixtures of them all.

Saturday October 26, 1996

Southampton 6 Manchester United 3

On first hearing this result most people went into that incredulous Victor Meldrew mode: 'I don't believe it!' And few would have blamed Alex Ferguson if he had adopted the same cantankerous attitude as the TV sitcom hero when trying to fathom what went wrong for his team.

Manchester United still probably don't believe it. But it happened at The Dell all right and marked eight days in which Manchester United lost two consecutive Premiership games and conceded 11 goals.

Before the kick-off, Southampton had won two from ten matches and, while not able to deny the glamorous appeal of a home game against Manchester United, the prospects of a favourable result for them belonged in the realms of fantasy.

Six minutes into proceedings and Southampton took a surprise lead. Eyal Berkovic, Southampton's Israeli signing, flicked a ball through to the unmarked Egil Ostenstadt and though Peter Schmeichel beat out the shot, Berkovic scored from the rebound.

Next it was the turn of the occasional footballing magician Matt Le Tissier. Berkovic opened the defence and Le Tissier executed a sweet chip to make it 2-0. By that stage Roy Keane had been sent off for a second bookable offence but, even so, few would have written off United and they enjoyed some respite when David Beckham scored from a free kick four minutes before half-time.

But in those telling last minutes of the half, United were caught again when Ostenstadt brushed aside the challenge of David May to make it 3-1. United, however, were still not out of it and more hope arrived in the shape of a May goal.

Southampton were not unduly worried and were content to absorb the increasingly frantic attempts of the visitors to score another – a situation exacerbated by the steady march of time. There were less than ten minutes remaining when Southampton delivered three decisive blows.

Gary Neville was caught in posession trying to take the ball forward from his own penalty area and Berkovic scored his second of the match. Two goals in four minutes for Ostenstadt not only completed his hat-trick but put Southampton 6-2 ahead.

Paul Scholes scored a third consolation goal for the visitors but the final scoreline of 6-3, coming after a 5-0 defeat at Newcastle, left many wondering about the effectiveness of Eric Cantona, the fitness of that defensive rock Gary Pallister and the potency of strikers Jordi Cruyff and Scholes. The European Cup was also seen as a distraction to United's Premiership ambitions.

Yet while Southampton fans will dine out on this 90 minutes for years to come, Manchester United went away chastened but a good deal wiser, their eventual fourth Premiership title in five years proving that their appetite cannot be dimmed by the occasional humiliation.

Celebrating a glorious hat-trick is Egil Ostenstadt

Southampton: Beasant, Van Gobbel, Lundekvam, Dryden, Dodd, Oakley, Berkovic, Neilson (Magilton 75min), Charlton (Potter 70min), Le Tissier (Watson 88min), Ostenstadt.

Manchester United: Schmeichel, G Neville, May, Pallister (Irwin 45min), P Neville, Beckham, Butt (McClair 17min), Keane (sent off 21min), Cantona, Cruyff (Solskjaer 83min), Scholes.

Referee: J Winter.

Attendance: 15,253.

Goals: Berkovic (6min) **1-0**, Le Tissier (35min) **2-0**, Beckham (41min) **2-1**, Ostenstadt (45min) **3-1**, May (56min) **3-2**, Berkovic (83min) **4-2**, Ostenstadt (85min) **5-2**, Ostenstadt (89min) **6-2**, Scholes (89min) **6-3**.

Saturday December 28, 1996

Newcastle United 7 Tottenham Hotspur 1

Hot-shot Les Ferdinand is mobbed by his mates (above) but he is still hungry for more (right)

Newcastle: Hislop, Watson, Peacock, Albert, Beresford, Gillespie (Clark 41min), Batty, Lee, Beardsley, Ferdinand, Shearer.
Tottenham: Walker, Carr, Calderwood, Campbell, Wilson, Howells, Fox, Nielsen, Sinton (Dozzell 45min, Rosenthal 54min), Iversen, Sheringham.
Referee: G Ashby.
Attendance: 36,308.
Goals: Shearer (20min) **1-0**, Ferdinand (22min) **2-0**, Ferdinand (59min) **3-0**, Lee (61min) **4-0**, Albert (79min) **5-0**, Shearer (82min) **6-0**, Lee (88min) **7-0**, Nielsen (89min) **7-1**.

Kevin Keegan was still the Newcastle manager but not only were these the last days of the year, they were the last days of a Keegan reign that had at times produced some truly inspiring attacking football, often at the expense of serious defensive work.

Yet if ever a result was to be a fitting epitaph for a manager, then this was it. Newcastle were rampant even by their standards and the trademark defensive lapse did not come until one minute from the end – by which time they were seven goals to the good.

The form book gave no hint of this massacre as Newcastle came into the match on the back of a dreadful run, six weeks without a Premiership win and four points from seven games. No wonder their fans were looking back at the end of the season and asking 'if only' as they finished second and seven points behind Manchester United. That might have earned them the second European Cup place but did little to soothe the eventual hurt in their losing title fight.

It took time for the Newcastle engine room to fire on all cylinders and the first goal did not arrive until the 20th minute when Alan Shearer broke through and, two minutes later, Les Ferdinand was also on target.

Spurs regrouped and held out until half-time but failed to use the break to reorganise themselves for a fight back. Instead it was the home side who came out as if playing for their lives.

Prompted by Peter Beardsley, playing and conducting affairs from his central attacking support role, Newcastle were irresistible. Ferdinand made it 3-0 after 59 minutes, Robert Lee was next to score, Philippe Albert scored the fifth and Shearer the sixth. Two minutes from time Robert Lee added the seventh.

Demoralised Tottenham scored a minute from time through Alan Nielsen but they had been torn apart by a Newcastle side which could and should have reached double figures.

It was a stylish way to end a drought, revived memories of Newcastle's great 5-0 win over Manchester United in the October and almost matched a record created in 1934 – the last time Newcastle had won a match by seven clear goals in the top flight when they beat Liverpool 9-2.

Saturday October 19, 1996

Chelsea 2 Wimbledon 4

In hindsight, Wimbledon would perhaps rather have lost this one and beaten Chelsea in the FA Cup semi-final. Nevertheless, this was a landmark win for Wimbledon, thoroughly deserved and proof that poverty of pocket counts for nothing when compared with the riches of an indomitable spirit.

Indeed, in 1996-97, Wimbledon were the Wimbledon we knew of old and a little bit more – at times daring to showboat without ever losing that essential steel. Almost overnight the Premiership's most unfashionable club became chic and won plaudits from the likes of Chelsea's manager Ruud Gullit and Manchester United's Alex Ferguson, and praise from that latter source is praise indeed.

Entering this match, Wimbledon had put behind them a nightmare start to the season which saw them lose their first three matches before embarking on a surge of six successive wins. If they were to beat Chelsea, they would set a club record for consecutive wins.

Chelsea, and these were the pre-Gianfranco Zola days, took to the field with Gianluca Vialli and Mark Hughes leading the attack and with a midfield including Craig Burley, Scott Minto and Roberto Di Matteo. The pre-match strategy was to pass through the Wimbledon midfield and defence. History has debunked that theory as being about as effective as Napoleon's march on Moscow.

Wimbledon were rock solid in defence and the attack had a cutting edge which glowed menacingly every time they moved forward. It took them just four minutes to draw first blood.

A typical long throw from Vinnie Jones bounced high over the Chelsea defence, leaving Robbie Earle the simple task of heading past a startled Kevin Hitchcock. Chelsea refused to let that get to them and were level after ten minutes through Minto, but Wimbledon were soon ahead again.

Neal Ardley took aim from a distance and benefited from a deflection which left Hitchcock stranded. That was how it stayed until half-time. Then Wimbledon killed the tie off with a peach of a goal from Marcus Gayle. He picked up a long clearance from Dean Blackwell and, though he had his back to goal, there was room to turn. He moved in on Steve Clarke, 'nutmegged' him then struck a precise but powerful left-foot shot past the goalkeeper.

Efan Ekoku wrapped it up with the fourth some 13 minutes later, skipping past the rash and lunging challenge of Franck Leboeuf before striking a telling shot past Hitchcock.

There was still time for Chelsea to gain a consolation goal when Vialli scored a penalty but even that could not take the gloss off a first-rate Wimbledon performance that encompassed their new spirit in every way, proving that they still do what they used to do better than anyone, but also hinting at a footballing maturity and an occasional sense of style that most would have thought was beyond them.

It also gave them seven wins in succession, a record of which to be proud but of little consolation when their dreams of qualifying for European football foundered as a hectic end of season caught up with their small, single-minded but ultimately overwhelmed squad.

The price Marcus Gayle has to pay for his super goal is a hug from Vinnie

Chelsea: Hitchcock, Johnsen, Leboeuf, Clarke, Petrescu, Burley (Spencer 55min), Newton (Wise 77min), Di Matteo, Minto (Gullit 55min), Hughes, Vialli.
Wimbledon: Sullivan, Cunningham, Blackwell, Perry, Kimble, Ardley, Jones, Earle, Leonhardsen, Ekoku (Holdsworth 90min), Gayle (Fear 90min).
Referee: D Elleray.
Attendance: 28,020.
Goals: Earle (4min) **0-1**, Minto (10min) **1-1**, Ardley (16min) **1-2**, Gayle (64min) **1-3**, Ekoku (77min) **1-4**, Vialli (pen) (85min) **2-4**.

Sunday May 11, 1997

Tottenham Hotspur 1 Coventry City 2

***Above:* Darren Huckerby in deadly combat with Sol Campbell. *Right:* The hero of Coventry's last stand, Steve Ogrizovic, and a loving team-mate**

Tottenham Hotspur: Baardsen, Vega, Scales, Campbell, Carr, Fox, Dozzell, Sinton (Clapham 22min), Edinburgh, McVeigh (Fenn 73min), Sheringham.
Coventry City: Ogrizovic, Telfer, Shaw, Williams, Burrows, Whelan (Jess 33min), McAllister, Richardson, Ndlovu, Huckerby, Dublin.
Referee: M Bodenham.
Attendance: 33,029.
Goals: Dublin (13min) **0-1**, Williams (38min) **0-2**, McVeigh (43min) **1-2**.

For a perfect sense of dramatic timing, no one does it quite like Coventry City. Ten times in the last 30 years they have reached the final match of the season with their future in the top division hanging by a thread – and ten times they have got away with it.

If anything, however, the thread at the end of the 1996-97 season was more frayed than ever because an outright win was not enough – they needed other results to go their way. Amazingly they did and Coventry breathed again as they pulled off a great escape so remarkable as to make Houdini feel like a fraud.

Coventry, with everything to play for, took the game from the first whistle to a Tottenham side ravaged by injury and their positive attitude was rewarded after 13 minutes when, completely with the run of play, they scored.

Gary McAllister played a short corner through Noel Whelan and his cross found Dion Dublin towering above a crowded penalty area. His header beat Espen Baardsen in the Spurs goal. Twenty-five minutes later, Coventry extended their lead through another corner. McAllister crossed again and this time Paul Williams was on hand to volley home.

That should have settled the nerves but Tottenham pulled a goal back two minutes before half-time, when a Teddy Sheringham free-kick hit the post and the rebounding ball was knocked in by Paul McVeigh.

Desperate to maintain the status quo of the scoreline, Coventry made what could have been a major error in the second half by opting to defend deep and the final 15 minutes was all one-way traffic, yet there was no way through. Ogrizovic twice pulled off stunning saves to deny Jason Dozzell and then spread himself to thwart Neale Fenn. When Spurs did get past him, Richard Shaw was there to clear the danger.

Time ticked down and the rest of football knew that if the result stayed the same Middlesbrough, who had drawn 1-1 at Leeds, and Sunderland, beaten 1-0 at Wimbledon, would be lost to the Premiership along with Nottingham Forest, relegated a week earlier.

It may not have been a classic in terms of sweet moves, blinding skills and great movement but for sheer human interest and for the nail-biting ride it gave spectators, even those with no allegiance to either club, it could not be beaten.

Saturday April 5, 1997

Manchester United 2 Derby County 3

This was a dead cert home banker. United would garner three points to make their passage towards the 1996-97 Championship all the smoother, with three points lost by a Derby team growing increasingly concerned by a looming fight for Premiership survival. Playing in an Old Trafford stadium dubbed the 'Theatre of Dreams', however, gave Derby a sense of purpose and a belief that dreams could come true – and how they did!

In the course of a season there will always be the underdog team that goes to Manchester United, scores one goal and then, through a blend of outrageous good fortune and dogged persistence, holds out for victory.

That was not true of Derby. They played with elan and belief. They were well worth their 1-0 advantage, deserved to be 2-0 up and the goal that made it 3-1 midway through the second half was footballing justice at its best.

United were badly off colour but visiting teams still need courage to take advantage and the simple truth is that Derby could have been 4-0 up at half-time and nobody who witnessed the action would have raised an eyebrow.

Ashley Ward gave the first hint of the shock to come when his scuffed shot bounced off the turf and over Peter Schmeichel's head. Next it was the turn of the debut boy, Paulo Wanchope. The 20-year-old Costa Rican had an assist in Ward's goal and now he scored one of his own.

Collecting the ball just inside his own half, he went round Phil Neville, beat Gary Pallister and then with some aplomb side-footed his shot past Schmeichel. That was how the score stayed until half-time when United received – judging by the way they came out in the second half – a flea in the ear.

Eric Cantona made it 2-1 a minute into the second half and United started to raise the ante. Just when it seemed they would get back into the game the defence froze. Pallister and Schmeichel both failed to take responsibility for a bouncing ball on the edge of the penalty area, allowing Dean Sturridge to ghost in and score.

Ole Gunnar Solskjaer reduced the arrears to one with a glorious volley after 75 minutes and though United huffed and puffed for the final 15 minutes, Derby were well worth their victory – a win that was perhaps the turning point of their season. Alex Ferguson described his defence as 'terrible' but even so the opposition has to be good enough to take advantage.

United are first on the ball with Phil Neville (above left) and Ryan Giggs (right), but the Rams came out on top in the end

Manchester United: Schmeichel, G Neville (Irwin 69min), Johnsen, Pallister (Scholes 85min), P Neville, Beckham, Keane, Butt (Solskjaer 45min), Giggs, Cantona, Cole.

Derby County: Poom, Laursen, McGrath, Dailly, C Powell, Trollope, Van der Laan, D Powell, Wanchope (Simpson 65min), Ward, Sturridge.

Referee: D Elleray.

Attendance: 55,243.

Goals: Ward (28min) **0-1**, Wanchope (35min) **0-2**, Cantona (46min) **1-2**, Sturridge (73min) **1-3**, Solskjaer (75min) **2-3**.

West Ham: Miklosko, Ferdinand, Hall, Bilic (Reiper 78min), Potts, Lomas (Boylan 89min), Moncur, Porfirio, Lazaradis (Bishop 82min), Hartson, Kitson.
Sheffield Wednesday: Pressman, Atherton, Walker, Stefanovic, Nolan, Whittingham (Blinker 45min), Pembridge, Carbone, Nicol (Oakes 45min), Booth, Hirst (sent off 60 min).
Referee: M Riley.
Attendance: 24,960.
Goals: Kitson (4min) **1-0**, Kitson (13min) **2-0**, Hartson (30min) **3-0**, Hartson (67min) **4-0**, Carbone (82min) **4-1**, Kitson (89min) **5-1**.

Saturday May 3, 1997

West Ham 5 Sheffield Wednesday 1

The calculators had been out in force. West Ham fans were scouring through the remaining fixtures of the season, awarding their side theoretical points here and there and reckoning that a win over Wednesday would go a long way to easing their relegation fears.

Wednesday on the other hand were looking back on a season that had seen them race out of the traps with four straight wins and, even at this late stage, still offered a glimmer of a Uefa Cup place for 1997-98.

According to Harry Redknapp, the West Ham manager, his side would have long since been consigned to the First Division had the club not splashed out on reinforcing the attack with the signing of Paul Kitson and John Hartson in the February. Even so, the best pre-match hopes for this encounter were for a tightly-fought and nervous home win.

But then Kitson produced the tonic to liberate his side when after just four minutes he put West Ham ahead. Less than ten minutes later he had added a second. This time Hartson climbed high to head down the ball for Kitson to score.

West Ham now swept forward, menacing with every attack, and the star of the show was Hartson, a player who had been nurtured at Luton by the Sheffield Wednesday manager David Pleat. The ginger-haired striker, who had been bought from Arsenal, stood as a beacon in attack. After half an hour, West Ham were 3-0 up when he scored his first of the afternoon and Wednesday were falling apart at the seams – a situation made worse when, on the hour, David Hirst was sent off for elbowing young Rio Ferdinand.

Hartson scored his second and West Ham's fourth seven minutes later and the win was in the bag. The home side were able to take the foot off the pedal and that allowed Wednesday a consolation goal, scored by Benito Carbone.

There was time for one more flourish from the Hammers. Hartson, of course, was at the centre of the attack and there was his new partner in crime, Kitson, on hand to complete his hat-trick and a convincing 5-1 victory.

Redknapp's investment had produced a gilt-edged return and certainly it was money spent just in time. It also left the finally relieved Hammers' supporters with time to wonder what effect these two would have had on the team's fortunes had they been bought earlier.

John Hartson in determined mood for the Hammers

Sunday February 2, 1997

Newcastle United 4 Leicester City 3

Leicester were in the Premiership by virtue of a last-minute extra-time play-off goal against Crystal Palace and were earmarked by many for a swift return to their roots. But in 1997, Leicester was the happening place in sport with all the local teams vying for attention.

Consider this: the cricket team were the 1996 county champions, the rugby side Pilkington Cup winners in 1997 and the football team much more than Premiership survivors and, as a bonus, holders of the Coca-Cola Cup.

Leicester finished the 1996-97 season ninth in the table and it is ironic that for all they achieved, their finest Premiership moment came in glorious defeat at Newcastle, who were under new management with Kenny Dalglish.

Newcastle, bubbling on the tide of local passion, came out with their usual goal-scoring intent and within three minutes were 1-0 up, thanks to a Robbie Elliott shot which went in via Julian Watts' boot. The tempo was raised a notch as Les Ferdinand, Alan Shearer and Robert Lee all went close or brought the best out of Kasey Keller, the visitors' goalkeeper.

The home side sensed that another goal would lead to a scoring riot but Leicester manfully held on until half-time then, ten minutes into the second half, were level as Matt Elliott rose to head home Garry Parker's cross.

This was the goal to transform the game. Leicester were now all-dominant and the Newcastle defence evaporated like the morning mist under a burning sky. Steve Claridge, the man whose goals had earned Leicester this quality Premiership fixture and later a trophy, beat Shaka Hislop from eight yards. Then Emile Heskey skipped down the wing and powered a low shot past him.

Newcastle looked dead and buried but, with less than 15 minutes remaining, hope was provided by Alan Shearer. David Ginola was fouled on the edge of the penalty area and Shearer hammered home the free kick. Six minutes later and Shearer, surrounded by defenders, opted for the audacious and scored by drilling home a goal, shooting through a defender's legs.

Leicester were horrified but could still hang on for the point. Some hope! Shearer was on fire and in the third minute of injury time Robert Lee and Lee Clark played a one-two, the cross was fired in and who should be on the end of it for a simple tap-in? Alan Shearer. Three points for Newcastle, three goals for Shearer in 13 minutes – and a game to remember.

Dalglish left St James' Park later that afternoon saying he now knew why Keegan's hair had gone grey. Leicester left ultimately disappointed by the end result but with confidence and self-belief in fine fettle.

Newcastle: Hislop, Albert, Peacock, Watson, Gillespie (Ginola 68min), Lee, Batty, R Elliott, Asprilla (Clark 87min), Shearer, Ferdinand.
Leicester: Keller, Grayson, Pior, M Elliott, Watts, Izzet, Taylor (Lawrence 80min), Lennon, Parker, Heskey, Claridge.
Referee: M Reed.
Attendance: 36,396
Goals: R Elliott (3min) **1-0**, M Elliott (55min) **1-1**, Claridge (60min) **1-2**, Heskey (68min) **1-3**, Shearer (77min) **2-3**, Shearer (83min) **3-3**, Shearer (90min) **4-3**.

Keith Gillespie is the split-second winner of this duel with Emile Heskey

The Business of Football – Part One

by Aubrey Ganguly

The zebras are out in force at the St James' watering hole!

It seems that cries of 'Up the City!' have taken on a new resonance these days. What with the number of clubs floated on the Stock Exchange, and the huge amounts of money that appear to be flooding into the sport, football now garners almost as much coverage in the financial pages as it does on the back pages.

Headlines such as 'United top the table' are as likely to refer to the League of Club Profitability as to the Premiership, while fans who previously showed their allegiance with the purchase of scarves, hats, mugs and calendars now have the opportunity to add club shares to the evidence of their devotion.

As with most sports, football enjoys peaks as well as troughs in its profile but the last few years have brought levels of attention rarely seen. The emergence of a credible England team, the rise of Fantasy Football, the 'laddish' culture trend, the quality of the Premiership and the fervour of Euro 96 – all have contributed to the success story.

All of which is very nice, but none of which explains exactly why the City has become so interested in the game. After all, nobody witnessed a rush of stock-market activity around football in 1966. So what has prompted the business world that the time is now right to invest?

The answer, of course, is money – and lots of it. Nothing interests the City more than profit, and in recent times there have been few more profitable areas than football. For example, from January 1996 to January 1997, the All Shares

Index, which indicates the average growth of shares, stayed practically level. A horizontal line on a graph proved that, while shares can go down as well as up, the market remains, on the whole, fairly steady.

In contrast, a graph of the Coopers and Lybrand Football Index for the same period resembled the north face of the Eiger – a steep, continuous climb. The accountants' measure of football stock over the 12-month period showed an increase in value of some 400 per cent. That's quite a return in just one year and more than enough incentive to encourage investors.

While Coopers have since issued a note of caution about these spectacular results, believing some clubs may be overvalued, it is clear that plenty of parties are keen to invest in the national game. Even some long-term investors, such as pension funds, have begun to move into football stocks – a sure sign that the sport bears at least some stability and credibility in the market.

Recognising this fact, merchant bankers Singer and Friedlander began their Football Fund early in 1997. An investment fund concentrating on a portfolio of football clubs and related businesses, the idea captured the imagination of many. Within 48 hours of launch, the bankers had pulled in more than £11 million in investments and, by March, more than 850,000 people had sent them money.

However, not everyone is enamoured with football's new-found friends in the City. Some fear that the interests of the boardroom may encroach on the interests of the team, with success being sacrificed for profit and potential match-winners being viewed as assets to be cashed in rather than to build on.

In reality this is unlikely to become a regular occurrence, if only because most boardrooms are aware that long-term financial gains are more easily attained with a club that achieves success on the pitch. Hence, a balance needs to be struck between business profit and football achievement and, as per the continent, any big-name departures are likely to be followed by new star attractions.

What most boardrooms are really concerned about is financial stability – developing a club that makes a reasonable profit year-in, year-out whether or not a trophy is won. After all, there are plenty of teams and only a handful of competitions and if financial success were dependent on the guarantee of silverware, few clubs would survive.

In England, the catalyst for change has also been commercial television. There were concerns when Sky took over the coverage of top-flight English football from domestic television. Would it be crass? Would the production values be amateurish? Would the game lose something?

As it transpired, the fears were mostly unjustified. In general, Sky's coverage has been excellent. Not only entertaining but innovative, and few would claim it has been anything less than a complete success. Even more significant is the vast amount of money Sky has brought to the game. The current broadcasting deal with Sky, together with the BBC's highlights package, is worth some £743 million in total to the Premiership and this influx of cash, together with the Taylor Report, has radically altered English football.

All-seater stadiums, big-name foreign signings, fewer quality English players going abroad – all are factors that have contributed to the rise in attendances and the increased financial security among Premier clubs. And fears that a wedge would be driven between Premiership and First Division have to some extent been allayed by the success of Leicester and Derby in the 1996-97 season.

As Giancarlo Galavotti, the London correspondent of *La Gazetta della Sport*, observed in an article for *The Times*: 'England is finally accepting football for what it really is: the most fascinating, spectacular money-spinner among popular entertainments; a goldmine of a sport. All the passions, madnesses and excesses that were once the exclusive prerogative of the fanatic Latin countries are now the norm in England. What a difference a business approach makes!'

Manchester United fans celebrate another title win . . .

. . . as Chelsea followers are all smiles on their Cup-happy day

The Business of Football – Part Two *by Aubrey Ganguly*

Ed De Goey, now at Chelsea, shows his agility for Feyenoord

So football is now seen as big business. Investment strategies and financial reports abound; profits go up, dividends grow and share prices rise. But how exactly do clubs make their money? And does your club get its fair share of the extra cash?

It's actually quite easy to see where the money is coming from and where it's going to, as there are only five major areas that affect a club's income:

TRANSFERS

While transfer fees can still provide a way of earning big money, in recent years Premiership clubs seem to be buying rather more than selling, at least as far as star names go.

The biggest deal to date in the Premiership remains the £15 million transfer of Alan Shearer from Blackburn to Newcastle, but the Bosman ruling appears to have encouraged clubs to buy younger players and put them under longer contracts. This makes sense from a business perspective because it ensures the club have the chance to recoup some of their initial outlay by selling on a player whilst he is still under contract. However, it can make fees appear higher than they really are.

For example, the various stories that floated around for a while in the summer of 1997, linking Brazilian wonder kid Ronaldo with any number of British clubs, may have quoted the transfer fee as £25 million but this would almost certainly have been for a 10-year contract, and would have included at least part of the cost of paying his salary. Also, at only 20 years old, he could almost certainly, bar injury, be sold on for as much, if not more, than he cost.

This seems to be the way forward for clubs. And while there will still be big-name transfers both to and from the continent, this may increasingly involve a player out of contract who can ensure any fee lines his pocket (and his agent's) rather than the club's. Chelsea are just one of the clubs who have taken advantage of the Bosman ruling, signing up a number of players pre-season, but rarely troubling their bank manager.

There has been some concern over the growing number of foreign imports into the Premiership, but as Chelsea's managing director Colin Hutchinson said following the club's fifth foreign signing of the summer: "It would be nice to buy one or two more English players but they're priced out of the market. For example, when we enquired about a certain English goalkeeper, we were quoted an asking price of £5 million. We subsequently signed Ed De Goey, a Dutch international 'keeper, for less than half that (£2.25 million)."

GATE MONEY

Fears that increased television coverage would adversely affect gates appear to be unfounded. The 1996-97 season saw the average attendance rise by almost 4%, with just under 11 million spectators in all at the Premiership's 380 games. That's 25% up on the attendances in the Premier League's first season in 1992-93.

Biggest rise of the year was the 32% increase at Old Trafford, where the extension of the north stand had lifted capacity to 55,300 (now at 56,387). The higher attendances ensured an additional amount of some £10 million in gate receipts.

Of course, there were big increases in attendances for the newly-promoted teams. The opportunity to watch Premiership football, week in, week out, pushed Derby's gate up by nearly 25% and Leicester's by 28.7%. Other clubs with significant increases included Wimbledon, whose improved fortunes on the pitch translated into a 20% upturn.

However, while season-ticket sales do aid stable finances, there are certain advantages to having some tickets available for sale on match day. From the purely financial side of things, 'casual' visitors are encouraged because they tend to buy more from the club shops, but there are other fundamental reasons for tickets to be on open sale. For a start, not everyone can afford a season ticket and there are plenty of fans, from shop workers to nurses, students to shift workers, who cannot make all the fixtures during the season.

As Tim Crabbe of the Football Supporters Association said: "A club may think it would lose money by leaving some tickets to be sold on the day, but in fact a block of a few thousand tickets would actually stimulate demand. As long as they are distributed fairly, tickets on open sale would bring more people and a greater cross-section of the community into matches."

But as football's popularity continues to grow, many clubs face a new dilemma – to move or not to move. With many grounds now so often at capacity, thoughts turn first to ground development and then to relocation. Among a number of clubs contemplating moves are Arsenal, Newcastle and Southampton, while Derby and Bolton completed their relocation for the 1997-98 season – yet another sign of the rapidly-changing face of football.

MERCHANDISING

These days, all clubs are aware of the value of merchandising and practically every Premiership side have a team store where fans can buy everything from away strips to bed linen.

Newcastle United not only have five stores dedicated to merchandising, but four mobile units to sell wares around the city, while Manchester United became the first club to announce that merchandising sales had exceeded gate receipts.

The days where merchandising consisted merely of scarves, hats and team shirts are long gone and these days the range of available items can enter the surreal. If baby bibs, slippers and knickers weren't enough, some clubs even offer bedroom furniture, wallpaper and curtains, while oven mitts and tea cosies are also proving popular.

But as the range of bizarre marketables continues to increase (club wines and spirits are one of the more recent crazes), one traditional item still tops the sales charts. The once humble kit remains the biggest money-spinner, although these days perhaps not so humble.

Worn not only by kids but their parents, shirts have become a staple of the casualwear market, as regular a sight in the high street as the football ground, and positively *de rigeur*, it seems, among Brits on holiday abroad. Estimates of how high sales reach are difficult, as most manufacturers are cagey about figures, but with some Premiership clubs earning in excess of £25 million from kit deals, you can be sure that a mountain of shirts is being sold.

Les Ferdinand, playing his part in helping to sell more Newcastle strips

Gary Lineker showing his crisp style for Barcelona

SPONSORS

As football's popularity continues to increase, club sponsorship offers an ever more attractive package to businesses. Putting the company's name and/or logo on a football shirt not only ensures that it is seen by tens of thousands of football fans every week but also by millions on television.

Sponsors range from breweries to electronic giants, car manufacturers to crisp makers, and deals can be worth anything from a couple of hundred thousand pounds to tens of millions.

Walkers Crisps, the Leicester-based company, have made great play of not only sponsoring the Leicester team but also using former local hero Gary Lineker in a series of television commercials that have seen sales of their crisps rocket. And the success of Martin O'Neill's team will certainly not have done the club any harm when it comes to negotiating a new contract with the company.

While in Tyneside, could there really be any other sponsor of the Toon's side than Newcastle Breweries? Between the Saturday afternoon at St. James' Park, the Saturday night at the pub and the Sunday-morning hangover, you really could 'eat, drink and sleep football' (to paraphrase another sponsor's commercial).

And it's not only teams that receive sponsorship. Individual players too can earn vast fortunes from their own sponsors. In recent years, players such as Les Ferdinand, David Beckham, Ian Wright and Alan Shearer (not to mention Monsieur Cantona) have all been used in successful campaigns that not only increase sales of whatever products are being promoted but also contribute to the general excitement that surrounds footballers and football these days.

Alan Shearer boosting Newcastle's bid for the big money

TELEVISION AND PRIZE MONEY

The current television deal with BSkyB ensures that half the TV revenue gained is shared between all 20 clubs. A further 25% is distributed according to the number of TV appearances and the remaining quarter is used as prize money.

Every Premier team receives prize money dependent on its final league position. For example, last season Manchester United earned £2,114,300 for finishing champions, while Newcastle in second place received £2,008,585. Tenth-place Tottenham were awarded £1,162,865, while even the relegated sides earned £317,145 (Sunderland) and £105,715 (Nottingham Forest).

On top of this, there is further money to be made if a club qualifies for Europe. Both Manchester and Newcastle United will benefit in the 1997-98 season from the Champions League, where television and prize money is enormous.

The five other English clubs in Europe – Arsenal, Liverpool, Chelsea, Aston Villa and Leicester – also stand to make considerable amounts should they progress in their respective tournaments, with television appearances worth up to £250,000 a time.

And of course on the not-so-distant horizon, pay-per-view television is almost in sight. A survey early in 1997 asked 400 people if they would be prepared to pay to watch football on television. Around 40% of viewers, asked if they would pay £10 for a top Premiership match, answered that they would. That sort of price would generate some £32 million in revenue for just one game.

The 20 Premiership teams are said to be looking closely at pay-per-view, and tests may well take place in the near future, with a more extensive service available by the year 2000. At present, it is thought that clubs would get to keep about half the income generated – a tidy sum, and likely to continue the current trend of finiancial growth in English football.

Soaring Salaries *by Ivan Speck*

For years Hollywood stars have received salaries with enough digits to double up as telephone numbers, but that sort of money is no longer their exclusive preserve. Sport is about big pay days, too. Fuelled by a global spectator market and an awareness that has put the players in a similar public spotlight as the heroes of the silver screen, the money being paid today to the main box-office draw is astronomical – and it's not bad for the supporting cast either.

There have always been big sports stars earning big money, their pay relative to their era – think of Jack Dempsey, of Joe DiMaggio, of Babe Ruth – yet maximum wage rules kept football in check.

Not so any more; now the sky is the limit. But if you think today's footballer is doing all right, just see what some of the other stars around the world are taking home.

Ryan Giggs

Paul Gascoigne

Naseem Hamed

Michael Jordan

ENGLAND – PREMIERSHIP FOOTBALLERS

ALAN SHEARER England's captain earns a basic salary of £800,000 per year. Adding in the £700,000 he receives in sponsorship from Umbro, Quaker Oats, Virgin and Gillette, and the healthy win and goal bonuses, Shearer's final salary is estimated to be £1.8 million per year.

RYAN GIGGS The Manchester United winger earned £800,000 in 1996, thanks in part to bonuses for winning the Premiership and FA Cup double. Sponsorship deals and royalties from his autobiography lifted his annual income to well over £1 million.

FABRIZIO RAVANELLI Middlesbrough's Italian star picked up £1.4 million during the 1996-97 season after his move from European champions Juventus.

ENGLISHMEN ABROAD

PAUL INCE The only high-profile Englishman plying his trade abroad in 1996-97, Ince had a £1.2 million contract with Inter Milan, a £500,000 deal to wear Adidas boots and lived in a £1 million mansion by Lake Como.

PAUL GASCOIGNE A marketing man's dream, Gascoigne currently earns £750,000 per year from Glasgow Rangers, but he is reputed to be worth over five times that figure when bonuses, signing-on fees and advertising commitments are taken into account. Even Gazza's often-changing hairstyles bring him financial rewards for each new coiffure to the tune of £20,000 from a national newspaper.

OTHER BRITISH SPORTSMEN

DAMON HILL The 1996 Formula One world champion made £5.5 million for driving his Williams-Renault to glory in the 16 Grands Prix. Personal sponsorship deals from Cellnet and Harrods took his earnings to nearly £7 million.

NASEEM HAMED Reputed to be worth as much as £12 million, Britain's double world boxing featherweight champion commands million-dollar purses every time he fights. Adidas, Sony, Joe Bloggs and Dime bar contracts make Hamed one of the country's richest sportsmen.

COLIN MONTGOMERIE Finishing top of the European golf tour in 1996 for the fourth successive year earned Montgomerie £720,000. He won another £275,000 on the US Tour, but sponsorship deals with Wilson clubs and Titleist balls take his annual salary to £2.5 million.

STEPHEN HENDRY Hendry has won over £5 million in prize money during his snooker career, but it is as much his earnings away from the table which have made his fortune. Exhibition appearances and a lucrative sponsorship deal with Sweater Shop make him more than £1 million per year.

THE REST OF THE WORLD

BASKETBALL Chicago Bulls star Michael Jordan earned a staggering $30.14 million in 1997. He is the highest-paid player in the NBA, where the average salary in the 1996-97 season was $2.2 million.

BASEBALL In April, Florida Marlins outfielder Gary Sheffield signed a six-year contract extension worth $61 million. Albert Belle of the Chicago White Sox earns $10 million per year. The 1997 average salary in Major League Baseball is $1.37 million.

ICE HOCKEY The highest-paid player in the NHL in 1996 was Mario Lemieux of the Pittsburgh Penguins, who earned $11.32 million. In 1995-96, the average salary was $892,000.

AMERICAN FOOTBALL Dallas Cowboys quarterback Trot Aikman earned $5.37 million in the 1996-97 season to make him the highest-paid player in the NFL. Miami's Dan Marino was just behind on $5.33 million, while the average pay was $795,000.

Then and Now . . .

This is a golden age for football. No longer does the game have stars, it has superstars – men who are huge box office, their pulling power so great that their names might almost glow above the title of their teams.

Every era has produced footballing gods like that; the real change has come in their projection to a willing public. In 60 short years, football has hardly changed. What has altered is the demand for today's stars.

Under those terms, football circa 1997 is light years ahead of football circa 1937. This is the story of now and then.

STAR PLAYER

Stanley Matthews, now Sir Stanley, did not score many goals – he managed three in 54 games for England – but in more than 700 games he created more goals than records could ever hope to track.

A Matthews appearance could put 20,000 on the gate, the crowd rattling through the turnstiles for a glimpse of his spectacular dribbling skills. As Sir Matt Busby said: "Matthews played football as if he was playing the Palladium."

Matthews was paid £8-a-week during his first spell at Stoke, where he made his debut in 1932, and earned less in a 33-year-career than Ryan Giggs in a couple of months.

He supplemented his income by holding head-tennis shows with his brother-in-law, Tommy Valence. And, later in his career, his boots were sponsored for £1,000-a-year by the Co-op. He also played exhibition games in South Africa for £25 a match.

"I'm not bitter about what I did or didn't earn," he said. "It's all relative, I wasn't a doctor or a surgeon. I haven't saved lives."

He never drank or smoked, drove nothing more exotic than a Ford Escort, and his restrained lifestyle helped him play until the age of 50.

BACK IN 1937. . .

THE LEAGUE

The top flight was made up of 22 teams and Manchester City were the reigning champions going into the 1937-38 season. Arsenal dominated the 1930s with five League Championships; once they were runners-up; twice FA Cup winners. There was a sign of things to come when their playing style was described as 'smash-and-grab football.'

THE WORLD CUP

Was played in 1938 in France where Italy beat Hungary 4-2 in the final. England did not compete.

TELEVISION

The first live match to be shown on September 16, Arsenal against Arsenal reserves, was such a success that the 1938 FA Cup Final was also televised live. Preston beat Huddersfield 1-0.

FOREIGN SIGNINGS

Barrow, then a League side, set a trend when they signed two Argentine players, Augustus Corps and Casco Rinaldi.

TRANSFERS

The biggest deal of 1938 was £14,500 paid by Arsenal to Wolves for Bryn Jones. The days of the £20,000 buy were still nine years away – in 1947 when Third Division Notts County paid Chelsea that amount for Tommy Lawton.

GROUNDS

Floodlights were not used until nearly two decades later but Arsenal's legendary manager Herbert Chapman had toyed with the idea. While visiting a friend in Austria, he watched a night match where headlights of 40 cars illuminated the field. Chapman had lanterns hung from the stands and invited the Press to a practice match at night, but could not convince the authorities to take up the idea.

RISING STAR

A 16-year-old Len Shackleton was working at Highbury as a grass-clipping groundsman in 1937 when he was told by Arsenal manager George Allison: "Go back to Yorkshire and get a job, you will never make the grade." He went on to dazzle crowds with his outrageous tricks, playing for Newcastle United and Sunderland. He scored 126 goals in 384 League appearances.

THE CARING GAME

There was no Professional Footballers Association in 1938, but FA president Charles Sutcliffe pledged to raise £100,000 for players who had fallen on hard times through injury.

MONEY

Stanley Matthews' £8-a-week could buy him a stadium-full of sweets, with a quarter-of-a-pound of Roses costing at pre-decimalisation rates 8p and Fruit Gums 2p. But on those wages he would have to save up a while for a car. In 1938, a basic Austin Seven would set him back £135. He could always afford marmalade, though, at 7p for a big jar. And if any of his fans wanted to immortalise the wonder of the wing in action, they could pick up a 'popular Brownie' camera for 30p. But they would have to be careful not to be blinded by the sparkle of his boots, provided by Kiwi polish at 6p a tin – and he was always scrupulously clean with Palmolive soap, a bargain at 3p!

from 1937 to 1997 *by Mark Oliver*

TODAY IN 1997 . . .

STAR PLAYERS

Ryan Giggs is not even the best-paid player in the Premiership, although Manchester United pay him more than £12,000-a-week, but he is one of the most marketable, having won a contract with Reebok for £8 million over six years.

In addition, he was also paid more than £500,000 to endorse Fuji Film, Quorn Burgers and Citroen Cars. And a mini-industry has grown around Ryan Giggs merchandise, such as books and posters.

He lives in a £250,000 house in a Manchester suburb and drives a top-of-the range Audi car. And he gets 2,000 letters a week from fans – 12,000 on Valentine's Day.

Top earner in the Premiership is probably England captain Alan Shearer, a goal-scoring phenomenon. His average is better than a goal every two games and he has easily been the Premiership's top scorer since it was formed in 1992. His total was 137 goals after five seasons.

"I can see a lot of people in him," said Bobby Charlton. "He reminds me of so many of all the greats, they all seem to be moulded into one."

Shearer's pay is probably more in a week than most people earn in a year and then there are lucrative sponsorship deals in place, including Lucozade and Braun shavers.

THE PREMIERSHIP

Only the following current Premiership teams were playing in the highest league 50 years ago: Arsenal, Bolton, Leeds United, Chelsea, Liverpool, Derby County, Everton and Leicester City. Indisputably, Manchester United are the major football force of the 1990s in England. They have won the Championship four times in five years and did the League and Cup 'double' of victories, in both 1994 and 1996. In Europe, they won the Cup Winners' Cup and reached the semi-finals of the European Cup in 1997.

WORLD CUP

Will be played in France in 1998.

TELEVISION

Sky satellite television screen up to 60 live Premiership matches in a season. BBC show the highlights and the two stations paid £743 million for the rights for four seasons, Sky's share being £640 million.

FOREIGN SIGNINGS

Arsenal signed five overseas players in a day – Marc Overmars (from Ajax), Emmanuel Petit and Gilles Grimandi (from Monaco), Luis Boamorte (from Sporting Lisbon) and Alberto Mendez-Rodriguez (from FC Feucht). Indeed, every Premiership club had foreign players in their 1997-98 line-up.

TRANSFERS

Alan Shearer set the seal on the biggest British club-to-club transfer when he left Blackburn Rovers for Newcastle for £15 million.

GROUNDS

Derby County and Bolton have moved to new grounds as have Sunderland, relegated at the end of the 1996-97 season.

RISEN STARS

Chris Waddle used to put the seasoning in sausages before his talent brought him international stardom. And both Stuart Pearce and Vinnie Jones were hod-carriers before becoming the 'hardmen' of 1990s football.

THE CARING GAME

Television stars Angus Deayton, Frank Skinner and Lenny Henry went on a 'Balls to Africa' tour for Comic Relief. The idea was to raise awareness of the African countries' problems and to demonstrate the universal language of football. But it also provided practical financial help – and footballs for villagers to enjoy the beautiful game.

MONEY

As more and more clubs floated themselves on the stockmarket, football began to feature prominently in the Financial Times as well as the sports pages. Prices have rocketed since the sepia-tinted, good-old-days of 1938. A basic Ford will cost about £8,000 and the price of Fruit Gums has shot up to 34p (new currency), while half-a-pound of Roses has increased to about £1.15. Cameras start at £19.99, but £700 camcorders are widely used these days. For a simple blast from the past, Palmolive soap is a pinch at 64p.

Golden Goals of the 1996-97 Season *by Jay Bigwood*

Goals – the very currency of football – come in all forms and ways; from the long-range shot, the predatory boot poke inside the six-yard box, the diving header or the sheer fluke of a deflection. They all count, but some are more special than others. JAY BIGWOOD here re-lives his chosen golden goals of the 1996-97 season.

David Beckham

August 17, 1996

Wimbledon 0 MANCHESTER UNITED 3

On the first day of the season and with his team already two goals up, David Beckham stole the headlines with a goal that will be remembered for many years to come and was certainly one of the best, if not THE best of the season. It was as spectacular as it was skilful, one to treasure and to savour, even after seeing it replayed for the umpteenth time.

With only seconds of the match remaining, Beckham received the ball 10 yards inside his own half. He took a couple of strides forward, looked up and noticed Wimbledon goalkeeper Neil Sullivan advancing off his line. With devastating accuracy, Beckham floated the ball over the hapless, back-pedalling Sullivan and into the unguarded net.

An amazing goal that kick-started a tremendous season for Beckham, who went on to score more spectacular goals over a period that saw him become a regular in the England team and a superstar of the game.

Richie Humphreys

August 17, 1996

SHEFFIELD WEDNESDAY 2 Aston Villa 1

Making his first start of his Sheffield Wednesday career, Humphreys became an instant hero with the fans by striking one of the sweetest goals of the season in an opening-day win over Aston Villa.

The 18-year-old's golden moment came in the 56th minute. A flicked header from Mark Pembridge found its way towards Humphreys. With no time to think, he met the ball firmly on the volley from 20 yards and sent it crashing into the net past the hapless Michael Oakes.

The goal lit up Hillsborough and ensured a permanent place for Humphreys in Wednesday's squad as their quest for a European place began well with four successive wins.

Karel Poborsky

September 7, 1996

Leeds United 0 MANCHESTER UNITED 4

Leeds' Elland Road is one of the Premiership's most intimidating grounds for visiting sides, especially with ex-idol Eric Cantona in the line-up, but the hostile atmosphere did nothing to stop the Reds powering to an overwhelming victory.

After tenacious midfield work from David Beckham, in the 77th minute, the loose ball reached Cantona. With the Leeds defence pushing up towards the halfway line, Cantona's pass and Poborsky's run were timed to perfection.

Still Poborksy had work to do. Faced with the on-rushing goalkeeper Nigel Martyn, Poborsky composed himself and beat him with a tremendous strike that flew inside Martyn's right-hand post.

Marcus Gayle

October 19, 1996

Chelsea 2 WIMBLEDON 4

A goal by Gayle was worthy of guaranteeing Wimbledon a club-record seventh successive Premiership win for the Dons.

After losing their first three Premiership matches, Wimbledon's surge up the table continued with a deserved win against the millionaires of Chelsea.

A long ball from defence found the head of Efan Ekoku. His nod down was collected by Gayle, who powered past the Chelsea defence before unleashing an unstoppable left-foot shot from 20 yards that flew into the top-right corner of Kevin Hitchcock's net.

David Ginola

October 20, 1996

NEWCASTLE UNITED 5 Manchester United 0

The clash of 1995-96's top two sides promised to be entertaining, but nobody could have predicted Newcastle's 5-0 victory.

The catalyst for the remarkable win was David Ginola's brilliant goal in the 30th minute that gave Newcastle a two-goal advantage.

Receiving a pass on the corner of the penalty area, Ginola turned sharply and curled a magnificent shot beyond Peter Schmeichel, who could only stand and admire the breathtaking skill of the Frenchman.

Dean Sturridge

December 7, 1996

Arsenal 2 DERBY COUNTY 2

Arsenal were beginning to start a very real Premiership challenge under Arsene Wenger, their new manager, but Derby shocked Highbury with an away draw that boasted one of the best strikes of the season from Dean Sturridge.

In the 62nd minute, with Derby trailing 1-0, Sturridge picked up a long clearance from defence. Hovering on the left wing, he had 40 yards to goal with no team-mate supporting him. It did not matter.

He beat Tony Adams with an excellent dummy and slammed a fierce 20-yard shot that flew past John Lukic and into the net, via the crossbar, to leave Highbury aghast and set up County for an excellent and deserved away point.

Eric Cantona

December 21, 1996

MANCHESTER UNITED 5 Sunderland 0

A five-goal mauling for Sunderland also saw one of the best goals of Eric Cantona's spectacular United career.

In the 79th minute, Cantona, already with one goal to his credit for the afternoon, gained possession just five yards inside the Sunderland half. He twisted, turned and tricked his way past two opponents before playing a one-two with Brian McClair.

By now McClair's pass left Cantona on the edge of the penalty area and, with goalkeeper Lionel Perez setting himself for the low shot, Cantona improvised as only he could.

His delicate chip was perfection, hitting the angle of crossbar and post to leave Perez stranded and Cantona soaking up the overwhelming applause from the United fans.

David Beckham

January 12, 1997

Tottenham Hotspur 1 MANCHESTER UNITED 2

Another spectacular long-range winner from Beckham, but this time delivered with an ironic twist. As a schoolboy, Beckham had trained with Tottenham but then left to join United, and how he made United fans grateful with a wonderful goal 15 minutes from time.

Tottenham looked to be holding United to a hard-earned point when Beckham received the ball on the halfway line and set off for goal. With space opening up for him, he hit a screamer which swerved viciously away from Ian Walker and into the top-left corner of the England goalkeeper's net.

Such moments, over in the blink of an eye, can make or break a season.

Faustino Asprilla

March 10, 1997

Liverpool 4 NEWCASTLE UNITED 3

For the second successive time, this fixture proved to be the match of the season, culminating in Liverpool's injury-time winner from Fowler.

It was hard luck on a Newcastle side that had clawed their way back from 3-0 down almost to snatch a point. Of the three goals in the comeback, their second showed the unquestionable skill of Faustino Asprilla.

David Ginola's magnificent 87th-minute pass put Asprilla through the Liverpool defence. With the ball at chest height and David James rushing out to meet him, Asprilla stuck out his right leg and lifted the ball over James and into the roof of the net for one of the most spectacular goals seen in the season.

Newcastle may have left the match empty-handed but they had more than played their part in a footballing spectacular, rich in thrills and spills and certain to be the centre point of many a reminiscence.

After the heartbreak of who lost or won, memories of the great goals are the jewels of the game to be handed down the generations.

Juninho

March 22, 1997

MIDDLESBROUGH 1 Chelsea 0

Middlesbrough were fighting a losing battle for their Premiership life and a victory was much needed against Ruud Gullit's Chelsea. The team was brimming with talent but not really gelling; however, the little Brazilian, as he did more than once during the season, won the game with a fantastic goal.

Juninho started the move in the 53rd minute, on the left touchline. He swerved past two defenders then advanced in-field before releasing Mikkel Beck down the left wing with a clever pass.

Instead of stopping to admire his work, Juninho continued his advance and when Beck's cross went into the area, the Brazilian's diving header at the near post gave Frode Grodas, in the Chelsea goal, no chance. Bryan Robson's team had collected three valuable points thanks to Juninho's vision, skill and bravery.

Paulo Wanchope

April 5, 1997

Manchester United 2 DERBY COUNTY 3

Derby were written off at Old Trafford by everyone but themselves. Instead they scored a truly memorable goal and collected three valuable points in their battle for Premiership survival.

Making his debut at the home of the champions did not scare Paulo Wanchope. Instead, 35 minutes into his Derby career, the Costa Rican scored an amazing goal. Stationed on the halfway line, wide on the right, he seemed to be running up a dark alley when faced with United's defensive line, but he shuffled his way past it and side-footed a right foot shot from the edge of the penalty area past a bemused Peter Schmeichel.

The Managers *by Aubrey Ganguly*

Passion personified by managers Gordon Strachan (Coventry) and Jim Smith (Derby)

Alex Ferguson in a familiar role with the Carling Premiership Trophy

A golf course somewhere in Britain. Kenny Dalglish and his former Liverpool and Scotland teammate Alan Hansen are enjoying a leisurely 18 holes. But just as Dalglish prepares to address the ball, his colleague interrupts with a question:

"Do you think I would have made a good football manager?"

On the face of it, a reasonable query. Hansen, after all, is not without experience. In a career that saw him win practically every honour in the game, he must have learned a thing or two. And he already enjoys something of a reputation for his post-match TV analyses.

But Dalglish pauses for less than a second: "Nah, not passionate enough," he sniffs, before returning to the shot at hand.

The laid-back Hansen takes the verdict with his customary cool detachment but the scene, from the BBC documentary 'The Sack Race', revealed one of the key elements for a successful managerial career. After all, when did you last hear Alex Ferguson described as 'laid-back'?

Despite a haul of trophies second to none in recent years, the Manchester United manager retains that vital element - a hunger for success. Now in his mid-fifties, he still arrives for work two hours before anyone else and is the last to leave. And if the down side of this is that he can appear a touch obsessive (witness his stopwatch antics on the touchline), it's hardly surprising. This is a job, after all, where you can win the title one season and then have the critics calling for your dismissal just a few months later – as happened to the United boss in 1995.

Of course, Ferguson survived the criticism that came following the sales of Ince, Kanchelskis and Hughes and went on to achieve the 'double-double'. But he had already established a good track record. Other managers have not been so fortunate because, quite simply, the modern game does not tolerate failure.

The last few seasons have seen one managerial casualty after another as clubs strive for instant success. Of the 20 teams who started the 1996-97 season, only two of them have kept the same manager since the Premiership began in 1992. One is Manchester United, the other is Wimbledon.

The south London club appointed Joe Kinnear in May 1992 on the back of one of the most bizarre CVs in football. From barrow boy in a fruit-and-veg market to training Sherpas on a mountain top, via five-a-sides with the King of Malaysia, Kinnear was perhaps the ideal candidate to take over the Crazy Gang.

Never afraid to call a spade a spade (or a journalist something far worse!), the former Tottenham and Republic of Ireland player set about transforming the club from a gritty bunch of survivors to a flourishing side capable of producing both attractive and effective football. Impressive performances in both the FA and Coca-Cola Cups, as well as the 1996-97 Premiership, were enough to earn the Dons' boss a 'Manager of the Year' award from Sky Television.

However, as Kinnear once stated that his ultimate ambition was to manage Tottenham Hotspur, his recent success won't have reassured Gerry Francis, who struggled at times with a squad wracked with injuries. To add to his woes, the 1996-97 season ended with striker Teddy Sheringham putting in a transfer request and the manager knows better results will be expected. Although, unlike some bosses, Francis at least has the reassurance of interests outside the game should it all go wrong – a flourishing antiques business – and he has already made it clear that he will walk away from football if the pressures get too great.

Fresh to face the Premiership challenge are Steve Coppell (above) and Danny Wilson

This is a course of action that Steve Coppell has already taken. Now back in his second spell as boss at Crystal Palace, Coppell hit the headlines in 1996 when he resigned from Manchester City after only six games, citing health reasons. His subsequent recovery saw a return to Selhurst Park and promotion for Palace via the play-offs. But, together with Barnsley's Danny Wilson and Bolton's Colin Todd, Coppell has one of the most difficult jobs in football: keeping a newly-promoted side in the Premiership for more than one season.

All three managers will be hoping to repeat the successes of Jim Smith and Martin O'Neill, who proved in the 1996-97 season that survival is possible if you organise your team to play to its strengths and invest wisely when financial resources are made available.

Jim Smith knew only too well that many saw Derby as relegation favourites in 1996-97. But with 37 years in the game, including 24 as a manager, he also knew how to approach the task of avoiding the drop. And the inspired addition of Aljosa Asanovic to an already well-organised side saw relegation comfortably avoided.

O'Neill went one better, not only escaping relegation but winning the Coca-Cola Cup. He seems to have instilled in his team his own tenacious attitude and, in doing so, has made Leicester a difficult team to beat.

If further proof is needed that good management can transform a club, you can look no further for an example than Danny Wilson, and Barnsley's metamorphosis from First Division also-rans to Premiership new boys.

In 1994, the club finished 18th in the First Division. Poor crowds, little money and few prospects are hardly the ingredients for future success and Wilson's appointment as manager that summer was certainly not regarded as a new dawn by the fans.

Chairman John Dennis was committed to investing in the development of the stadium and made it clear to Wilson that, at least initially, any success would have to be coached rather than bought. Unfazed, Wilson encouraged his team to play entertaining football and give the fans something to cheer about. The former Bury, Chesterfield, Nottingham Forest, Brighton, Luton, Sheffield Wednesday and

Martin O'Neill and Alex Ferguson tasted success in 1996-97

Northern Ireland player believed that results would come if the players were prepared to combine a relaxed passing game with disciplined defending.

It may sound Utopian but the following season Barnsley finished tenth, the next they were up to sixth – all without spending any money on new players – and then came the fairy-tale ending that even their fans could hardly believe. Barnsley won promotion and entered the top flight for the first time in their history. In doing so, Danny Wilson has proved what is possible when a manager gets the best from his team.

It's a trick Harry Redknapp and Gordon Strachan might appreciate. Both managers suffered with teams that failed to follow instructions and only late surges kept West Ham and Coventry in the Premiership.

Of course, Strachan's countryman George Graham never looked that likely to face the drop at Leeds. After all, it's hard to lose games if you never concede goals. But while the former Arsenal boss has again proved that he can build a defence, he still has some way to go before Leeds achieve the kind of success seen at Highbury in the late 1980s.

Arsene Wenger, Arsenal's French lieutenant

Meanwhile, as Graham attempts to turn Leeds into his former side, his former side are busy undergoing a transformation of their own. Since Arsene Wenger arrived in north London, Arsenal have become (gulp, whisper it!) entertaining. The French revolution in N5 appears to please both fans and players, with some of the Arsenal squad dating back to the Graham era now playing the best football of their career.

On the other side of the Thames, renovations are also going on at Chelsea. While Ken Bates turns Stamford Bridge into Disneyland, with an ever-increasing number of chalets, hotels and leisure complexes planned, manager Ruud Gullit has introduced a continental approach and a European flavour to the side, and has reaped rewards in the FA Cup.

Less spectacularly, Brian Little has been busy turning Aston Villa into an efficient outfit and David Pleat is attempting the same at Sheffield Wednesday. However, while the jury is still out on the developments at Blackburn, Everton and Southampton, they could soon reach a verdict on Roy Evans.

Roy Evans aims to keep the Anfield flag flying

The Liverpool boss knows that after coming close, but not close enough, to the Premiership title in the last few years, time may be running out. Liverpool are not a club that enjoy being out of the limelight. And while Evans has created an attractive and, on their day, exceptional team, consistency and backbone are necessities that he'll have to instill if they are to attain the kind of success enjoyed in the days of Shankly and Paisley.

Or, of course, Kenny Dalglish, which is where we came in. The former Liverpool and Blackburn manager's record is second only to Alex Ferguson's in the modern era, and with both of them involved in the Champions League, Dalglish poses the biggest threat to the United manager's crown.

Another in the long line of canny Scottish managers, Dalglish has already shown at St. James' that he'll take no prisoners in his quest to achieve honours.

Nonetheless, he was still a bit harsh with Hansen.

Cult Heroes and Crowd Pleasers *by Chris Dighton*

Take one loyal servant, one cult hero, add nine other men and what do you have? The answer: a football team. Up and down the land, from the Sunday lunchtime O'Boozers XI through to the Manchester Uniteds of this world, the ingredients, in varying degrees, are the same.

There are Premiership players who have been with their club for what seems like forever and a day. The idea of, say, Tottenham being without Gary Mabbutt is akin to the ravens deserting the Tower of London.

Mabbutt and Spurs came together in the 1982-83 season when he joined them from Bristol Rovers and since then the milestones have been ticked off; 100 games played, 200, 300 then 400. On and on it goes through the pain and hurt of outrageous fortune to both club and self.

Steve Ogrizovic, Coventry's 'keeper for 12 years and more

The most loyal of them all tend to be goalkeepers. And perhaps this is because age gives them a lease of life a good many years beyond that of the outfield player. Secondly, the nature of the job makes them possessive. They own their own penalty areas, they own the No 1 shirt and they are not moving for anyone.

Running down Premiership records of club appearances, you often find the men with a good record for one-club appearances are goalkeepers. Steve Ogrizovic joined Coventry in the 1984-85 season and has recorded more than 450 games with the first team. Neville Southall entered stage centre for Everton in the 1981-82 season and by the end of the 1996-97 campaign had gone past 550 appearances for the club. Nigel Martyn arrived at Leeds United after more than 250 games for Crystal Palace and will probably become an Elland Road fixture.

If absolute proof of the goalkeep-

O'Leary

Callaghan

Cork

Big Jack

THE FAITHFUL

TEAM	PLAYER/APPEARANCES/SEASONS		
ARSENAL	David O'Leary	558	1975-93
ASTON VILLA	Charlie Aitken	561	1961-76
BARNSLEY	Barry Murphy	514	1962-78
BLACKBURN ROVERS	Derek Fazackerley	596	1970-86
BOLTON WANDERERS	Eddie Hopkinson	519	1956-70
CHELSEA	Ron Harris	655	1962-80
COVENTRY CITY	George Curtis	486	1956-70
CRYSTAL PALACE	Jim Cannon	571	1973-88
DERBY COUNTY	Kevin Hector	486	1966-78
EVERTON	Neville Southall	566	1981-
LEEDS UNITED	Jack Charlton	629	1953-73
LEICESTER CITY	Adam Black	528	1920-35
LIVERPOOL	Ian Callaghan	640	1960-78
MANCHESTER UNITED	Bobby Charlton	606	1956-73
NEWCASTLE UNITED	Jim Lawrence	432	1904-22
SHEFFIELD WEDNESDAY	Andy Wilson	502	1900-20
SOUTHAMPTON	Terry Paine	713	1956-74
TOTTENHAM HOTSPUR	Steve Perryman	655	1969-86
WEST HAM UNITED	Billy Bonds	663	1967-88
WIMBLEDON	Alan Cork	439	1977-92

ers' longevity was needed, it came in the 1996-97 season when Peter Shilton, in his late 40s, played his 1000th match – the milestone passed with Leyton Orient. Shilton's epic career – and there can be no other description for it – kicked off before England won the World Cup in 1966 and has gone on and on and on, proving conclusively where there is a will, there is a way.

During that time, Shilton was a fixture at a number of clubs: he made almost 300 League appearances for Leicester, 100-plus for Stoke, 200 and more for both Nottingham Forest and Derby County and almost 200 for Southampton. Throw in another half-dozen clubs or so where he has filled in between the posts and you have a one-man living history of modern professional football.

Out on the pitch are other durable servants and no-one stands out as more special than Tony Adams. He came through the Arsenal ranks

Sir Bobby

Paine

Southall

Bonds

Tony Adams stands out in the crowd, a special Arsenal favourite since the mid-eighties

Evergreen at Everton, Dave Watson is still a pin-up at Goodison

and debuted in the first team in the 1983-84 season. And there he has stayed. Now in his early 30s, there is no reason why Adams cannot carry on for Arsenal for a good few years yet and take his tally well over the 400 mark.

Intriguingly, Manchester United, a club perceived as buyers of instant disposable talent, have inspired remarkable allegiance to the cause. Steve Bruce, who left for Birmingham at the end of the 1995-96 season, clocked up more than 300 appearances, as had Brian McClair. Gary Pallister was around the same mark while Denis Irwin broke the 250 barrier.

In the fever of football the constant factor is the club. The fans know players and managers drift like so many corks in an ocean but when a man stays and gives his all, scoffing at talk of big-money moves and ambitions not fulfilled by his present team, then he is a pearl to be treasured.

All but a handful of clubs boast players who have worn the same colours for more than 200 matches. West Ham's Steve Potts, John Barnes at Liverpool, Leicester's Steve Walsh and Dave Watson at Everton are all in the 300 club. Honourable mention too for the members of the 200 club – men like Neil Redfearn at Barnsley, Chelsea club captain Steve Clarke, Colin Hendry in two spells at Blackburn and David Hirst for Sheffield Wednesday.

Every club, it seems, has a player who will run and run. Casting through the Premiership sides of today reveals that Southampton have had the king of the one-club men in Terry Paine, who between 1956 and 1974 played 713 League games for the club. Paine, capped 19 times by England, moved from Southampton to Hereford United where he ended his League career and in a nice act of symmetry announced his retirement in October 1976 – before a final game against Southampton.

The call for an encore, however, could not be resisted. Paine reappeared to fight Hereford's corner in a relegation battle and finally hung up his boots with 824 League matches in all to his credit.

Paine stands alone in the 700 club but there are some tough warriors in the 600 class. Ron 'Chopper' Harris at Chelsea clocked up 655 in 18 years at the club, Jack Charlton had 629 outings for Leeds United, brother Bobby 606 for Manchester United, Ian Callaghan 640 for Liverpool, Steve Perryman 655 for Tottenham and Billy Bonds 663 at West Ham.

Yet of all the record holders, those players who have bridged the generations, only one man has spanned the football revolution which led to the Premiership. David O'Leary made himself into Mr Arsenal, as dependable as the Bank of England when it came to the time for the buck to stop with the Arsenal defence. On 558 occasions he pulled on the famous Gunners shirt for a League match and six times he wore the colours in Premiership action – although he started just one of those matches.

Club captain Vinnie Jones demonstrates that never-say-die Wimbledon spirit

Long after their legs have given out, the loyal men are remembered by their clubs, canonised in programmes and recalled, sometimes through gritted teeth, by rivals' supporters. There can be fewer REAL honours in football.

Yet if the stamina is not up to carving footballing immortality via this route there is an alternative – become a cult hero. More often than not, however, the two go together in today's Premiership. The cult hero is a bit special and every team has one – a man who has become legend in his own playing time.

Come rain or shine, win, lose or draw, the cult hero can do no wrong, his every good move cherished, every mistake instantly forgiven and forgotten. What is the secret of this devoted and blind affection?

There is no ready answer. True, the cult heroes of today all have some common features but much of the aura has to do with the time and the place.

Vinnie Jones at Wimbledon is revered for his never say die attitude and his raw aggression but, above all that, a perceived devotion to the Dons, even though he has had spells at Leeds United, Sheffield United and Chelsea. Wimbledon fans, even during his three-and-a-bit seasons away, always regarded Vinnie as their man. And when he eventually came back, a whole flock of sheep was sacrificed to celebrate their prodigal's return. He has passed, in total, the 200 appearances barrier to score on the loyalty front as well.

Over at Upton Park, Julian Dicks received much the same treatment after he wandered off for a brief sojourn at Liverpool before returning more revered than ever by the West Ham faithful.

Yet for all their hardness, the snarling confrontations on the pitch, and occasionally off it too, both those men reveal slightly vulnerable, private-public faces which serve to make them more human and endear them to fans. Dicks, it is said by his wife Kay, is a domestic kitten not afraid of doing the washing-up.

Matt Le Tissier at Southampton is a different kettle of fish and the analogy

Paul McGrath, a survivor in the true sense of the word

is apt. His critics would say he is a big fish in a small pond at The Dell and he has sold himself short by not seeking to stretch his talents at one of the big clubs who would trample one another underfoot in the stampede to sign him.

But try explaining that to Southampton fans. Le Tissier is a class act who not only produces moments of sublime magic on the pitch but he has stayed faithful to the Saints since making his first-team debut in 1986. Modest about his talents, he seems positively reluctant to seek richer pastures and has gone through the 300 League appearance barrier at a canter – although the Paine marker is almost certainly out of sight.

There is also a talismanic quality to Le Tissier which is easier to explain. The fact used to be that if he was not in the side, Southampton stood no chance of winning – as proven by the results. The sequence was only broken in 1996 when Derby were beaten 3-1 at The Dell just before Christmas.

Le Tissier is all things to Southampton followers. Loyal, footballing magician and scorer of great goals. What more could you want at a club which down the years has fought countless battles against relegation and survived? Le Tissier has The Dell crowd eating out of his hand and the day will surely come when a stand is built in his honour.

Paul McGrath, who spent the 1996-97 season at Derby County, is one who has become a legend both for his determination on the pitch and for his lifestyle. Whoever he has served he has done them proud, from Manchester United, Aston Villa through to Derby. Age should have finished him, as should his dodgy knees. But McGrath is a survivor in the truest sense of the word.

The Republic of Ireland player had a reputation for high living, for going absent without leave and for being so physically shot that all he could manage was to play the matches and go home. But did he, when it came to a game of football, ever let anyone down? Never.

Favourites old and new . . . Le Tissier a Saint forever and Zola in his first fantastic spell at the Bridge

Then there are the instant cult heroes made by the indefinable force of personality, aided and abetted by a world-class reputation. In itself that is not enough because the burden of expectation can bring many a great player to his knees. Gianfranco Zola at Chelsea, however, has gracefully skated past the pitfalls and enhanced his standing by living up to his billing. That is no easy task in the face of the in-bred cynicism of the English and a still-evident, deep mistrust of foreign imports to the game who are too often viewed as being here to take the money and run.

That of course could not be said of Juninho, diminutive of size, a giant of heart. Crowd pleasing is about skill and daring; it is about making up for your shortcomings with heartfelt determination; it is about devotion to club and fans.

David Ginola and Faustino Asprilla could weave magic for Newcastle and be darlings of the crowd for weeks on end and Robbie Fowler could bang in goals from now until the end of time – yet none of these three quite makes it to cult hero status. The same too is true of Gary Lineker, one of the finest strikers to have appeared for England. Cult heroes revive memories of great moments for their club as well as moments of high humour and sometimes bitter disappointment. They are, for the period of their employment, the living, breathing, vibrant colour of their club.

Ultimately the essential make-up of the cult hero is about having a star aura, a quality that cannot be manufactured or learned. Quite simply it is called panache. You are, or you are not, born to be a cult hero. You have or you don't have the lungs, legs and will to be the most loyal of servants.

Supporters' Clubs *by Iain Spragg*

Football is caught in a fast flow of change that is sweeping away tradition and history and shedding the image of the manager's faithful old sheepskin jacket. Carnaby Street chic circa 1960s will not do in the techno 1990s. But some things never change.

The Premiership now boasts some of the game's biggest and brightest stars from around the globe; in Alan Shearer, a £15-million striker who is the envy of the world; and a league which is compared favourably with the best Italy, Spain or Germany can offer. New stadiums have sprouted up around the country offering high-tech facilities, but one thing which hasn't been transformed beyond recognition in the football revolution is the fan – the lifeblood of the game.

All over the country, there are still thousands upon thousands of diehard devotees who live and breathe the dramas of their club. Life revolves around the team; a good or bad week is defined by the 90 minutes of football played on the Saturday.

This army of fans are some of the most dedicated, if not fanatical, in the world and many are members of the supporters' clubs where they find kindred spirits to whom the fortunes of the team are almost a matter of life and death.

Every Premiership club has at least one supporters' club, so that the like-minded can get together to celebrate or commiserate and they are not just parochial. All over the world are groups of fans who band together to share their enthusiasm and passion for their club. Liverpool can boast a supporters' club in Malaysia, Manchester United one in New York, and Coventry City one in the Philippines. Australia is a hot-bed for the long-distant fan who is as emotionally involved with his or her side as ever. The ties that bind span many an ocean.

These days you can get married on the pitch of your favourite club and the number of requests for the ashes of the dearly departed to be spread on pitches is rising by the week. Football is, as you see, a life-and-death matter.

In England, however, the traditional perception of the supporters' club is little more than an association for arranging match tickets and cheap travel to away games. Few people realise how active the supporters' clubs are – it is not just on match days that they benefit the fans.

The Football Supporters Association (FSA), formed in the wake of the Heysel tragedy in 1985, is a nationwide organisation which typifies the more involved, often political, role that supporters' groups are now taking in the game. Best summed up as a consumer pressure group for fans, the FSA offers an outlet for the voice of supporters to be heard by the game's governing bodies. One of the FSA's major campaigning successes was its part in the removal of perimeter fencing at grounds, in the interests of safety, during the Lord Justice Taylor inquiry following the Hillsborough disaster.

It was also to the forefront when the controversy over the now-abandoned ID card scheme erupted, collecting 250,000 fans' signatures in protest – a perfect illustration of how the FSA has acted as the supporters' collective voice at a time when they were not being heard. The FSA also maintains a register of solicitors who are clued up on football law so that any fan can be sure he will get the right legal representation.

Another prominent fans' group which ensures the grassroots of football are not overlooked is the National Federation of Football Supporters' Clubs (NFFSC), which celebrated its 70th anniversary in January 1997 and is also a part of the Advisory Group Against Racism and Intimidation.

In recent years the NFFSC has successfully campaigned for a minimum 10 per cent ticket allocation for visiting fans at Premiership matches and continues to support standing areas at grounds where the fans want it, arguing that terracing is not inherently dangerous and that people standing on seats presents its own dangers.

Away from the politics of the game, however, supporters' clubs are just as active socially. Sometimes hundreds of miles away from their beloved clubs, fans still gather together to debate and celebrate the exploits of their team.

The Association of Provincial Football Supporters' Club in London (APFSCIL) boasts member clubs from Southampton to Sheffield and Barnsley to Blackburn, who have joined together because of their love of football.

Formed in the mid-1970s, APFSCIL has grown from a handful of supporters' groups to a 54-member body which now represents over 8,000 fans in the capital and is a social focal point for its many members. In addition to London-wide pool and darts leagues, APFSCIL runs numerous football leagues and an annual five-a-side tournament, which gives the member clubs an opportunity to avenge defeats suffered by their teams in the 'other' league.

The annual presentation evening, held at The Oval cricket ground in south London, is the highlight of the year and has attracted the likes of Mick McCarthy, the Republic of Ireland manager, and Brendon Batson, the chief executive of the PFA, in recent years.

The growth of supporters' groups like FSA and APFSCIL, both politically and socially, reflects the healthy state of football in England today but also ensures the fans are not forgotten as the game becomes increasingly commercialised and glamorous.

Supporters' clubs are vital if football is to continue to enjoy its rebirth in the eyes of the public. They guarantee the fans have a say in how the game is run, as well as providing fun and games away from the dramas on the pitch. Few would disagree that happier fans make for a happier sport.

Mick McCarthy and (below) Brendon Batson enjoyed fun with the fans at their annual get-together

Brits Abroad

by Sarah Winterburn

Paul Ince, hard at work on his Italian job

Gossip and rumour . . . football thrives on them as much as it thrives on goals. Yet the talk, in both pub and on paper, is often more fantasy than reality. After all, if some of the rumours circulating during the 1996-97 Premiership season are to be believed, it would not have been surprising to see Ryan Giggs playing in the famous colours of Inter Milan while avoiding a fierce tackle from David Beckham – who would be clad in the black-and-white of Juventus. A classic case, you might say, of the Englishman abroad and the Welshman abroad – exports worth their weight in footballing gold.

After all, John Charles ploughed that furrow back in the 1956-57 season when he quadrupled his maximum English wage of £15 per week, collected a signing-on fee of £10,000 and was involved in a £65,000 record-breaking transfer from Leeds United to Juventus.

The reality of the 1996-97 season, however, was that Ryan Giggs was playing in the traditional red of Manchester United and failing to avoid tackles from Borussia Dortmund's Paul Lambert, the ex-St Mirren and Motherwell midfielder lining up in the colours of the German champions alongside rather more familiar names like Karl-Heinz Riedle, Matthias Sammer and Paolo Sousa.

Lambert is one of the few British players to be plying his trade on the continent, because despite a steady stream of rumours about our home-grown football talent being exported, the actual trade in British players and managers is less brisk than it has been in the past. The pattern has changed.

Back at the start of the 1990s, the likes of Paul Gascoigne, David Platt, Ian Rush and Des Walker wanted to play quality football for quality money – so they went to Italy. Times have changed and today the biggest money may well be found in Newcastle or Manchester, and, if Italian culture proves to be a lure, then Stamford Bridge is probably a more apt destination.

The strength and sheer magnitude of English football may have stemmed the flow of big-name talent out of the country, but the new open era in Europe has also allowed some of Britain's lesser-known footmen to scale previously unassailable heights.

Followers of British clubs in Europe have seen Lambert help Borussia Dortmund to stifle Manchester United and he then went on to win a European Cup winner's medal when Dortmund beat Juventus 3-1 in the final. Another Scotsman abroad, John Colllins, helped Monaco to destroy Newcastle United in the Uefa Cup.

"I'm lucky to be a footballer at the time of the Bosman business," says Collins, Scotland international and regular in the Monaco side. "It's the best thing that could have happened to me."

Collins was signed by the French club on a free transfer after Euro 96, Celtic being forced to let him go at the end of his contract after turning down £2 million offers from Middlesbrough, Chelsea and Everton during the season. The deal left Celtic not only penniless but minus one of their most experienced players. The Bosman ruling had shifted the goalposts and player-power was all strong. Collins, after a word from Glenn Hoddle in the ear of his former club Monaco, made a move to one of France's classier sides.

The winner in all this, as if you need to be told, is Collins. His game has clearly benefited from the move away from the internal wranglings of Celtic and the fierce competition of Glasgow for the more serene surroundings of Monaco, under the guidance of Jean Tigana. Newcastle would certainly agree with that, for Collins played more than a bit-part in their European downfall.

Another man who has certainly grabbed a new opportunity with firmly outstretched hands is Tony Cascarino, sometimes an object of derision in his native country but a well-respected striker in his adopted home of France. We remember the name and the stories of how he was once bought for a set of tracksuits but, over the last few years, mention of Cascarino has led to that 'where is he now?' question.

He was given a free transfer by Chelsea in 1994 but did not relish the idea of ending his career with Lincoln City. The thought of going, initially, to Marseille was a good deal more appetising.

"In England I never did myself justice," says Cascarino, now with another French club, Nancy. "Perhaps I didn't take it seriously enough. But in those days, I just sat back and said to myself: 'Nice job, good pay, a few goals. Enjoy it'.

Tony Cascarino, in fierce action here for the Republic of Ireland, opted for a quieter life in France

"I realised on leaving Chelsea that I had to do something. Marseille represented my last chance. I knew that if I didn't do it with Marseille there were not a lot of options left open to me. I'm chuffed with what I've done here, not just scoring goals and making a success of the move but the way I've fitted in and learned to live a different life.

"It's lovely to open your windows in December and see the sun streaming through. I wasn't the most enthusiastic when it came to training, but I get up in the morning now and really look forward to it. In England I'd go for a beer or two after training. There's none of that in France.

"Maybe I could have done more for Chelsea, but that is all in the past. It would be great to prove something to people back home, but I am just thinking about what I could do over here. I have no thoughts about going back to England. I have no ambitions at all in that direction – I'm just enjoying what I am doing here."

Far outweighing the rumours of an exodus to foreign fields has been the return of Paul Ince, England's only current international to be playing overseas in the 1996-97 season. He joined Inter Milan in 1995 and his return was a constant source of speculation from the minute he touched down on Italian soil.

Even so, Ince himself never claimed he was unhappy playing in Italy. During one interview there, he said: "The Italian fans idolise me, they love me. Playing

Bobby Robson and yet another trophy. It's the European Cup-Winners' Cup bound for Barcelona

in Italy has helped me a lot. It has taught me to stand on my feet a little more than I used to."

Many factors had to be considered before, finally, he agreed to join Liverpool in July 1997 for a fee of £4.2 million.

The football trade movement has not just been restricted to players. Managers have also criss-crossed Europe. England has attracted the Dutchman Ruud Gullit, who took Chelsea to a memorable FA Cup triumph, and the Frenchman Arsene Wenger, who has stamped his mark on Arsenal and shaped them for the future.

But perhaps the most remarkable story is that of Roy Hodgson, back at home and in charge of Blackburn Rovers. His is an adventure of a footballer who never even became a journeyman professional but, as a coach, he has been one of the leading lights and was, until the end of the 1996-97 season, Ince's boss in Milan.

Hodgson first coached in South Africa, had an unhappy stint at Bristol City but then made his mark with Orebero in Sweden. He took them to the second division championship then moved to Malmo, where his success made the footballing world sit up and look. First Malmo gave Inter Milan a scare in the 1988 European Cup and then, in 1989, they beat the Italian giants.

Hodgson moved to Switzerland and struggled with the football politics, but he still ended up on the rise, being appointed national coach and leading the country to the World Cup – for the first time since 1966 and beating Italy in the qualifying stages.

Inter, who had not been managed by an Englishman since Jesse Carver in the middle 1950s, came calling but such is the intensity of the job that nothing other than win-after-win is acceptable and third place in Serie A, where they finished, is not good enough. Any slip leads to the gears of the rumour mill grinding noisily and that sort of result leads to deafening calls for the coach's head.

Bobby Robson knows all about that too. He won the European Cup Winners' Cup, the Spanish Cup and the Spanish League Cup with Barcelona in 1996-97 and had a track record which had seen him transform Ipswich in England, lead England to a World Cup semi-final and then perform wonders with Porto in Portugal.

Yet 1996-97 was regarded by the Barcelona faithful as a year of underachievement. Why? Because Real Madrid won the Spanish League title and Barcelona finished second!

The lure to go abroad, however, will not fade. Graeme Souness saved Southampton from relegation from the Premiership in May 1997 and then quit the club to take charge at Torino in Italy. There seems to be no end to the traffic both back and forth across the Channel and into a Europe with no frontiers.

For the time being the Premiership is without doubt one of the best, if not THE best, league in the world, the place where the top stars want to play. Yet for some players a sense of adventure will prove too great a bait; the desire to head for new lands and seek a fortune will be a pull like the tide, too hard to resist.

England is the place to be but, even so, one feels there's some corner of a foreign football field that is forever England.

Roy Hodgson, back home after years of success abroad

New Carling Premiership Stars

by Sarah Winterburn

Three to watch: Chris Perry of Wimbledon (left), Stephen Hughes of Arsenal (top) and Leicester's Emile Heskey

In a year when readers of *The Sun* grew accustomed to seeing the word 'samba' on their back pages, and readers of the *Telegraph* frequently shook hands with 'foreign influx' while perusing their sports pull-out, perhaps the real Premiership revelations were the Brits who played for the league's less fashionable clubs.

Wimbledon and Leicester were the 'unlikely lads' who tasted success beyond anything their respective followers could have hoped, and the men behind the results were not £6 million signings from Inter Milan or free transfers from Barcelona with £40,000 a-week price tags, but young British players who now find themselves on the brink of international selection after holding their own in the best league in the world.

At Leicester all the talk is of Emile 'Bruno' Heskey, the Bruno coming from

Neil Sullivan rose from the Wimbledon junior ranks to 'keeper for Scotland

his stature, determination and fighting spirit. This nickname does no justice to his speed, intelligence and talent. Frank Bruno never looked this promising.

"Every time I see him he looks to have improved and at this stage that is the most important thing," says Gary Lineker of the man challenging his crown as the most talented striker to emerge from Filbert Street. "He is so quick and strong. He has tremendous talent and potential. Leicester can't go and buy an Alan Shearer but they've got one of their own."

Heskey is still only a teenager but earns £3,000 a week after signing a two-and-a-half year deal with his hometown club – pledging his immediate future to them despite interest from top clubs in the country. His future may eventually lie elsewhere, but he has probably ensured that his first full England appearance will be made as a Leicester player.

"Heskey is one of the outstanding talents in this country and it has given us peace of mind – and him as well – to know he is with us for a good while," says manager Martin O'Neill of his most astounding protege. "I know he's happy here because he's getting games regularly, which might not be the case if he were with one of the bigger clubs. We will look after him. He knows that."

Heskey's attitude is rare in someone so young, rejecting the lure of the big money, big lights and big rewards of other clubs for the safety and consistency of life at Leicester.

"When I was 15, the most I thought I'd be getting at this stage was a run in the reserves," says Heskey. "I realise that young players can do too much too quickly and then burn out, but I'm confident that won't happen to me.

"I'm from Leicester and I only lived down the road from this place, even though I supported Liverpool as a boy and hero-worshipped John Barnes. I couldn't be playing higher than the Premiership anyway, and by living at home I can keep my feet on the ground with my family and friends around me."

Also thumbing their noses at the critics are Wimbledon, always the first name on the betting list for relegation, but in 1996-97 there was a different story to be told at Selhurst Park as the Dons' band of Merry Men all hit form at exactly the same time. Foremost among these are a couple of players whose potential was never in question, but the realisation was far, far better than the promise.

In goal was Neil Sullivan, a man who had risen up through the junior ranks at Wimbledon. At the beginning of the season he was an object of derision as he was beaten from some distance by first David Beckham and then David Batty. But by the Spring, there was little laughter as he became a part of the Scotland set-up and was acknowledged as one of the finest young goalkeepers in the country.

"In a funny way, the Beckham goal has been the making of me. I shot to fame because of it," says Sullivan. "Suddenly everyone knew my name. People were watching me to see what would happen next and I kept four or five clean sheets on the trot."

One fan is Alex Ferguson, no mean judge of young talent himself. He is also impressed with the Dons' defender Chris Perry, tipping him for a place in the England team in the not-too-distant future. He said: "If it was down to me I wouldn't hesitate to put him in the England squad. He's class and I really believe he could play at international level."

"Alex would be on the phone to me like a shot if he thought we'd consider selling Chrissy Perry and he's got three England defenders at the club," says Perry's manager Joe Kinnear. "Not much chance of us letting him go, though. There are not many centre-halves as consistent as Chris in the Premiership. He's got pace, great judgement and jumps like a stag for such a small lad."

Ferguson may have more than an eye on the prime candidate to become only the second Wimbledon player to represent England, but he has more than his own share of young talent to keep him busy. Although the names of Scholes, Butt and Beckham are now achingly familiar to anyone who has seen his team destroyed by United, in 1996-97 they made the important move from squad members to becoming regular starters for England.

Frank Leboeuf has more glory in his sights at Chelsea

David Beckham signalled his intent for the season with his halfway-line lob of Neil Sullivan in the opening game. The following month he made his debut appearance in the England side, adding international caps to his collection of championship medals. He is now seen as the future of the English midfield – a fine accolade for a man barely out of his teens.

"Beckham is ahead of his age," says England coach Glenn Hoddle. "My theory about experience is nothing to do with grey hair. It's about whether you can be experienced in doing the right things. You can be that at a very young age."

Hoddle's respect clearly stretches to Beckham's teammate Nicky Butt, the England coach giving him his first international cap in the friendly against Mexico. And with Paul Scholes proving he has the consistency to deserve a regular Premiership berth, it can only be a matter of time before the third young gun takes the step up.

But in a Manchester United side full of skilful internationals, these young players are forced to strain for the zenith of their game in order to earn respect. For Lee Bowyer the situation is a little different – he shines in a Leeds team not noted for its flair, but rather for its grit. However, he has made the most of a difficult situation and has himself featured in the full England squad.

One name which may not be in Glenn Hoddle's mind now but could feature in the near future is Arsenal's Stephen Hughes. He may only have been in the reckoning at Arsenal for a matter of months, but he has proved impervious to the pressures of playing in the Premiership. For whatever the pressure facing a young Brit, the stress must be multiplied when you come attached to a pricetag.

"On my debut for Arsenal, against Sheffield Wednesday, my knees were trembling as I sat on the bench," says Patrick Vieira. "I wanted so badly to play,

***Overleaf:* Emile Heskey on the attack**

WALKERS
CRISPS

to get out there and show my new team what I could do. Then the singing started and I was almost too excited to play well."

But play well he did, and has continued to do so. Across the capital two more new arrivals have become the darlings of Stamford Bridge. Franck Leboeuf's arrival may not have created the same hoo-ha as that of Gianfranco Zola, but close watchers of Chelsea will note that his contribution has been equal to that of the little Italian.

"Chelsea believe in me," said Zola on his arrival at the club. "This is a great opportunity for me and for my career. I am not bothered where Chelsea ask me to play. I want to play where I can do the best job possible for my team."

One player who arrived without so much as a welcoming fanfare, bought almost entirely as striking back-up, was Manchester United's Ole Gunnar Solskjaer. Few could have predicted the impact that the Norwegian with the babyface would have on a team which already boasted a large handful of international superstars.

But perhaps the biggest impact made by any 'continental' player was Fabrizio Ravanelli at Middlesbrough, who was reputed to be earning £42,000 a week. Controversy surrounded the Italian every step of the way, the silver-haired striker sparking rumours of his departure before he had barely got his north-east bearings. But Ravanelli's respect for Bryan Robson saw him give his all in the 1996-97 season.

"One of the reasons I joined this club is because of him," said Ravanelli. "He has a standing in the world of soccer. He would not allow people like me simply to take their wages and not give blood for the cause. I will be happy to give blood for Middlesbrough."

That sort of dedication for such a struggling outfit cannot purely be the work of £42,000 a week, and the 1996-97 season's work of Aljosa Asanovic at Derby and Eyal Berkovich at Southampton are also proof that a player of true quality shines through whatever the talents of his teammates.

And as long as these success stories outweigh the Nikola Jerkan and Orlando Trustfull stories, the word 'samba' will become as familiar a term in the football dictionary as 'a game of two halves'.

David Beckham shooting for more glory with United

Ravanelli was the shining star at Middlesbrough with goals galore in his debut season

Ins and Outs – The £2m+ Carling Premiership Transfers

Alan Shearer – £15 million

Juninho – £12 million

Dennis Bergkamp – £7.5million

Andy Cole – £7 million

PLAYER	FROM	TO	FEE	DATE
Alan Shearer	Blackburn	Newcastle	£15m	Aug 96
Juninho	Middlesbro'	Atletico Madrid	£12m	Jun 97
Stan Collymore	Nott'm For.	Liverpool	£8.5m	Jun 95
Andrei Kanchelskis	Everton	Fiorentina	£8m	Jan 97
Paul Ince	Man Utd	Inter Milan	£7.5m	Jun 95
Dennis Bergkamp	Inter Milan	Arsenal	£7.5m	Jun 95
Andy Cole	Newcastle	Man Utd	£7m	Jan 95
Fabrizio Ravanelli	Juventus	Middlesbro'	£7m	Jul 96
Stan Collymore	Liverpool	Aston Villa	£7m	May 97
Marc Overmars	Ajax	Arsenal	£7m	Jun 97
Faustino Asprilla	Parma	Newcastle	£6.7m	Feb 96
Les Ferdinand	QPR	Newcastle	£6m	Jun 95
Les Ferdinand	Newcastle	Tottenham	£6m	Jul 97
Nick Barmby	Middlesbro'	Everton	£5.75m	Oct 96
Nick Barmby	Tottenham	Middlesbro'	£5.25m	Aug 95
Chris Sutton	Norwich	Blackburn	£5m	Jul 94
Andrei Kanchelskis	Man Utd	Everton	£5m	Jul 95
Paul Merson	Arsenal	Middlesbro'	£5m	Jul 97
Graeme Le Saux	Blackburn	Chelsea	£5m	Aug 97
Henning Berg	Blackburn	Man Utd	£5m	Aug 97
Roberto Di Matteo	Lazio	Chelsea	£4.9m	Jul 96
David Platt	Sampdoria	Arsenal	£4.75m	Jul 95
Juninho	Soa Paulo	Middlesbro'	£4.75m	Oct 95
Chris Armstrong	Crystal P.	Tottenham	£4.5m	Jun 95

Roberto Ravanelli – £7 million

Teddy Sheringham– £3.5 million

Faustino Asprilla – £6.7 million

PLAYER	FROM	TO	FEE	DATE
Jason McAteer	Bolton	Liverpool	£4.5m	Sep 95
Tomas Brolin	Parma	Leeds	£4.5m	Nov 95
Lee Sharpe	Man Utd	Leeds	£4.5m	Aug 96
Slaven Bilic	West Ham	Everton	£4.5m	May 97
Lee Sharpe	Man Utd	Leeds	£4.5m	Aug 96
Gianfranco Zola	Parma	Chelsea	£4.5m	Nov 96
Pierre v. Hooijdonk	Celtic	Nott'm For.	£4.5m	Mar 97
Alessandro Pistone	Inter Milan	Newcastle	£4.5m	Jul 97
Ruel Fox	Newcastle	Tottenham	£4.2m	Oct 95
Paul Ince	Inter Milan	Liverpool	£4.2m	Jul 97
Emerson	Porto	Middlesbro'	£4m	May 96
Duncan Ferguson	Rangers	Everton	£4m	Dec 94
Warren Barton	Wimbledon	Newcastle	£4m	Jun 95
Sasa Curcic	Bolton	Aston Villa	£4m	Aug 96
Roy Keane	Nott'm For.	Man Utd	£3.75m	Jul 93
David Batty	Blackburn	Newcastle	£3.75m	Feb 96
Ramon Vega	Cagliari	Tottenham	£3.75m	Jan 97
Oyvind Leonhardsen	Wimbledon	Liverpool	£3.75m	Jun 97
Phil Babb	Coventry	Liverpool	£3.6m	Sep 94
John Scales	Wimbledon	Liverpool	£3.5m	Sep 94
Savo Milosevic	P.Belgrade	Aston Villa	£3.5m	Jun 95
Gary Speed	Leeds	Everton	£3.5m	Jun 96
Karel Poborsky	Sl.Prague	Man Utd	£3.5m	Aug 96
Patrick Vieira	AC Milan	Arsenal	£3.5m	Aug 96
Patrik Berger	B.Dortmund	Liverpool	£3.5m	Aug 96
Teddy Sheringham	Tottenham	Man Utd	£3.5m	Jun 97
Tony Yeboah	E.Frankfurt	Leeds	£3.4m	Jan 95
Alan Shearer	Southampton	Blackburn	£3.3m	Jul 92
John Hartson	Arsenal	West Ham	£3.3m	Feb 97
Mark Draper	Leicester	Aston Villa	£3.25m	Jul 95
David Hopkin	Crystal Palace	Leeds	£3.25m	Jul 97
Georghe Popescu	Tottenham	Barcelona	£3.2m	May 95
Garry Flitcroft	Man City	Blackburn	£3.2m	Mar 96

Les Ferdinand – £6 million

Nick Barmby – £5.75 million

Graeme Le Saux – £5 million

Roberto Di Matteo – £4.9 million

Paul Ince – £4.2 million

PLAYER	FROM	TO	FEE	DATE
Daniel Amokachi	Bruges	Everton	£3m	Aug 94
Gary McAllister	Leeds	Coventry	£3m	Jul 96
Emmanuel Petit	Monaco	Arsenal	£3m	Jun 97
Stephane Henchoz	Hamburg	Blackburn	£3m	Jun 97
Georghe Popescu	PSV Eind.	Tottenham	£2.9m	Sep 94
Chris Coleman	Crystal P.	Blackburn	£2.8m	Dec 95
Lois Boa Morte	Sporting Lisbon	Arsenal	£2.8m	Jun 97
Andy Sinton	QPR	Sheff Wed	£2.75m	Aug 93
David Batty	Leeds	Blackburn	£2.75m	Oct 93
Brian Deane	Sheff Utd	Leeds	£2.7m	Jul 93
Des Walker	Sampdoria	Sheff Wed	£2.7m	Jul 93
Paul Warhurst	Sheff Wed	Blackburn	£2.7m	Sep 93
Darren Peacock	QPR	Newcastle	£2.7m	Mar 94
Stefan Schwarz	Arsenal	Fiorentina	£2.7m	Jul 95
Andy Booth	H'dersfield	Sheff Wed	£2.7m	Jul 96
Steffen Iversen	Rosenborg	Tottenham	£2.7m	Nov 96
Gianluca Festa	Inter Milan	Middlesbro'	£2.7m	Jan 97
Philippe Albert	Anderlecht	Newcastle	£2.65m	Aug 94
Carlton Palmer	Sheff Wed	Leeds	£2.6m	Jun 94
Illie Dumitrescu	Bucharest	Tottenham	£2.6m	Jul 94
Lee Bowyer	Charlton	Leeds	£2.6m	Jul 96
Benito Carbone	Inter Milan	Sheff. Wed.	£2.6m	Oct 96
John Scales	Liverpool	Tottenham	£2.6m	Dec 96
David Ginola	Newcastle	Tottenham	£2.6m	Jul 97
Terry Phelan	Wimbledon	Man City	£2.5m	Aug 92
Kevin Gallacher	Coventry	Blackburn	£2.5m	Mar 93
Neil Ruddock	Tottenham	Liverpool	£2.5m	Jul 93
Bryan Roy	Foggia	Nott'm F	£2.5m	Jun 94
John Hartson	Luton	Arsenal	£2.5m	Jan 95
Gareth Southgate	Crystal P.	Aston Villa	£2.5m	Jun 95
Kevin Campbell	Arsenal	Leeds	£2.5m	Jun 95
David Ginola	Paris St G.	Newcastle	£2.5m	Jul 95
Chris Bart-Williams	Sheff Wed	Nott'm For	£2.5m	Aug 95
Franck Leboeuf	Strasbourg	Chelsea	£2.5m	Jun 96
Darko Kovacevic	Sheff Wed	R Sociedad	£2.5m	Jul 96
Gary Breen	Birmingham	Coventry	£2.5m	Jan 97
Per Pedersen	Odense	Blackburn	£2.5m	Feb 97
Jan Thomasson	Heerenveen	Newcastle	£2.5m	Apr 97
Lee Clark	Newcastle	Sunderland	£2.5m	Jun 97
Martin Dahlin	Roma	Blackburn	£2.5m	Jul 97
Craig Burley	Chelsea	Celtic	£2.5m	Jul 97
Florin Raducioiu	Espanol	West Ham	£2.4m	Jul 96
Paul Kitson	Newcastle	West Ham	£2.3m	Feb 97
Dan Petrescu	Sheff Wed	Chelsea	£2.3m	Oct 95
Nigel Clough	Nott'm F	Liverpool	£2.275m	Jun 93
Nigel Martyn	Crystal Palace	Leeds	£2.25m	Jul 96
Celestine Babayoro	Anderlecht	Chelsea	£2.25m	Apr 97
Ed de Goey	Feyenoord	Chelsea	£2.25m	Jun 97
Robbie Elliott	Newcastle	Bolton	£2.2m	Jul 97
Vinny Samways	Tottenham	Everton	£2.2m	Aug 94
Gilles Grimandi	Monaco	Arsenal	£2m	Jun 97
Jimmy Hasselbaink	Boavista	Leeds	£2m	Jun 97

The Bargain Basement – Transfers under £1m

PLAYER	FROM	TO	FEE	DATE
John Lukic	Leeds	Arsenal	Free	Jul 96
Scott Oakes	Luton	Sheff. Wed.	£425,000	Jul 96
Richard Dryden	Bristol C.	Southampton	£150,000	Jul 96
Wayne Collins	Crewe	Sheff. Wed.	£650,000	Aug 96
Jordi Cruyff	Barcelona	Man. Utd.	£800,000	Aug 96
Espen Baardsen	S.F.Blackhawks	Tottenham	Free	Aug 96
Graham Potter	Stoke	Southampton	£250,000	Aug 96
Remi Garde	Strasbourg	Arsenal	Free	Aug 96
Kasey Keller	Millwall	Leicester	£900,000	Aug 96
Spencer Prior	Norwich	Leicester	£600,000	Aug 96
Robbie Slater	West Ham	Southampton	£250,000	Aug 96
Ian Marshall	Ipswich	Leicester	£800,000	Sep 96
Claus Lundekvan	SK Brann	Southampton	£400,000	Sep 96
Egil Ostenstadt	V. Stavanger	Southampton	£900,000	Sep 96
Gunner Halle	Oldham	Leeds	£475,000	Dec 96
Terry Phelan	Chelsea	Everton	£850,000	Dec 96
Maik Taylor	Barnet	Southampton	£500,000	Jan 97
Claus Thomsen	Ipswich	Everton	£900,000	Jan 97
Alex Yevtushok	Dnepropetrosk	Coventry	£800,000	Jan 97
Robert Ullathorne	Osasuna	Leicester	£600,000	Feb 97
Steve Guppy	Port Vale	Leicester	£850,000	Feb 97
Mick Evans	Plymouth	Southampton	£500,000	Mar 97
Nicolas Anelka	P.St.Germain	Arsenal	£500,000	Mar 97
Danny Granville	Cambridge	Chelsea	£300,000	Mar 97
Alex Manninger	Casino Graz	Arsenal	£400,000	Mar 97
Mart Poom	Flora Tallin	Derby	£500,000	Mar 97
Pierre Laurent	Bastia	Leeds	£500,000	Mar 97
David Billington	Peterborough	Sheff. Wed.	£500,000	Mar 97
Derek Lilley	Morton	Leeds	£500,000	Mar 97
David Robertson	Rangers	Leeds	£500,000	May 97
Stefano Eranio	AC Milan	Derby	Free	May 97
Kevin Davies	Chesterfield	Southampton	£750,000	May 97
Jonathan Hunt	Birmingham	Derby	£400,000	May 97
Lars Lees	B. Leverkusen	Barnsley	£250,000	Jun 97
Simon Howarth	Cardiff	Coventry	£500,000	Jun 97
Gustavo Poyet	Real Zaragoza	Chelsea	Free	Jun 97
John Barnes	Liverpool	Newcastle	Free	Aug 97
Ian Rush	Leeds	Newcastle	Free	Aug 97

John Lukic – free

Danny Granville – £300,000

The Art of Training – Sol Campbell

by Jay Bigwood

Young boys used to want to be train drivers. Not any more. To a knee-high sock they all want to be footballers. And it is not difficult to see why. Becoming a professional footballer is one of the most glamorous jobs going – Saturday-afternoon heroes, weekday idols and, by night, stars smoothly circulating in the world of showbiz and pop music.

It does not end there. Beamed into homes in all his glory by Sky TV, today's footballer is as high profile as they come; as a player brave, strong and flattered by the camera lens. Bathos and pathos in a split second. Then there is the spin-off as a marketable commodity. Alan Shearer uses Braun shavers, David Ginola drives Renault cars and Ryan Giggs munches Quorn Burgers. If the stars are not plying their trade on the football pitch, they can often be found on the catwalk modelling the latest fashions, dating members of the Spice Girls and hosting television programmes.

Sol Campbell wins the argument with Neil Lennon

In terms of public profile the success of Euro 96 in England helped project footballers past pop stars on the gossip pages and into the national consciousness. But what are professional footballers actually put through during a normal week? Is life really as glittering as it seems?

The Tottenham and England defender Sol Campbell is one of the new breed, certainly a star of today and more than likely of tomorrow. By the age of 22, he was established as a Premiership player and also as an England international, who has already played in a major international tournament, Euro 96.

Campbell's long journey started at school in Newham, Essex, and with a local Sunday side called Rippleway. He had trials with Essex Schools but was not selected. Spurs, however, saw the potential and signed him up, when he was 14, for their School of Excellence. From there he progressed through the youth and reserve ranks at White Hart Lane to his present position as one of the most sought-after English defenders in the country. The England caps have been slowly accumulated but for all that he has been a regular in the national squad for the last two seasons.

And Campbell knows more about that other side of the glamorous life than most – the sweat and the pain of training, the hours of hard graft that make a star. Just how do systems and methods change as you climb the football ladder?

According to Campbell the difference in training drills is slight, but it's the time you have to perfect the skills that is the most noticeable change between playing for your club and your country.

"The major difference is you can train two or three hours at your club, go home and start again the next day, but with England you're there all the time," he says. "I prefer to train and then go home and relax with my family, but it's an unbelievable honour to train with the country's best players.

"It's more like a training camp with England. You train, go back to your room, possibly have a sleep, and then you might watch a video later in the day where you go over a few things – like the last game or to look at the opponents in preparation for the forthcoming match."

National coach Glenn Hoddle surveys the scene at Bisham Abbey

Campbell made his England debut in May 1996 against Hungary and admits that staying with the squad has positive and negative sides. "Sometimes, especially when you're young, you get restless," he says, "but you just tune yourself into the way of things and after a while you get used to it.

"It can get boring from time to time, but you're with players from other clubs whom you rarely see, so most of the time, if you're not training, you are socialising and enjoying a laugh with the rest of the squad. There is definitely a club atmosphere whenever you're in the England squad."

So what is a normal day at Bisham Abbey under the control of national coach Glenn Hoddle really like?

"The morning is normally quite gentle and then you train for perhaps two or three hours in the afternoon," says Campbell. "You do the same exercises and drills as you would at your club. The difference is that you get more time allocated per day – for warm-ups and warm-downs, ball work and possession play.

"And when you're not training you have briefings, talks about tactics, videos to watch. It's more on-going than Tottenham, and I think the four or five days is enough to fit everything in."

Time for celebration for goal-scoring Sol

The senior England players are sometimes joined by the potential stars of tomorrow, the players from the under-21 squad, who are drafted in for the experience that might hold them in good stead for the future. Men who have had the opportunity include Lee Bowyer of Leeds and Rio Ferdinand at West Ham.

Campbell agrees whole-heartedly with that because it gives youngsters a taste of national training. "I think it's a good thing because these players can get an early taste of what the training is all about," he says.

But such an environment can leave the less demonstrative players feeling a little humble. Not that Campbell has such a problem. He has bags of confidence and is not intimidated by rubbing shoulders and tackling some of the established stars of the England side. In spite of his relative youth, Campbell has learned something new with every day in the business.

He has been in the Tottenham first team for the last four years and admits that many factors go into establishing a place in the side, attitude to training playing a big part in making a favourable impression.

"If you don't feel comfortable with the jokes and the wind-ups from the other players it takes longer to relax, but the more games you play the better you are going to feel," he says. "It was a hard step up for me from the youth team to training with the older players, but they help you to feel comfortable."

But doesn't a 17-year-old boy stand in awe of experienced international players such as Gary Lineker, Paul Gascoigne and Gary Mabbutt?

"No, you don't feel overshadowed by them," he says. "You just want to concentrate on playing and showing them what you can do, both on the training field and on the pitch."

The main difference between preparing for a match with England and preparing with Tottenham has, according to Campbell, nothing to do with the mechanics of the game but public expectation.

"The media attention is very different," he says. "When you train at Tottenham you don't normally see the journalists until two days before a game, but with England they are there every other day. With England you've got to be prepared for that because you are in the spotlight representing your country."

They were all around when Sol was a rookie . . . Lineker, Mabbutt and Gazza

The continuing influx and influence of the foreign players and managers suggests that it will not be long before the Premiership clubs adopt a more continental approach to training – for example, turning out for two sessions in a day. Campbell believes that would be a move in the right direction.

"I would be happy doing training in the morning and afternoon for two days a week," he says. "It's good that you do more ball work because you need that on a Saturday in a match. Two sessions would mean that training is less rushed because you don't have to cram everything in to the morning session."

For England and for Tottenham, the publicly-perceived easy glory for today's Premiership stars is the product of a labour of love and a toil of sweat. Stars have to earn their stripes.

The Carling Premiership Teams – Facts and Figures

ARSENAL – The Premiership History

Patrick Vieira

1996-97 PRE-SEASON: Bruce Rioch is sacked days before the season starts and then Arsenal court the Frenchman Arsene Wenger, who for contract reasons cannot join the club until November. Patrick Vieira signs from AC Milan for £3.5 million along with Remi Garde from Strasbourg.

THE SEASON: A win and defeat are followed by a series of Premiership draws which, for a club expected to set the pace, is not satisfactory. Worse follows when Arsenal are knocked out of the Uefa Cup at the first hurdle, losing 6-4 on aggregate to Borussia Monchengladbach.

The shock of that and the arrival of Wenger – caretaker manager Stewart Houston moves to QPR – sparks a revival that sees the Gunners climb the table and, by the turn of the year, they are close to mounting a real title challenge.

That fades – as do hopes for the second spot and a European Champions' League place – on the back of successive home defeats by Manchester United and Wimbledon and, despite a strong finish, too much ground has been lost.

Ian Wright

Even so a European place and the impact of Vieira along with the the form of Dennis Bergkamp and Ian Wright suggest that Wenger is moulding the side he wants and one that will be a greater force in 1997-98.

Best win: 4-1 at home to Sheffield Wednesday in September; worst defeat 2-0 at Liverpool in August. Top scorer: Ian Wright (23).

Arsenal facts and figures

CLUB ADDRESS: Arsenal Stadium, Highbury, London N5 1BU.

TELEPHONE: 0171-704 4000

FAX: 0171-704 4001

CLUBLINE: 0891-20 20 20

The club was formed in 1886, turning professional in 1893.

PREVIOUS GROUNDS: Plumstead Common, Sportsman Ground, Manor Ground, Invicta Ground.

The club was previously called Dial Square, Royal Arsenal and Woolwich Arsenal.

RECORD ATTENDANCE: 73,295 v Sunderland, Div 1, March 1935.

BIGGEST WIN: 12-0 v Loughborough Town, Div 2, March 1900.

BIGGEST DEFEAT: 0-8 v Loughborough Town, Div 2, December 1896.

TOP LEAGUE SCORER IN A SEASON: Ted Drake (42), 1934-35.

HIGHEST AGGREGATE SCORER: Cliff Bastin (178), 1930-46.

MOST CAPPED PLAYER: Kenny Sansom (86) for England.

STARS OF YESTERYEAR: Alex James (1929-37), Cliff Bastin (1930-46), Ted Drake (1934-39), Joe Mercer (1946-54), Don Howe (1964-66), Liam Brady (1973-80), Frank Stapleton (1973-80).

GREAT MANAGERS: Herbert Chapman (1925-34), Tom Whittaker (1947-1956), Bertie Mee (1966-76), George Graham (1986-95).

HONOURS: 1929-30 – FA Cup winners, 1930-31 – First Division champions, 1932-33 – First Division champions, 1933-34 – First Division champions, 1934-35 – First Division champions, 1935-36 – FA Cup winners, 1937-38 – First Division champions, 1947-48 – First Division champions, 1949-50 – FA Cup winners, 1952-53 – First Division champions, 1969-70 – Fairs Cup winners, 1970-71 – First Division champions, FA Cup winners, 1978-79 – FA Cup winners, 1986-87 – League Cup winners, 1988-89 – First Division champions, 1990-91 – First Division champions, 1992-93 – FA Cup winners, League Cup winners, 1993-94 – European Cup-Winners' Cup winners.

PREMIER MANAGERS: George Graham 1986-95, Bruce Rioch 1995-96, Arsene Wenger 1996-

1992-93

PRE-SEASON: Arsenal sell David Rocastle to Leeds for £2 million and Andy Cole to Bristol City for only £500,000. Cole would later go to Newcastle for £1.75 million and Manchester United for £7 million.

THE SEASON: Arsenal's first Premier League game is at Norwich, where they lose 4-2 after leading 2-0. They record their first victory at Anfield, where Wright scores his first of 15 League goals.

In November, Arsenal top the table after six consecutive victories but slip to ninth by the end of the year. In February, they strengthen their defence by signing Martin Keown from Everton for £2 million and Arsenal finish their first Premier season in tenth position. They have 56 points from 42 matches, having recorded 15 wins and 11 draws.

Best wins 3-0 against Coventry in November and Crystal Palace in May; worst defeat 3-0 at Leeds in November. Top scorer: Ian Wright (15).

1993-94

PRE-SEASON: Arsenal pay £1 million to Crystal Palace for the midfielder, Eddie McGoldrick.

THE SEASON: Arsenal finish fourth but are still 21 points behind the champions, Manchester United.

A disappointing start to the campaign when losing 3-0 at home to Coventry is halted by a win in the North London derby, thanks to an Ian Wright goal. They continue to improve and rise up the Premiership to finish the season with 17 draws. Only 13 goals are conceded away from home, which is testimony to their solid defence.

Best wins 5-1 and 4-0 over Ipswich Town; worst defeat 3-0 at home to Coventry City. Top scorer: Ian Wright (23).

1994-95

PRE-SEASON: Stefan Schwarz is the only new face, joining from Benfica for £1.75 milion.

THE SEASON: Events off the field overshadow those on it. George Graham loses his manager's position in February after investigations by the FA into allegations of illegal transfer deals. Earlier Paul Merson reveals his drink, drugs and gambling problems and leaves the game for a few months to rehabilitate. Arsenal miss his skill in midfield.

Wright again finishes the season as top scorer but Arsenal are marooned in mid-table. New arrivals towards the end of the season, John Hartson, Chris Kiwomya and Glenn Helder, cannot bring a dramatic change and the club record only 13 wins for the season.

Best win 5-1 at home to Norwich in April; worst defeat 3-0 away at Liverpool. Top scorer: Ian Wright (18).

1995-96

PRE-SEASON: Bruce Rioch is appointed manager and Arsenal sign Dennis Bergkamp for £7.5 million from Inter Milan and David Platt, home from Sampdoria, for £4.75 million.

THE SEASON: European football for the 1996-97 season is guaranteed in the last match as Bergkamp scores the winning goal in a 2-1 victory over already relegated Bolton. Arsenal finish fifth.

Unbeaten in their first seven games, they suffer their first defeat 1-0 at Chelsea. Home victories over eventual champions Manchester United and second-placed Newcastle show what might have been but for unexpected defeats, away at Bolton and Sheffield Wednesday and at home to Everton.

Best wins: 3-0 away at Leeds and Wimbledon and home to QPR; worst defeats 3-1 at Liverpool and home to Wimbledon. Top scorer: Ian Wright (15).

ARSENAL
Supporters' Club Best XI Since 1993 (5-3-2)

Supporter/Manager: Arthur Phillips

DAVID SEAMAN – England's first choice 'keeper signed from QPR in May 1990 for £1.3 million.

LEE DIXON – Consistent former England right back who joined from Stoke City in January 1988 for £400,000.

TONY ADAMS – Towering international defender who began his career as a Gunners' trainee, turning pro in January 1984.

STEVE BOULD – Reliable centre back signed from Stoke for £390,000 in June 1988.

NIGEL WINTERBURN – Evergreen left back who has enjoyed a decade at Highbury since his £407,000 move from Wimbledon.

MARTIN KEOWN – Tireless defender or midfielder signed from Everton for £2 million in February 1993.

PAUL MERSON – Enigmatic England midfielder who began as an Arsenal apprentice, turning professional in December 1985.

PATRICK VIEIRA – Long-striding French international who arrived at Highbury from AC Milan in August 1996 for £3.5 million.

JOHN JENSEN – Durable Danish international who left Arsenal for his former club Brondby in 1996.

IAN WRIGHT – Aggressive and prolific striker who signed from Crystal Palace for £2.5 million in September 1991.

DENNIS BERGKAMP – Stylish Dutch international who joined Arsenal from Inter Milan in July 1995 for £7.5 million.

ASTON VILLA – The Premiership History

Fernando Nelson

Sasa Curcic

Dwight Yorke

1996-97 PRE-SEASON: Brian Little sets his sights on the Premiership title and buys two quality foreigners. Portuguese defender Fernando Nelson comes in from Sporting Lisbon for £1.75 million and Serbian midfield dynamo Sasa Curcic arrives from Bolton for £4 million.

THE SEASON: The best-laid plans go awry in a season of chronic under-achievement for Villa. They flatter to deceive, never more so than in the Uefa Cup where they go out on away goals to Swedish part-timers Helsingborgs.

Villa's fine run of form at the end of the previous season, which had many experts tipping them as dark horses for the Championship, surfaces in fits and starts. Indeed, they briefly threaten to mount a title challenge when their 5-0 thrashing of Wimbledon, three days before Christmas, takes them second.

It proves to be a false dawn, though, as Villa slip away. A lack of goals is the problem. They find the net only eight times in their next 12 games, winning only three of those matches.

Qualifying for a place in the Uefa Cup hangs by a thread and depends on a win in their last game of the season at home to Southampton. The eventual 1-0 victory lifts them to fifth place with 61 points and assures them of European club football in the 1997-98 season.

Best win 5-0 over Wimbledon at Villa Park; worst defeat 3-0 at Liverpool in January. Top scorer: Dwight Yorke (17).

Aston Villa facts and figures

CLUB ADDRESS: Villa Park, Trinity Road, Birmingham B6 6HE.

TELEPHONE: 0121-327 2299

FAX: 0121-322 2107

CLUBCALL: 0891 121148

The club was formed in 1874, turning professional in 1896.

PREVIOUS GROUNDS: Aston Park and Perry Barr.

RECORD ATTENDANCE: 76,588 v Derby County, FA Cup 6th rnd, March 1946.

BIGGEST WIN: 13-0 v Wednesbury Old Ath in FA Cup 1st rnd, October 1886.

BIGGEST DEFEAT: 1-8 v Blackburn in FA Cup 3rd rnd, February 1889.

TOP LEAGUE SCORER IN A SEASON: 'Pongo' Waring (49), 1930-31.

HIGHEST AGGREGATE SCORER: Billy Walker (244), 1919-34.

MOST CAPPED PLAYER: Paul McGrath (80) for Republic of Ireland.

STARS OF YESTERYEAR: Harry Hampton (1904-20), Frank Barson (1919-22), Billy Walker (1919-34), 'Pongo' Waring (1927-35), Peter McParland (1952-62), Andy Gray (1975-79 and 1985-87).

GREAT MANAGERS: Eric Houghton (1953-58), Ron Saunders (1974-82), Tony Barton (1982-84).

HONOURS: 1886-87 – FA Cup winners, 1893-94 – First Division champions, 1894-95 – FA Cup winners, 1895-96 – First Division champions 1896-97 – First Division champions, FA Cup winners, 1898-99, 1899-1900 – First Division champions, 1904-05 – FA Cup winners, 1909-10 – First Division champions, 1912-13, 1919-20 – FA Cup winners, 1937-38 – Second Division champions, 1956-57 – FA Cup winners, 1959-60 – Second Division champions, 1960-61 – League Cup winners, 1971-72 – Third Division champions, 1974-75, 1976-77 – League Cup winners, 1980-81 – First Division champions, 1981-82 – European Cup winners, 1993-94, 1995-96 – League Cup winners.

PREMIER MANAGERS: Ron Atkinson 1991-94, Brian Little 1994-

1992-93

PRE-SEASON: Ron Atkinson strengthens the Villa squad when he signs Republic of Ireland international Ray Houghton from Liverpool for £825,000.

THE SEASON: Aston Villa draw their opening three Premier League games 1-1. Newcomer Dalian Atkinson scores their goal in each game. A run of only five defeats in their first 27 matches sees them climb to second by February.

Striker Dean Saunders is bought from Liverpool at a cost of £2.3 million. Villa are in a three-horse race for the title with Norwich and Manchester United but after a spell at the top, Atkinson's side slide following defeats by Blackburn, Oldham and QPR. Villa finish the season runners-up to United with 74 points.

Best win 5-1 v Middlesbrough in September; worst defeat 3-0 at Blackburn in late April. Top scorer: Dean Saunders (13).

1993-94

PRE-SEASON: Ron Atkinson adds more fire-power by buying Guy Whittingham from Portsmouth for £1.2 million, and Chelsea's aggressive midfielder Andy Townsend for £2.1 million.

THE SEASON: Villa fail to live up to the promise of the 1992-93 campaign. They are too inconsistent to mount a serious title challenge although Saunders and Atkinson continue to score goals but the defence is unexpectedly generous, conceding 50.

The season ends with Villa in tenth place on 57 points, having lost 15 of their 42 games, eight of those at Villa Park.

Best win 5-0 v Swindon in October; worst defeat 3-1 at Old Trafford against the champions Manchester United. Top scorer: Dean Saunders (10).

1994-95

PRE-SEASON: Villa look for improved strength up front with the surprising capture of Gladiators star John Fashanu for £1.35 million from Wimbledon.

THE SEASON: Villa's defensive woes continue and Ron Atkinson is dismissed in November following a run of nine matches without a win.

Villa old boy Brian Little takes over and immediately buys Tommy Johnson and Gary Charles from Derby in an effort to pull Villa away from the relegation zone. Five points from their last three games, including a priceless victory over Liverpool, save them as they finish the season in 18th place, one above relegation, with 48 points.

Best win 3-0 v Chelsea in December: worst defeat 4-0 at the hands of Leeds. Top scorer: Dean Saunders (15).

1995-96

PRE-SEASON: New faces aplenty at Villa Park, including Leicester midfielder Mark Draper, Crystal Palace defender Gareth Southgate and striker Savo Milosevic (Partizan Belgrade) for a total outlay of £9.25 million.

THE SEASON: Villa enjoy a renaissance in Brian Little's first full season. A 3-1 victory over Manchester United on the opening day sets the tone and home form is good throughout – just three defeats all season.

Villa's best moments come in the Coca-Cola Cup, where they triumph with an emphatic 3-0 victory over Leeds in the final. Inspired by Dwight Yorke's splendid goal-scoring feats, Villa also reach the FA Cup semi-final and finish fourth in the Premiership table with 63 points.

Best win 4-1 over Coventry at Villa Park in December; worst defeat 3-0 at Liverpool in March. Top scorer: Dwight Yorke (17).

ASTON VILLA
Supporters' Club Best XI Since 1993 (4-3-3)

Supporter/Manager: Ray Hodgetts

MARK BOSNICH – Australian international 'keeper who began his career with Sydney Croatia.

GARY CHARLES – Pacy and skilful full-back signed from Derby County in January 1995.

PAUL McGRATH – Ever-reliable Republic of Ireland defender who later joined Derby County.

GARETH SOUTHGATE – Versatile England defender signed from Crystal Palace for £2.5 million in June 1995.

ALAN WRIGHT – Attacking full-back signed from Blackburn Rovers in March 1995 for a bargain £1 million.

KEVIN RICHARDSON – Veteran midfielder who left Villa Park for Coventry in January 1995.

IAN TAYLOR – Powerful midfielder who started his career with Port Vale and joined Villa from Sheffield Wednesday in December 1994.

ANDY TOWNSEND – Capped over 60 times by the Republic of Ireland, Townsend joined Villa from Chelsea in July 1993 for £2.1 million.

DWIGHT YORKE – Trinidad and Tobagan international striker who was voted Villa 'Player of the Year' for 1995-96.

SAVO MILOSEVIC – Mercurial Serbian international who signed from Partizan Belgrade for £3.5 million in June 1995.

DALIAN ATKINSON – Athletic striker who signed for £1.6 million in July 1991 after a brief spell with Sheffield Wednesday.

Neil Redfearn

BARNSLEY – The Pre-Premiership Years

1996-97

PRE-SEASON: In a surprise move, Andy Payton leaves for Yorkshire rivals Huddersfield in a £350,000 deal. Danny Wilson replaces him with Paul Wilkinson on a free transfer from Middlesbrough.

THE SEASON: The greatest season in Barnsley's 110-year history as they win promotion to England's top division for the first time. The Tykes stay the course to pip Wolves for the second automatic promotion spot.

Despite a blistering start in which they win their opening five matches, the key moment comes in early October when Wilson signs John Hendrie from Middlesbrough, a 'steal' at £250,000.

Hendrie's goals and leadership keep Barnsley in the top three all season although he doesn't finish as the Tykes' leading scorer. That honour goes to skipper Neil Redfearn, who fires home several crucial free-kicks and penalties in his tally of 17 goals.

With experts tipping them to fade away, Barnsley do the opposite. They are unbeaten in March, winning four of their seven matches. They beat off the challenge of so-called more fashionable clubs to finish runners-up to Bolton with 80 points.

Best win 4-0 v Charlton in April; worst defeat 5-1 on the final day at Oxford. Top scorer: Neil Redfearn (17).

John Hendrie

Barnsley facts and figures

Club address: Oakwell Ground, Grove Street, Barnsley, South Yorkshire s71 1et.

Telephone: 01226 211211

Fax: 01226 211444

Clubcall: 0891 121152

The club was formed in 1887, turning professional in 1888.

Previous grounds: None.

The club was previously called Barnsley St Peter's.

Record attendance: 40,255 v Stoke City, FA Cup 5th rnd, February 1936.

Biggest win: 9-0 v Loughborough Town, Division 2, January 1899.

Biggest defeat: 0-9 v Notts County, Division 2, November 1927.

Top League scorer in a season: Cecil McCormack (33), 1950-51.

Highest aggregate scorer: Ernest Hine, League and Cup (130), 1921-26 and 1934-38.

Most capped player: Gerry Taggart (35) for Northern Ireland.

Stars of yesteryear: Ernest Hine (1921-26 and 1934-38), Sid 'Skinner' Normanton (1947-53), Charlie Williams (1954-58), Barry Murphy (1962-78), Mick McCarthy (1977-84).

Great managers: Arthur Fairclough (1904-12 and 1929-30), Angus Seed (1937-53), Allan Clarke (1978-80 and 1985-89), Danny Wilson (1994-).

Honours: 1911-12 – FA Cup winners, 1933-34, 1938-39, 1954-55 – Division 3 (N) champions.

Recent Managers: Mel Machin 1989-93, Viv Anderson 1993-94, Danny Wilson 1994-

1992-93

PRE-SEASON: Mel Machin resists the temptation to enter the transfer market, insisting his side can improve on the previous season's 16th position.

THE SEASON: The Tykes begin the campaign disastrously with six defeats in their first nine League matches. They climb off the bottom with a 3-0 win over Luton in October.

By March, they stand on the fringes of the play-off zone but slip back with a disappointing end to the season. Defensive frailties away from home cost them 41 goals in 23 matches.

One man who does not see the season's end is manager Machin, sacked the day before Barnsley's final match against Swindon. His team finish 13th with 60 points.

Best win 5-1 at home to Bristol Rovers in November; worst defeat 6-0 to champions Newcastle in April. Top scorer: Wayne Biggins (14).

1993-94

PRE-SEASON: Viv Anderson takes over as player-manager and buys Danny Wilson from Sheffield Wednesday for £200,000, using him as a player and his right-hand man behind the scenes.

THE SEASON: Barnsley have to be grateful to their away form for keeping them afloat in the First Division as they lose seven of their first nine League matches at Oakwell.

They beat Peterborough 1-0 in December to avoid slipping to the foot of the table. New signing Andy Payton, a £300,000 part-exchange capture from Celtic, scores the winner.

The Tykes finally find home comforts to their liking in March when four straight wins lift them away from the relegation zone. They finish 18th with 55 points.

Best win 4-0 over Sunderland in March; worst defeats 5-0 at Luton and Middlesbrough. Top scorers: Neil Redfearn and Andy Payton (12).

1994-95

PRE-SEASON: Another managerial change as Viv Anderson leaves to become Bryan Robson's assistant at Middlesbrough. Danny Wilson takes over at Oakwell.

THE SEASON: Scoring goals is a problem for the Tykes early on as they slip to 20th, but five victories in six matches lift them into the promotion frame by November.

A 4-1 Boxing Day win over Grimsby sends them third and dreaming of the Premiership. Inconsistency then robs them of the dream.

Convincing defeats of Reading and Sunderland in March bring them back into the frame but another dip and a poor run in April sees them miss out on the play-offs by one place in a season where only the top side – Middlesbrough – are automatically promoted. Barnsley finish sixth with 72 points.

Best wins 4-1 v Grimsby and Millwall; worst defeat 6-1 at Tranmere in November. Top scorer: Andy Liddell (13).

1995-96

PRE-SEASON: It's all quiet on the Oakwell transfer front except for Northern Ireland defender Gerry Taggart's £1.5 million move to Bolton.

THE SEASON: Barnsley start off with all guns blazing, netting 10 goals in their first four games. A 2-0 victory over Derby in late September keeps them in third place.

That's as good as it gets for the Tykes, though. Just two wins in their next 14 League matches has them anxiously looking over their shoulders at the relegation pack.

The arrival of Dutch midfielder Arjan de Zeeuw steadies the ship and Barnsley finish in a comfortable tenth position with 60 points.

Best win 3-0 over Huddersfield in March; worst defeat 5-0 at Birmingham in September. Top scorer: Andy Payton (17).

BARNSLEY Supporters' Club Best XI Since 1993 (4-4-2)

Supporter/Manager: Alan Bloore

DAVID WATSON – Former England Under-21 'keeper who began his professional career with Barnsley in July 1992.

MATTY APPLEBY – Versatile defender or midfielder who signed from Darlington after starting as a trainee with Newcastle United.

NICK EADEN – Right-sided defender who began his football career with Barnsley juniors before graduating to the professional ranks.

NEIL THOMPSON – Stylish left-back who had spells with Hull, Scarborough and Ipswich before arriving at Oakwell.

ARJAN DE ZEEUW – Dutch central defender who joined Barnsley from Telstar for £250,000 in November 1995.

NEIL REDFEARN – Well-travelled midfielder who signed from Oldham Athletic for £150,000 in August 1991.

DARREN SHERIDAN – Hard-tackling midfielder who started his professional career with Barnsley in 1993.

MARTIN BULLOCK – Skilful midfielder who was signed from Eastwood Town in August 1993 for £15,000.

STEVE DAVIS – Former England Youth player who started out with Crewe before moving to Oakwell in July 1991.

PAUL WILKINSON – Fearless front runner who had eight other League clubs before moving to Barnsley in 1996.

JOHN HENDRIE – Scottish striker whose pace and determination have made him a constant threat to defences.

Tim Flowers

BLACKBURN ROVERS – The Premiership History

1996-97

PRE-SEASON: The Blackburn faithful are horrified at the end of July when an era ends and Alan Shearer leaves Ewood Park for Newcastle in a world-record £15 million deal.

THE SEASON: Shearer's departure hangs like a cloud over Rovers. After 10 Premiership matches without a win, manager Ray Harford resigns in late October after the club lose to lowly Stockport County in the Coca-Cola Cup. Tony Parkes takes over as caretaker.

Rovers record their first victory in Parkes' second game in charge, 3-0 over Liverpool. They finally climb off the bottom of the table with a 1-1 draw at home to Chelsea on November 16, and a 2-0 win at Everton on New Year's Day lifts them out of the relegation zone.

That win over Everton was their only success in any competition away from home during the season but five successive home Premiership wins from November through to March 1 ease the pressure.

Chris Sutton

Uncertainty surrounds their new manager. Sampdoria coach Sven-Goran Eriksson agrees to join Rovers at the end of the season, then backs out much to the displeasure of chairman Jack Walker. Internazionale's Roy Hodgson is lined up instead.

Blackburn assure their Premiership status with a 4-1 win over Sheffield Wednesday in late April. They finish on 42 points in 13th place.

Best win 4-0 v Coventry in January; worst defeat 4-2 at home to Leicester on the final day of the season. Top scorer: Chris Sutton (11).

Blackburn facts and figures

CLUB ADDRESS: Ewood Park, Blackburn, Lancashire BB2 4JF.

TELEPHONE: 01254-698888

FAX: 01254-671042

CLUBCALL: 0891 121179

The club was formed in 1875, turning professional in 1880.

PREVIOUS GROUNDS: In 1875-76 the club was a nomad side, in 1876 home matches were played at Oozehead Ground, 1877 Pleasington Cricket Ground, 1878 Alexandra Meadows, 1881 Leamington Road, 1890 Ewood Park.

RECORD ATTENDANCE: 61,783 v Bolton Wanderers, FA Cup 6th rnd, March 1929.

BIGGEST WIN: 11-0 v Rossendale, FA Cup 1st rnd, October 1884.

BIGGEST DEFEAT: 0-8 v Arsenal, Div 1, February 1933.

TOP LEAGUE SCORER IN A SEASON: Ted Harper (43), 1925-26.

HIGHEST AGGREGATE SCORER: Simon Garner, (168), 1978-92.

MOST CAPPED PLAYER: Bob Crompton (41) for England.

STARS OF YESTERYEAR: Bobby Langton (1946-47 and 1953-55), Bill Eckersley (1947-60), Ronnie Clayton (1950-68), Bryan Douglas (1954-68), Andy McEvoy (1958-66), Simon Garner (1978-92).

GREAT MANAGERS: Thomas Mitchell (1884-96), Jack Marshall (1960-67), Howard Kendall (1979-81), Kenny Dalglish (1991-95).

HONOURS: 1883-84, 1884-85, 1885-86, 1889-90, 1890-91 – FA Cup winners, 1911-12, 1913-14 – First Division champions, 1927-28 – FA Cup winners, 1938-39 – Second Division champions, 1974-75 – Third Division champions, 1994-95 – Premiership champions.

PREMIER MANAGERS: Kenny Dalglish 1991-95, Ray Harford 1995-96, Tony Parkes (Caretaker) 1996-97, Roy Hodgson 1997-

1992-93

PRE-SEASON: Newly promoted to the Premiership, Blackburn splash out a British record £3.3 million for Southampton striker Alan Shearer.

THE SEASON: The season begins with a 3-3 draw at Crystal Palace, Stuart Ripley scoring Blackburn's first goal and Alan Shearer adding the other two as the club go on to challenge for the title.

They finish the season in storming style, winning eight of their last ten games and averaging three goals per game. Blackburn finish in a highly-satisfying fourth place with 71 points.

Best win 7-1 at home to Norwich in early October; worst defeat 5-2 at Leeds in April. Top scorer: Alan Shearer (16).

1993-94

PRE-SEASON: After a season of settling down in the top flight, Kenny Dalglish is happy with his expensively-acquired squad. In addition to Shearer, his signings have been Paul Warhurst (£2.7 million), Kevin Gallacher (£2.5 million) and Tim Flowers (£2 million).

THE SEASON: Rovers continue their rise to the top. Shearer's form is red hot as Blackburn threaten to win the title, only to falter on the run-in after winning 13 successive home matches. They, do however, take four points from Manchester United – the eventual champions and FA Cup winners.

Shearer scores 31 goals, including one hat-trick, as Blackburn finish the season in second place with 84 points.

Best wins, both 3-0, away at Everton and home to Wimbledon; worst defeat ironically by Wimbledon six weeks later by 4-1. Top scorer: Alan Shearer (31).

1994-95

PRE-SEASON: The club pay Norwich City £5 million for Chris Sutton in July 1994, beating off the challenge of Arsenal and Manchester United.

THE SEASON: Sutton's partnership with Shearer (predictably the pair become known as the SAS) inspires Blackburn to their first Championship for 81 years. They score 49 Premiership goals between them.

Rovers' success is built on their impressive home form. They win 17 and draw two of their 21 League matches at Ewood Park. They stumble in the Championship run-in but still clinch the title by a single point on the final Sunday of the season. Rovers are beaten 2-1 by Liverpool but rivals Manchester United can only manage a draw at West Ham. They finish with 89 points.

Best win 4-0 at home to Coventry in August; worst defeat 3-1 at Tottenham in February. Top scorer: Alan Shearer (34).

1995-96

PRE-SEASON: Manager Kenny Dalglish moves upstairs to become technical director, leaving his assistant Ray Harford to take over team affairs.

THE SEASON: Rovers soon discover that retaining the title is harder than winning it in the first place. Despite an opening-day victory over QPR, the defending champions do not win a second Premiership match until late September when they demolish Coventry 5-1. Graeme Le Saux suffers a broken leg in December and misses the rest of the season.

With an early European Champions' League exit, the only bright spot in a disappointing campaign is the form of Shearer. He nets four hat-tricks, all at Ewood Park. Rovers finish seventh with 61 points.

Best win 7-0 thrashing of Nottingham Forest in November; worst defeat 5-0 at Coventry City. Top scorer: Alan Shearer (31).

BLACKBURN
Supporters' Club Best XI Since 1993 (4-3-3)

Supporter/Manager: Jim Norris

TIM FLOWERS – England 'keeper who joined Rovers in November 1993 for £2.4 million from Southampton.

HENNING BERG – Versatile Norwegian international signed from Lillestrom in January 1993 for £400,000.

COLIN HENDRY – Rock-solid Scottish centre back who is enjoying his second spell at Ewood Park.

KEVIN MORAN – Dublin-born Eire defender who began his illustrious career with Manchester United.

GRAEME LE SAUX – Composed England left back who signed from Chelsea in March 1993.

TIM SHERWOOD – Abrasive ball-winning midfielder who moved to Ewood Park from Norwich for £500,000 in February 1992.

DAVID BATTY – Energetic Yorkshireman who has since joined Newcastle for £3.75 million after three seasons with Rovers.

GORDON COWANS – Graceful midfielder who signed for Blackburn in November 1991 from Aston Villa for a bargain £200,000.

KEVIN GALLACHER – Industrious Scottish striker who began his career with Dundee United, arriving at Rovers in March 1993 via Coventry for a fee of £2.5 million.

ALAN SHEARER – Amazingly prolific England striker who joined Newcastle for a world record £15 million in August 1996.

CHRIS SUTTON – Rangy striker or central defender who arrived at Rovers for a then British record £5 million from Norwich in July 1994.

BOLTON WANDERERS – The Premiership History

John McGinlay

Gerry Taggart

1996-97

PRE-SEASON: The omens are not good as Alan Stubbs joins Celtic for £3.5 million and Sasa Curcic leaves for Aston Villa in a £4 million deal. Danes Per Frandsen and Michael Johansen come at a combined cost of £2.28 million.

THE SEASON: Bolton treat their supporters to a season of total dominance as they bounce back to the Premiership in style.

A 2-0 victory over Portsmouth sends them top in mid-September. It is a position they never relinquish. Bolton's modern-day Cup pedigree is proved again as they beat Chelsea in the Coca-Cola Cup and then trounce Tottenham 6-1 in the next round.

They record seven successive League victories between December and February to establish themselves as the class act of the First Division.

Bolton say goodbye to Burnden Park with a 4-1 victory over Charlton. They finish on 98 points, 18 clear of second-placed Barnsley and become the first team for 21 years to score 100 League goals. Only a 90th-minute equaliser from Tranmere striker Lee Jones prevents them making it a 'century double' with 100 points.

Best win 7-0 mauling of Swindon in March; worst defeat 5-2 at Southend in September. Top scorer: John McGinlay (24).

Bolton facts and figures

CLUB ADDRESS: The Reebok Stadium, Mansell Way, Horwich, Bolton BL6.
TELEPHONE: 01204 389200
FAX: 01204 698899
CLUBCALL: 0891 121164
The club was formed in 1874, turning professional in 1880.
PREVIOUS GROUNDS: Park Recreation Ground, Cockle's Field, Pike's Lane, Burnden Park. The club was previously called Christ Church FC.
RECORD ATTENDANCE: 69,912 v Manchester City, FA Cup 5th rnd, February 1933.
BIGGEST WIN: 13-0 v Sheffield Utd, FA Cup 2nd rnd, February 1890.
BIGGEST DEFEAT: 1-9 v Preston NE, FA Cup 2nd rnd, December 1887.
TOP LEAGUE SCORER IN A SEASON: Joe Smith (38), 1920-21.
HIGHEST AGGREGATE SCORER: Nat Lofthouse, League and Cup (285), 1946-61.
MOST CAPPED PLAYER: Nat Lofthouse (33) for England.
STARS OF YESTERYEAR: Nat Lofthouse (1946-61), Doug Holden (1951-62), Eddie Hopkinson (1956-70), Francis Lee (1960-67), Peter Reid (1974-83).
GREAT MANAGERS: Charles Foweraker (1919-44), Bill Ridding (1951-68), Ian Greaves (1974-80).
HONOURS: 1908-09 – Second Division champions, 1923, 1926, 1929, 1958 – FA Cup winners, 1972-73 – Third Division champions 1977-78 – Second Division champions, 1996-97 – First Division champions.
RECENT MANAGERS: Bruce Rioch 1992-95, Roy McFarland 1995-96, Colin Todd 1996-

1992-93

PRE-SEASON: With Bolton languishing in the Second Division, Bruce Rioch and Colin Todd are handed the task of steering the club back to the big time at the expense of the sacked Phil Neal.

THE SEASON: Rioch turns around results at Burnden Park with the inspired signing of John McGinlay from Millwall in September.

McGinlay and fellow Scot Andy Walker score 42 League goals between them as Bolton rise from 18th in late October to surge towards promotion. They beat Liverpool 2-0 at Anfield in a memorable FA Cup run and claim the runners-up spot behind Stoke in the final week, finishing with 90 points.

Best wins 5-0 v Bradford and Chester; worst defeat 3-1 at West Brom in January. Top scorer: Andy Walker (26).

1993-94

PRE-SEASON: Rioch strengthens his squad by signing Owen Coyle from Airdrie, Jimmy Phillips from Middlesbrough and Alan Thompson from Newcastle, for £250,000 each.

THE SEASON: Poor away form costs the Trotters their chance of a second successive promotion. Away from Burnden Park they lose 12 times and that record consigns Bolton to a place among the also-rans.

It is all in stark contrast to their magnificent FA Cup form. Bolton dump Premiership sides Everton, Arsenal and Aston Villa on their way to the quarter-finals, where they lose 1-0 to Oldham. Bolton finish in 14th place in the First Division with 59 points.

Best win 4-0 v Millwall in October; worst defeat 3-0 at Charlton in August. Top scorer: John McGinlay (25).

1994-95

PRE-SEASON: Andy Walker leaves for Celtic. He is replaced at Bolton by Finnish striker Mixu Paatelainen, a £350,000 signing from Aberdeen.

THE SEASON: A memorable season as Wanderers win promotion to the Premiership and reach the Coca-Cola Cup final.

Successive 5-1 home wins over Charlton and Wolves take them top in February, but they win only one of their last seven matches to finish third behind Middlesbrough with 77 points. Disappointment then turns to joy for Bolton as they come from 2-0 behind to defeat Reading 4-3 after extra time in a pulsating play-off final at Wembley.

Best wins 5-1 v Charlton and Wolves; worst defeat 3-0 by Barnsley at Oakwell. Top scorer: John McGinlay (16).

1995-96

PRE-SEASON: Bruce Rioch cannot resist the lure of the manager's job at Arsenal. Bolton appoint Roy McFarland in his place and buy Gerry Taggart from Barnsley for £1.5 million.

THE SEASON: Wanderers struggle from start to finish in the Premiership. Never out of the bottom three, they slip to the foot of the table after losing 1-0 at Southampton in November.

To make matters worse, they lose influential midfielder Jason McAteer to Liverpool for £4.5 million. McFarland is sacked on January 2 and his assistant Colin Todd takes over. Despite a spirited revival in March inspired by £1 million Serbian midfielder Sasa Curcic, Bolton finish bottom on 29 points, nine adrift of safety. They lose 25 of their 38 matches.

Best win 4-1 at Middlesbrough in February; worst defeat 6-0 at home by Manchester United a week later. Top scorer: John McGinlay (6).

BOLTON
Supporters' Club Best XI Since 1993
(3-4-1-2)

Supporter/Manager: Nick Holt

KEITH BRANAGAN – Agile goal-keeper signed on a free transfer from Millwall in July 1992.

GERRY TAGGART – Northern Ireland international centre back who left Barnsley for Wanderers for £1.5 million in August 1995.

CHRIS FAIRCLOUGH – Well-travelled defender who began his career with Nottingham Forest, joining Bolton from Leeds in July 1995.

ALAN STUBBS – Elegant defender who started his career with Bolton before a £3.5m switch to Celtic in May 1996.

JASON McATEER – Dynamic mid-fielder or wing back who left for Liverpool after three seasons with Bolton.

PER FRANDSEN – Dutch interna-tional who arrived at Burden Park in 1996 from FC Copenhagen.

ALAN THOMPSON – Mercurial winger who started out as a trainee at Newcastle, joining Bolton in July 1993 for £250,000.

SCOTT SELLARS – Experienced midfielder who was bought from Newcastle for £750,000 in December 1995.

SASA CURCIC – Silky Yugoslavian international signed from Partizan Belgrade in October 1995 for £1 million.

NATHAN BLAKE – Prolific Welsh international marksman who enjoyed spells at Cardiff and Sheffield United.

JOHN McGINLAY – Committed Scottish striker who arrived at Bolton from Millwall in August 1992 for a bargain £125,000.

CHELSEA – The Premiership History

Roberto Di Matteo

1996-97

PRE-SEASON: The managerial reins are taken over by Ruud Gullit, who immediately persuades Gianluca Vialli to join from European Cup winners Juventus on a free transfer under the Bosman ruling. Chelsea's foreign legion grows when Franck LeBoeuf moves to London from Strasbourg and Roberto Di Matteo comes in from Lazio.

THE SEASON: Di Matteo gets the season off to the perfect start with a goal on his home debut against Middlesbrough. Five unbeaten matches establish them as a team to watch.

Tragedy strikes in October with the death of vice-chairman Matthew Harding in a helicopter crash on the way back from watching Chelsea at Bolton in a Coca-Cola Cup tie.

Gullit lifts some of the gloom two weeks later with the signing of the season – Gianfranco Zola from Parma for £4.5 million. The tiny Italian strikes up an immediate rapport with his minder Mark Hughes.

Together they inspire Chelsea to a 2-0 FA Cup Final triumph over Middlesbrough, their first major honour for 26 years. In the Premiership, the Blues finish in a creditable sixth place with 59 points, at times producing some of the most exciting and incisive football in the division.

Zola ends a wonderful debut season by being voted 'Player of the Year' by the football writers.

Best win 6-2 goal feast v Southampton in March; worst defeat 5-1 at Liverpool in September. Top scorer: Gianluca Vialli (9).

Frank Leboeuf

Steve Clarke

Chelsea facts and figures

CLUB ADDRESS: Stamford Bridge, London SW6 1HS.

TELEPHONE: 0171-385 5545

FAX: 0171-381 4831

CLUBCALL: 0891 121159

The club was formed in 1905, turning professional in the same year.

PREVIOUS GROUNDS: None.

RECORD ATTENDANCE: 82,905 v Arsenal, Div 1, October 1935.

BIGGEST WIN: 13-0 v Jeunesse Hautcharage, European Cup-Winners Cup, September 1971.

BIGGEST DEFEAT: 1-8 v Wolverhampton Wanderers, Div 1, September 1953.

TOP LEAGUE SCORER IN A SEASON: Jimmy Greaves (41), 1960-61.

HIGHEST AGGREGATE SCORER: Bobby Tambling (202), 1959-70.

MOST CAPPED PLAYER: Ray Wilkins 24 (84) for England.

STARS OF YESTERYEAR: Hughie Gallacher (1930-34), Jimmy Greaves (1957-61), Peter Bonetti (1959-78), Bobby Tambling (1959-70), Terry Venables (1960-66), Ron Harris (1961-80), Peter Osgood (1964-74), Ray Wilkins (1973-79).

GREAT MANAGERS: Billy Birrell (1939-52), Ted Drake (1952-61), Tommy Docherty (1962-67), Dave Sexton (1967-74), Glenn Hoddle (1993-96).

HONOURS: 1954-55 – First Division champions, 1964-65 – League Cup winners, 1969-70 - FA Cup winners, 1970-71 – European Cup-Winners' Cup winners, 1983-84, 1988-89 – Second Division champions, 1996-97 FA Cup winners.

PREMIER MANAGERS: Ian Porterfield 1991-93, David Webb 1993, Glenn Hoddle 1993-96, Ruud Gullit 1996-

1992-93

PRE-SEASON: Ian Porterfield adds experience to his squad in the form of Mal Donaghy, Mick Harford and Robert Fleck.

THE SEASON: Newly-promoted Chelsea's debut in the Premiership is not impressive, as they fail to win any of their first four games. Things then improve and, with the help of eight goals from Harford, they enter December in fourth place.

A disastrous run of 12 games without a win sees the Blues drop to 11th and costs Ian Porterfield his job. Former Stamford Bridge hero David Webb is put in charge until the end of the season. The return to form of Tony Cascarino helps settle the nerves and Chelsea finish 11th with 56 points.

Best win 4-0 v Middlesbrough in April; worst defeats 4-2 at Manchester City and Sheffield United. Top scorer: Mick Harford (9).

1993-94

PRE-SEASON: Chairman Ken Bates prises Glenn Hoddle away from Swindon to take over as player-manager. His first move is to sell Andy Townsend to Aston Villa and buy Gavin Peacock from Newcastle.

THE SEASON: A season of under-achievement for Chelsea, whose form is erratic. A 1-0 victory over Liverpool in September brings joy before a run of 11 games without a win as Christmas approaches.

The arrival of Mark Stein, from Stoke, helps to improve the position as he scores 11 goals in nine games and Chelsea finish in 14th position with 51 points. Their salvation is the FA Cup. They reach the final only to lose 4-0 to Manchester United, but as United also achieve the double, the Blues are guaranteed a European place.

Best win 4-2 against Everton in January; worst defeat 4-1 at Leeds in November. Top scorer: Mark Stein (13).

1994-95

PRE-SEASON: Glenn Hoddle ends David Rocastle's unhappy spell at Manchester City by bringing him to Stamford Bridge for £1.25 million and Paul Furlong arrives from Watford.

THE SEASON: Chelsea begin the season promising much with three straight wins. Another mid-season slump sees them drop to 13th by February but they prove themselves as a quality cup team, reaching the semi-final of the European Cup Winners' Cup.

The goals dry up in the Premiership, though, as Chelsea finish 11th with 54 points. A home record of won 7, drawn 7, lost 7 tells its own story.

Best win 4-0 v Leicester in October; worst defeats 3-0 at Norwich, Aston Villa and Leeds. Top scorer: John Spencer (11).

1995-96

PRE-SEASON: Hoddle begins Chelsea's transformation into London's glamour club by signing dreadlocked Dutch superstar Ruud Gullit from Sampdoria on a free transfer and Mark Hughes from Manchester United for £1.5 million.

THE SEASON: The Hoddle jigsaw is slowly falling into place. After a stuttering start, Hughes proves to be an astute buy with four goals in seven matches as Chelsea climb to the top half.

Allegations of boardroom bickering between chairman Ken Bates and director Matthew Harding take over the Chelsea headlines before the pair appear to make their peace with a public reconciliation. Wing-backs Terry Phelan and Dan Petrescu join from Manchester City and Sheffield Wednesday respectively. Chelsea reach the FA Cup semi-final but their league form remains patchy. They finish 11th with 50 points. Glenn Hoddle leaves to become the England coach.

Best win 5-0 at home to Middlesbrough in February; worst defeat 4-1 at home to Manchester United. Top scorer: John Spencer (13).

CHELSEA
Supporters' Club Best XI Since 1993 (5-3-2)

Supporter/Manager: Malcolm Carle

DIMITRI KHARINE – Russian international 'keeper who joined Chelsea from CSKA Moscow in December 1992 for a modest £200,000.

GLENN HODDLE – Mercurial international midfielder who has since become England coach.

MICHAEL DUBERRY – Hugely promising defender who started his career as a Chelsea trainee, turning professional in June 1993.

FRANCK LEBOEUF – Cultured French central defender who signed from Strasbourg after an impressive Euro 96.

DAN PETRESCU – Experienced Romanian full-back who has played for Genoa and Sheffield Wednesday.

STEVE CLARKE – Reliable Scottish international who has been at Stamford Bridge for more than a decade.

RUUD GULLIT – Visionary Dutch international who became Chelsea manager following Glenn Hoddle's appointment as England coach.

DENNIS WISE – England midfielder who signed for Chelsea from Wimbledon for £1.6 million in July 1990.

ROBERTO DI MATTEO – Skilful Italian midfielder who left Lazio in July 1996 for £4.9 million.

GIANFRANCO ZOLA – Magical Italian striker who joined the Stamford Bridge side for £4.5 million in November 1996.

MARK HUGHES – Bustling Welsh striker who signed for Chelsea from Manchester United in July 1995 for £1.5 million.

COVENTRY CITY – The Premiership History

1996-97

PRE-SEASON: Gary McAllister joins from Leeds United for £3 million and Regis Genaux, a Belgian international, also signs but struggles to make the side.

THE SEASON: A familiar pattern for Coventry as they lose four and draw one of their first five matches. With the side struggling at the bottom of the Premiership and a near-fortune having been spent to improve the situation, Ron Atkinson moves aside in November, handing control of the team to Gordon Strachan.

Strachan quickly makes an impact, inspiring the Sky Blues to four vital successive Premiership wins in December. The highlight is a 3-1 victory at his former club Leeds on Boxing Day.

But the new year does not herald a new dawn – more a return to the bad old ways. A run of poor results has relegation looming more threateningly than ever for Coventry. Even the signing of Darren Huckerby, for £1 million from Newcastle, does little to lift the gloom.

Then an unexpected 2-1 win away at Liverpool in March, followed by a 3-1 home win over Chelsea, brings hope and not for the first time Coventry's future depends on their success in the last match of the season. They win 2-1 at Tottenham, results go their way and for the tenth time in 30 years they have preserved top-flight status at the death.

Best win 3-0 at home over Middlesbrough in December; worst defeats, all away, 4-0 by Middesbrough in September, Blackburn in January and Newcastle in March. Top scorer: Dion Dublin (13).

Above left: Noel Whelan

Left: Gary McAllister

Coventry facts and figures

CLUB ADDRESS: Highfield Road Stadium, King Richard Street, Coventry CV2 4FW.
TELEPHONE: 01203 234000
FAX: 01203 630318
CLUBLINE: 0891 121166
The club was formed in 1883, turning professional in 1893.
PREVIOUS GROUNDS: Binley Road, and Stoke Road.
The club was previously called Singers FC.
RECORD ATTENDANCE: 51,455 v Wolves, Div 2, April 1967.
BIGGEST WIN: 9-0 v Bristol City, Div 3 South, April 1934.
BIGGEST DEFEATS: 2-11 v Berwick Rangers, FA Cup, November 1901, 2-10 v Norwich, Div 3 South, March 1930.
TOP LEAGUE SCORER IN A SEASON: Clarrie Bourton (49), 1931-32.
HIGHEST AGGREGATE SCORER: Clarrie Bourton (181), 1931-37.
MOST CAPPED PLAYERS: Dave Clements 21 (48) for Northern Ireland and Ronnie Rees 21 (39) for Wales.
STARS OF YESTERYEAR: Clarrie Bourton (1931-37), Reg Matthews (1950-56), George Curtis (1956-70), Ronnie Rees (1962-67), Bill Glazier (1964-75), Mick Coop (1966-80), Ernie Hunt (1967-73), Willie Carr (1967-74), Denis Mortimer (1969-75), Ian Wallace (1976-80), Mark Hateley (1978-83).
GREAT MANAGERS: Harry Storer (1931-45 and 1948-53), Jimmy Hill (1961-67), Noel Cantwell (1968-72), Gordon Milne (1974-81), John Sillett (1987-90).
HONOURS: 1935-36 – Third Division (South) champions, 1963-64 – Third Division champions, 1966-67 – Second Division champions, 1986-87 – FA Cup winners.
PREMIER MANAGERS: Bobby Gould 1992-93, Phil Neal 1993-95, Ron Atkinson 1995-1996, Gordon Strachan 1997-

1992-93

PRE-SEASON: It is all change at the top. Bobby Gould returns to the club as joint manager with Don Howe, Howe resigns and Phil Neal takes charge as Gould's assistant. Phil Babb and John Williams come in; Paul Furlong and Kevin Drinkell leave.

THE SEASON: Coventry are typically inconsistent, winning six of their first eight Premiership matches, but crash out of the League Cup to Third Division Scarborough.

Gould buys Mick Quinn from Newcastle for £250,000 in December and he scores ten in his first six matches. City slump at the end of the season to finish 15th with 52 points, just three points above relegated Crystal Palace. They lose ten matches at Highfield Road.

Best win 5-1 thrashing of Liverpool in December; worst defeat 5-0 at champions-to-be Manchester United nine days later. Top scorer: Mick Quinn (17).

1993-94

PRE-SEASON: City sell defender Andy Pearce to Sheffield Wednesday for £500,000 and sign the old warrior Mick Harford from Sunderland.

THE SEASON: By their standards, Coventry enjoy a stable season. Off the pitch, they are rocked by the resignation of Bobby Gould just ten minutes after a 5-1 defeat at QPR. Phil Neal takes over.

The discovery of the season is Zimbabwean striker Peter Ndlovu, who assumes the goalscoring responsibility from out-of-form Quinn. Coventry finish 11th with 56 points.

Best win 4-0 against Manchester City in February; worst defeat 5-1 at QPR. Top scorer: Peter Ndlovu (11).

1994-95

PRE-SEASON: American World Cup star Cobi Jones arrives at Highfield Road for £300,000. Wolves midfielder Paul Cook joins him just three days before the season kicks off.

THE SEASON: A bleak beginning as Coventry lose both opening away games 4-0, at Newcastle and Blackburn. Then in the space of seven September days, the club receives a record fee of £3.6 million as Liverpool buy Phil Babb, then spend a club-record £2 million on Manchester United's Dion Dublin.

Despite a mid-season revival, City slip back into the bottom three in February. Phil Neal is sacked as manager and replaced by Ron Atkinson, who saves the club from the drop. He buys Kevin Richardson from Aston Villa and immediately makes him club captain. They finish 16th with 50 points, having scored just 44 goals.

Best win 4-2 against relegation-bound Leicester; worst defeat 5-1 Christmas stuffing at Sheffield Wednesday. Top scorer: Dion Dublin (16).

1995-96

PRE-SEASON: Atkinson spends £3.15 million in an attempt to transform Coventry into contenders for a place in Europe. He buys Marques Isaias, Paul Telfer and John Salako.

THE SEASON: Coventry become one of the Premiership's big spenders as the squad is enlarged by the arrivals of Noel Whelan, Richard Shaw, Eoin Jess and Liam Daish. They cost £7 million. Even so Coventry still spend the season battling to avoid relegation.

A leaky defence concedes 60 goals but tightens up just in time with successive clean sheets in the last three games as they save their place in the Premiership with a last-day 0-0 draw against Leeds. Coventry finish 16th, level on 38 points with Manchester City, who go down because of an inferior goal average.

Best win 5-0 hammering of Blackburn in December, avenging their worst defeat 5-1 at the hands of the 1994-95 champions in September. Top scorer: Dion Dublin (16).

COVENTRY
Supporters' Club Best XI Since 1993 (5-3-2)

Supporter/Manager: Terry Potts

STEVE OGRIZOVIC – Long-serving Coventry 'keeper who joined the Sky Blues for just £70,000 from Shrewsbury Town back in June 1984.

PHIL BABB – Pacy left-sided defender who has since moved to Liverpool for £3.6 million.

RICHARD SHAW – Competitive and versatile defender who was signed from Crystal Palace in November 1995.

PETER ATHERTON – Durable former England Under-21 defender who has since moved to Sheffield Wednesday for £800,000.

PAUL WILLIAMS – Muscular defender signed from Derby County in August 1995.

BRIAN BORROWS – Consistent central defender who joined Coventry from Bolton after starting his career with Everton.

PETER NDLOVU – Zimbabwean international striker who signed from Highlanders in August 1991 for a bargain £10,000.

ROY WEGERLE – Tricky South African-born American international signed from Blackburn Rovers for £1 million.

JOHN WILLIAMS – Speedy striker who moved on to Wycombe for £150,000 in September 1995.

DARREN HUCKERBY – Electric striker with an intuitive eye for goal, signed from Newcastle in November 1996 for £1 million.

DION DUBLIN – Inspirational Coventry skipper who left Manchester United for Highfield Road in September 1994 for £2 million.

David Hopkin

CRYSTAL PALACE – The Premiership History

1996-97

PRE-SEASON: After the First Division play-off agony of the previous season, when Palace finished third then missed out in the play-offs, not much changes – except goalkeeper Nigel Martyn moves to Leeds United for £2.25 million and Palace replace him with Chris Day, from Tottenham.

THE SEASON: A discouraging result but encouraging performance as Palace open with a 1-0 defeat at Birmingham City, and from then until late November they lose just one match.

Along the way there are some stunning wins, including successive 6-1 victories – away at Reading and then home to Southend. Palace also come back from being 2-0 down to draw 2-2 with the team of the First Division, Bolton Wanderers.

Palace climb to second in the table but from November through until late January the season goes stale: six defeats, three draws and one win produce six points out of a possible 30.

Worse, in February manager Dave Bassett leaves the club to join Nottingham Forest and Steve Coppell, who had a short and controversial stay at Manchester City, returns to Selhurst Park. Andy Linighan is signed from Arsenal to tighten the defence and Palace start battling for a place in the play-offs – which they achieve by finishing sixth.

Wolves are beaten 4-3 on aggregate in the play-off semi-final and Palace then face Sheffield United at Wembley for a Premiership place. The match looks set for extra time when David Hopkin, the Palace skipper, scores a stunning goal, erasing memories of their 2-1 defeat by Leicester City in the previous season – again with a last-minute goal.

Best wins 6-1 at Reading and 6-1 at home to Southend; worst defeat 3-0 at Sheffield United in April. Top scorer: Bruce Dyer (18).

Bruce Dyer

Crystal Palace facts and figures

CLUB ADDRESS: Selhurst Park, London SE25 6PU
TELEPHONE: 0181-768 6000
FAX: 0181-771 5311
CLUBCALL: 0891 400333
The club was formed in 1905, turning professional the same year.
PREVIOUS GROUNDS: Crystal Palace, Herne Hill, The Nest
RECORD ATTENDANCE: 51,482 v Burnley, Division 2, May 1979.
BIGGEST WIN: 9-0 v Barrow – Division 4, October 1959.
BIGGEST DEFEATS: 0-9 v Burnley, FA Cup 2nd rnd replay, February 1909 and v Liverpool – Division 1, September 1990.
TOP LEAGUE SCORER IN A SEASON: Peter Simpson (46), 1930-31.
HIGHEST AGGREGATE SCORER: Peter Simpson (166), 1929-34.
MOST CAPPED PLAYER: Eric Young 19 (21) for Wales.
STARS OF YESTERYEAR: Johnny Byrne (1956-61 and 1966-67), John Jackson (1964-73), Gerry Queen (1969-72), Jim Cannon (1973-88), Peter Taylor (1973-76), Kenny Sansom (1974-79), Ian Wright (1985-91).
GREAT MANAGERS: Eddie Goodman (1907-25), Bert Head (1966-72), Malcolm Allison (1972-76), Terry Venables (1976-80), Steve Coppell (1984-93) and (1997-).
HONOURS: 1920-21 – Division 3 (S) champions, 1978-79 – Division 2 champions, 1993-94 – Division 1 champions.
RECENT MANAGERS: Steve Coppell 1984-93, Alan Smith 1993-95, Ray Lewington & Peter Nicholas 1995-96, Dave Bassett 1996-97, Steve Coppell 1997-

1992-93

PRE-SEASON: Palace, having finished tenth in the previous season, enter the first Premier League season with a tried and tested squad.

THE SEASON: An opening 3-3 draw with newly-promoted Blackburn, parading Alan Shearer for the first time, paves the way for three more draws – and that is to be the cause of the Palace downfall.

They draw 16 matches but still collect 49 points only to be relegated on goal difference as Oldham, who have to win their last three matches, do just that. Relegation is made certain as Ian Wright scores for Arsenal against his old club in the final match of the season.

Steve Coppell, the Palace manager for the previous nine years, resigns and Alan Smith is appointed in his place.

Best win 4-1 at home to Middlesbrough in April; worst defeat 5-0 at Liverpool in November. Top scorer: Chris Armstrong (15).

1993-94

PRE-SEASON: The Palace players, relegated the previous season, stay faithful to the club under new manager Alan Smith.

THE SEASON: A slow start after a 0-0 opening-day home draw with Tranmere and 2-0 defeat at Bristol Rovers picks up with a 2-0 victory over Nottingham Forest.

From then on Palace blaze a trail through the First Division, promoted and champions well before the season is over. The success is built on the prolific goal-scoring of Chris Armstrong but Palace end with a surprise 2-0 home defeat by Watford. Even so the celebratory Premiership T-shirts "We're back, we told you so" still fit snugly.

Best win 5-1 at home to Portsmouth in August; worst defeat 3-0 away to Millwall in January. Top scorer: Chris Armstrong (22).

1994-95

PRE-SEASON: Palace are back in the Premiership after a season away but Alan Smith's loyal charges are in for a rude shock.

THE SEASON: A 6-1 home defeat by Liverpool on the opening day sets the tone for a season in which Palace finish in the last four of everything – the Coca-Cola Cup (beaten by Liverpool), the FA Cup (beaten by Manchester United) and the fourth relegation spot. A lack of goals is to cost them dear.

A run of four wins in October through to November offers some reprieve but it is always an uphill struggle and Palace finish by going to Newcastle needing to win if they are to escape above Aston Villa. They lose 3-2. Ray Houghton, signed from Aston Villa, stabilises the side but arrives too late to save the club. Smith resigns as manager.

Best win 4-1 away to Coventry City in November; worst defeat 6-1 at home to Liverpool. Top scorer: Chris Armstrong (10).

1995-96

PRE-SEASON: Relegated from the Premiership, Palace see the squad break up. Gareth Southgate moves to Aston Villa, while Richard Shaw and John Salako go to Coventry City and Chris Armstrong to Tottenham Hotspur. Palace adopt a continental approach with Ray Lewington and Peter Nicholas as first-team coaches.

THE SEASON: Palace appear hung over and struggle in the lower reaches of the table until, in February, Dave Bassett – the former Sheffield United boss – takes charge and brings about a major transformation. Palace lose once in 21 matches and climb from 20th to third in the table.

They just fail to pip Derby County in the race for automatic promotion but reach the play-off final against Leicester City, where Steve Claridge's goal in the last seconds of extra time ruins the day for the south Londoners.

Best win: 5-0 at home to Grimsby in March; worst defeat 3-0 at Huddersfield in February. Top scorer: Dougie Freedman (20).

CRYSTAL PALACE
Supporters' Club
Best XI Since 1993
(4-3-3)

Supporter/Manager: Colin Reynolds

NIGEL MARTYN – England 'shot-stopper' who enjoyed seven seasons at Palace after signing from Bristol Rovers for £1 million.

MARC EDWORTHY – Attacking full-back who signed for Palace in June 1995 for £350,000 from Plymouth Argyle.

ANDY THORN – Seasoned central defender who spent five years at Selhurst Park before returning for a second spell at Wimbledon.

GARETH SOUTHGATE – Assured and versatile defender who joined Aston Villa for £2.5 million in June 1995.

RICHARD SHAW – Strong defender who began his career as a Palace apprentice before joining Coventry in 1995.

DAVID HOPKIN – Scottish winger who moved from Chelsea to Palace in July 1995 for £850,000.

ANDY ROBERTS – England Under-21 midfielder who signed from Millwall in July 1995 for £1.8 million.

JOHN SALAKO – Erratic but sometimes brilliant winger who joined Coventry in August 1995 for £1.5 million.

MARK BRIGHT – Accomplished striker who scored over 100 goals at Selhurst Park during his six-year stay.

CHRIS ARMSTRONG – Quick and elusive striker who signed for Tottenham for £4.5 million in June 1995.

SIMON RODGER – Strong-tackling midfielder or winger who joined from Bognor Regis Town in 1990 for just £1,000.

DERBY COUNTY – The Premiership History

Dean Sturridge

Darryl Powell

Christian Dailly

1996-97

PRE-SEASON: Aware that his side are being tipped as favourites for relegation, manager Jim Smith responds by signing Croatian midfielder Aljosa Asanovic for £950,000 from Hadjuk Split. Jacob Laursen, Danny Griffin and Christian Dailly also arrive.

THE SEASON: Derby's overseas contingent, Asanovic, Laursen and Igor Stimac, are in superb form as the Rams confound the critics by comfortably avoiding the drop.

A 2-1 win at struggling Blackburn earns them a first Premiership win but they are reliant on a solid defence to overcome goalscoring problems early in the campaign. Much of the credit is heaped on the 38-year-old shoulders of Paul McGrath, who signs from Aston Villa in a £200,000 deal.

Victory over Coventry on November 30 lifts Derby briefly into the top ten but the highlight of the season is a thrilling 3-2 victory over Manchester United at Old Trafford in which Costa Rican international Paulo Wanchope scores a memorable debut goal.

That victory ends any jitters in the scramble to avoid relegation and there are also victories over Aston Villa and away at Coventry City.

County end the season with an emotional farewell to the Baseball Ground, their home for 103 years. They finish 12th with 46 points. In the cups, they are beaten by finalists Middlesbrough in the FA Cup and by Luton in the Coca-Cola.

Best win 4-2 v Tottenham in March; worst defeat a 6-1 pummeling at Middlesbrough two weeks earlier. Top scorer: Dean Sturridge (11).

Derby County facts and figures

CLUB ADDRESS: Pride Park Stadium, Pride Park, Derby DE24 8XL

TELEPHONE: 01332 667503

FAX: 01332 667519

CLUBLINE: 0891 121187

The club was formed in 1884, turning professional the same year.

PREVIOUS GROUNDS: Racecourse Ground, Baseball Ground.

RECORD ATTENDANCE: 41,826 v Tottenham, Div 1, September 1969.

BIGGEST WIN: 12-0 v Finn Harps, Uefa Cup 1st Rnd, September 1976.

BIGGEST DEFEAT: 2-11 v Everton, FA Cup 1st Rnd, 1889-90.

TOP LEAGUE SCORERS IN A SEASON: Jack Bowers (37), 1930-31, Ray Straw (37), 1956-57.

HIGHEST AGGREGATE SCORER: Steve Bloomer (331), 1892-1906 and 1910-14.

MOST CAPPED PLAYER: Peter Shilton 34 (125) for England.

STARS OF YESTERYEAR: Steve Bloomer (1892-1906 and 1910-14), Tommy Cooper (1925-34), Peter Doherty (1945-46), Raich Carter (1945-48), Kevin Hector (1966-78 and 1980-82), John O'Hare (1967-74), Roy McFarland (1967-80), Dave Mackay (1968-70), Archie Gemmill (1970-77), Colin Todd (1971-78).

GREAT MANAGERS: Jimmy Methven (1906-22), Harry Storer (1955-62), Brian Clough (1967-73), Dave Mackay (1973-76), Jim Smith (1995-).

HONOURS: 1911-12, 1914-15 – Division 2 champions, 1945-46 – FA Cup winners, 1956-57 - Division 3 North champions, 1968-69 – Division 2 champions, 1971-72, 1974-75 - Division 1 champions, 1986-87 – Division 2 champions.

PREMIER MANAGER: Jim Smith 1995-

1992-93

PRE-SEASON: The future looks bright for County, with millionaire director Lionel Pickering determined to buy his way into the Premier League.

THE SEASON: Manager Arthur Cox reacts to Derby's disastrous start by signing defensive colossus Craig Short for a club record £2.5 million from Notts County.

The struggling Rams sort out their away form with seven consecutive victories, but it is a different story at home, where they lose ten League games. They reach the quarter-finals of the FA Cup and the final of the Anglo-Italian. However, it is no compensation for eighth position in the First Division. Derby's 66 points leave them ten short of a play-off place.

Best win 7-0 thrashing of Southend in the Coca-Cola Cup in October; worst defeat 3-0 at Portsmouth in April. Top scorer: Paul Kitson (23).

1993-94

PRE-SEASON: The new arrivals at the Baseball Ground are Gary Charles from Nottingham Forest and Sheffield Wednesday's American midfielder John Harkes.

THE SEASON: Despite an opening-day 5-0 win over Sunderland, their best start for 79 years, Derby again under-achieve.

Cox resigns in October with chronic back trouble and his assistant Roy McFarland takes over.

County finish fourth with 71 points and then suffer the heartache of losing 2-1 to Midlands rivals Leicester in the play-off final at Wembley.

Best win is that 5-0 success at Sunderland; worst defeats are 4-0 losses against Wolves and Tranmere. Top scorers: Marco Gabbiadini and Tommy Johnson (15).

1994-95

PRE-SEASON: Lionel Pickering decides enough is enough and puts away his cheque book. In a pivotal move for the club's future, Roy McFarland is told to succeed or else.

THE SEASON: McFarland's job prospects are not helped by a return of just one point from the first four matches.

Pickering's patience runs out and he tells his manager to sell. Paul Kitson moves to Newcastle for £2.25 million, Tommy Johnson and Gary Charles leave for Aston Villa in a combined £2.9 million deal. With Derby wallowing in mid-table, Roy McFarland is sacked in April. Despite a late surge, managerless County finish in ninth position with 66 points.

Best win 5-0 hammering of play-off bound Tranmere in April; worst defeat 4-1 at Millwall in August. Top scorer: Marco Gabbiadini (13).

1995-96

PRE-SEASON: New manager Jim Smith's knowledge of the lower leagues is apparent when he signs midfielders Robin van der Laan and Darryl Powell from Port Vale and Portsmouth respectively. Club captain Craig Short moves to Everton for £2.4 million.

THE SEASON: Smith shows his managerial pedigree by steering Derby back to the top flight after a five-year absence.

With the Rams languishing in 17th place after a 5-1 thrashing at Tranmere in November, promotion appears to be nothing but a pipedream. Incredibly, though, Derby are eight points clear at the top by January following a run of 10 wins in 11 games. Sunderland and Crystal Palace catch up in the spring and the Rams need to beat Palace in their penultimate match to assure themselves of promotion. They do, 2-1, and finish as runners-up with 79 points.

Best win 6-2 on Easter Monday against Tranmere, avenging their worst defeat 5-1 at Tranmere five months earlier. Top scorer: Dean Sturridge (20).

DERBY COUNTY Supporters' Club Best XI Since 1993 (5-3-2)

Supporter/Manager: Granville Gigg

MARTIN TAYLOR – 'Keeper signed from local club Mile Oak Rovers in July 1986 and has made over 100 league appearances for the Rams.

JACOB LAURSEN – Danish international defender who signed from Silkeborg for £500,000 after Euro 96.

CRAIG SHORT – Imposing central defender who moved to Everton in July 1995 in a £2.4 million deal.

IGOR STIMAC – Abrasive Croatian defender who arrived at the Baseball Ground in October 1995 for £1.57 million from Hadjuk Split.

PAUL McGRATH – Seemingly indestructible Eire defender who was snapped up by Derby for a mere £200,000 in October 1996.

CHRIS POWELL – Assured left-sided defender who joined from Southend in January 1996 for £750,000.

PAUL WILLIAMS – Burly defender or midfielder who signed for Coventry in August 1995 for £975,000.

ROBIN VAN DER LAAN – Fiery Dutch midfielder who joined Derby for £475,000 from Port Vale in August 1995.

ALJOSA ASANOVIC – Gifted Croatian midfielder who has played throughout Europe and cost Derby £950,000.

DEAN STURRIDGE – Pacy striker who began his career as a Derby trainee, turning professional in July 1991.

MARCO GABBIADINI – Combative striker who signed for Derby in January 1992 from Crystal Palace for £1.2 million.

EVERTON – The Premiership History

Gary Speed

1996-97

PRE-SEASON: Joe Royle signs midfielder Gary Speed (£3.5 million) from Leeds and goalkeeper Paul Gerrard (£1.5 million) from Oldham to underpin a championship challenge. Gary Ablett and Barry Horne both move to Birmingham.

THE SEASON: A frustrating season for the blue half of Merseyside. Everton are expected to be in the hunt for honours but they win just one of their first seven Premiership matches and are dumped out of the Coca-Cola Cup by York City.

The arrival of England forward Nick Barmby in a club record £5.75 million transfer from Middlesbrough briefly sparks a revival in which the high point is a 7-1 drubbing of Southampton.

Duncan Ferguson

From then on it is mainly downhill. Six successive league defeats around Christmas end any thoughts of silverware and the departure of Andrei Kanchelskis to Fiorentina for £8 million signals the end for Royle. He resigns when permission to sign two unknown Norwegians is refused.

Stalwart skipper Dave Watson takes over the reins as temporary player-manager and steers the side clear of relegation. Everton finish 15th with 42 points.

Best win 7-1 v Southampton in November; worst defeat 4-0 at Wimbledon in September. Top scorer: Duncan Ferguson (10).

Everton facts and figures

CLUB ADDRESS: Goodison Park, Liverpool L4 4EL.

TELEPHONE: 0151-330 2200

FAX: 0151-523 9666

CLUBCALL: 0891 121199

The club was formed in 1878, turning professional in 1885.

PREVIOUS GROUNDS: Stanley Park, Priory Road, Anfield Road.

The club was previously called St Domingo FC.

RECORD ATTENDANCE: 78,299 v Liverpool, Div 1, September 1948.

BIGGEST WIN: 11-2 v Derby County, FA Cup 1st rnd, January 1890.

BIGGEST DEFEAT: 4-10 v Tottenham Hotspur, Div 1, October 1958.

TOP LEAGUE SCORER IN A SEASON: William 'Dixie' Dean (60), 1927-28.

HIGHEST AGGREGATE SCORER: William 'Dixie' Dean (377), 1925-37.

MOST CAPPED PLAYER: Neville Southall (91 at end of March 1997) for Wales.

STARS OF YESTERYEAR: William 'Dixie' Dean (1925-37), Ted Sagar (1929-52), Tommy Lawton (1936-39), Brian Labone (1957-71), Bobby Collins (1959-62), Alex Young (1960-67), Joe Royle (1965-74), Alan Ball (1966-71), Bob Latchford (1973-81), Andy Gray (1983-85), Gary Lineker (1985-86).

GREAT MANAGERS: William Cuff (1901-18), Thomas McIntosh (1919-35), Theo Kelly (1936-48), Cliff Britton (1948-56), Harry Catterick (1961-73), Howard Kendall (1981-87, 1990-93 and 1997-).

HONOURS: 1890-91 – First Division champions, 1906 – FA Cup winners, 1914-15, 1927-28 – First Division champions, 1930-31 – Second Division champions, 1931-32 – First Division champions, 1933 – FA Cup winners, 1938-39 – First Division champions, 1962-63 – First Division champions, 1966 – FA Cup winners, 1969-70 – First Division champions, 1984 – FA Cup winners, 1984-85 – First Division champions, European Cup Winners' Cup winners, 1986-87 – First Division champions, 1995 – FA Cup winners.

PREMIER MANAGERS: Howard Kendall 1990-93, Mike Walker 1994, Joe Royle 1994-97, Dave Watson (Caretaker player-manager) 1997, Howard Kendall 1997-

1992-93

PRE-SEASON: In July the club reveals it has debts of £3.6 million but still spends £500,000 to sign striker Paul Rideout from Rangers.

THE SEASON: A 1-1 home draw with Sheffield Wednesday is followed by a stunning 3-0 win at Manchester United, who were to end the season as champions.

Everton's form suffers afterwards, though, and the club go six home matches without a victory. Their away form is not much better. The Blues are left hovering around the relegation area and, while never in serious danger, they are not too far away from trouble. They end the season 13th with 53 points.

Best win 5-2 at Manchester City; worst defeat 5-3 at home by QPR. Top scorer: Tony Cottee (12).

1993-94

PRE-SEASON: Peter Beardsley moves to Newcastle but Graham Stuart arrives from Chelsea for £850,000.

THE SEASON: Another flying start sees Everton win 2-0 at Southampton and follow up with home wins over Manchester City and Sheffield United. In the first published table, they are second – behind Liverpool. Another mid-season slump prompts the resignation of manager Howard Kendall. Norwich manager Mike Walker takes over but cannot prevent a slide into the relegation zone.

Everton play their last match of the season at home to Wimbledon needing a victory. They trail 2-0 after only 20 minutes, but miraculously come back to win 3-2 with Graham Stuart scoring twice. They are saved when Sheffield United lose to a late goal at Chelsea.

Best win 6-2 v Swindon in January; worst defeat 5-1 by Norwich at Goodison Park in September. Top scorer: Tony Cottee (16).

1994-95

PRE-SEASON: Mike Walker spends heavily, bringing in Vinny Samways from Tottenham for £2.2 million and Nigerian striker Daniel Amokachi from Bruges for £3 million.

THE SEASON: Everton make a disastrous start to their Premiership campaign. It takes them 13 matches to record their first win – a 1-0 home victory over West Ham. Walker is fired in mid-November and Joe Royle, the former Goodison playing hero and manager at Oldham for over 10 years, makes a triumphant return.

Royle works the oracle. Liverpool are beaten in his first match in charge and Everton ease away from the relegation zone with the help of Duncan Ferguson, who joins the club initially on loan from Rangers. They cap the season with an FA Cup Final victory over Manchester United. In the league they finish 15th with 50 points.

Best win 4-1 at home to Ipswich Town in December; worst defeat 4-0 at Manchester City in August. Top scorer: Paul Rideout (13).

1995-96

PRE-SEASON: Joe Royle makes one major purchase, signing Andrei Kanchelskis from Manchester United for £5 million.

THE SEASON: Expectations are high at Goodison but patchy early-season form sees Everton drop out of the title chase. To make matters worse, Duncan Ferguson receives a jail sentence for an assault on an opponent, dating back to his days in Scotland.

The Blues finish with four victories out of six but results go against them on the final day of the season and they miss out on a Uefa Cup place. They end up sixth with 61 points and the satisfaction of having won 2-1 at arch rivals Liverpool.

Best win 4-0 at home to Midddlesbrough; worst defeat 3-1 at home to Newcastle in October and away to QPR in April. Top scorer: Andrei Kanchelskis (16).

EVERTON Supporters' Club Best XI Since 1993 (4-3-3)

Supporter/Manager: Jim King

NEVILLE SOUTHALL – Evergreen Welsh international 'keeper who has played over 600 games for Everton since signing from Bury in July 1981.

MATTHEW JACKSON – Versatile defender who arrived at Goodison for £600,000 from Luton in October 1991.

DAVE WATSON – Aggressive former England defender who was signed for only £900,000 in August 1986 from Norwich.

DAVID UNSWORTH – Influential England defender who started out as an Everton trainee, turning professional in June 1992.

ANDY HINCHCLIFFE – Attacking left back who left Manchester City for Goodison in July 1990 for £800,000.

JOHN EBBRELL – Competitive midfielder who left Everton to join Sheffield United in February 1997 for £1 million.

IAN SNODIN – Well-travelled midfielder who played over 200 games during his seven-year spell with Everton.

GARY SPEED – Athletic Welsh winger signed from Leeds United for £3.5 million in June 1996.

ANDREI KANCHELSKIS – Incredibly quick Ukranian winger who moved to Italy to join Fiorentina for £8 million in January 1997.

DUNCAN FERGUSON – Tall Scottish striker who signed for Everton for £4 million from Rangers in October 1994.

TONY COTTEE – Former England striker who scored 99 goals for Everton in his six seasons at Goodison.

Lee Bowyer

LEEDS UNITED – The Premiership History

1996-97 PRE-SEASON: Howard Wilkinson has a summer clearance sale at Elland Road. Gary Speed goes to Everton, John Lukic leaves for Arsenal and, most surprisingly, captain Gary McAllister is sold to Coventry. Joining are Liverpool legend Ian Rush (on a free transfer), Charlton youngster Lee Bowyer, Crystal Palace 'keeper Nigel Martyn and Manchester United winger Lee Sharpe for a combined £9.35 million. Striker Tony Yeboah is out with a knee injury.

THE SEASON: Leeds' shapeless start to the season costs Wilkinson his job. A 4-0 home defeat by Manchester United is the final straw.

The man asked to bring the glory days back to Elland Road is George Graham, returning to the game after being banned for a year following the "bung inquiry" controversy. Leeds lose five of the first six matches and Graham realises he has a major job on his hands.

The first priority is to tighten a creaky defence and Leeds become the grinders of the Premiership. Fourteen of their final 23 matches have one goal or none in them. Nine of them are 0-0 draws and goalkeeper Martyn is king of the clean sheets with 20 in Premiership games.

Graham signs Gunnar Halle from Oldham and Robert Molenaar from FC Volendam, but it is the form of Martyn in goal which proves the biggest factor in their miserly defence.

Leeds now have that Graham-look and the season, while not wholly satisfactory, is a major step in re-shaping the club's playing style for future success.

Best wins 3-0 v Sunderland and Leicester; worst defeats 4-0 by Manchester United and Liverpool. Top scorers: Lee Sharpe and Brian Deane (5).

Nigel Martyn

Leeds facts and figures

CLUB ADDRESS: Elland Road, Leeds LS11 0ES.
TELEPHONE: 0113-226 6000
FAX: 0113-272 0370
CLUBCALL: 0891 121180
The club was formed in 1919, following the disbandment of Leeds City, turning professional in 1920.
PREVIOUS GROUNDS: None.
RECORD ATTENDANCE: 57,892 v Sunderland, FA Cup 5th rnd replay, March 1967.
BIGGEST WIN: 10-0 v Lyn (Oslo) in European Cup, September 1969.
BIGGEST DEFEAT: 1-8 v Stoke City in Div 1, August 1934.
TOP LEAGUE SCORER IN A SEASON: John Charles (42), 1953-54.
HIGHEST AGGREGATE SCORER: Peter Lorimer (238), 1965-79 and 1983-86.
MOST CAPPED PLAYER: Billy Bremner (54) for Scotland.
STARS OF YESTERYEAR: John Charles (1948-56 and 1962), Jackie Charlton (1952-72), Billy Bremner (1959-76), Norman Hunter (1961-76), Johnny Giles (1963-74), Gordon Strachan (1989-95).
GREAT MANAGERS: Arthur Fairclough (1920-27), Don Revie (1961-74), Howard Wilkinson (1988-96).
HONOURS: 1923-24 – Second Division champions, 1963-64 – Second Division champions, 1967-68 – League Cup winners, European Fairs Cup winners, 1968-69 – First Division champions, 1970-71 – European Fairs Cup winners, 1971-72 – FA Cup winners, 1973-74 - First Division champions, 1989-90 – Second Division champions, 1991-92 – First Division champions.
PREMIER MANAGERS: Howard Wilkinson 1988-96, George Graham 1996-

1992-93

PRE-SEASON: After winning the First Division championship in 1991-92, Howard Wilkinson strengthens his squad with midfielders Scott Sellars (£950,000 from Blackburn) and David Rocastle (£2 million from Arsenal). Neither player settles at Elland Road.

THE SEASON: The champions frustrate their supporters with a season of Jekyll and Hyde performances. They dominate teams at home, but fail to register a single Premiership victory away from Elland Road.

Heavy defeats at Ipswich, Manchester City and Middlesbrough see them languishing at the lower end of the table. In November, Wilkinson angers the supporters by selling Eric Cantona to Manchester United for £1.2 million. He does not replace him. Leeds crash out of the European Cup to Glasgow Rangers and end the season in a lowly 17th position with only 51 points.

Best win 5-0 v Tottenham in August; worst defeat 4-0 at Manchester City and at Tottenham. Top scorer: Lee Chapman (15).

1993-94

PRE-SEASON: Wilkinson sells his top scorer, Lee Chapman, to Portsmouth for £250,000, replacing him with Brian Deane from Sheffield United for £2.7 million.

THE SEASON:Leeds fail to win any of their first three away games and appear set for another frustrating campaign. The return of Rod Wallace to the side coincides with a change in their fortunes, however, and a run of 14 games without defeat sees them climb to second.

In October, David Batty is sold to Blackburn for £2.75 million while David White arrives from Sheffield United. But when Wallace is injured the goals dry up. United drop to fifth, where they stay until the end of the season.

Best win 5-0 v Swindon on the final day; worst defeat 4-0 at home to Norwich in August. Top scorer: Rod Wallace (17).

1994-95

PRE-SEASON: Howard Wilkinson buys Carlton Palmer and Nigel Worthington from Sheffield Wednesday and brings Phil Masinga over from South Africa.

THE SEASON: Youngster Noel Whelan impresses early on, scoring six times in 11 games to push Leeds up to sixth, but he then loses his sparkle and Leeds go four games over the Christmas period without a goal.

Wilkinson responds by signing Ghanaian international Tony Yeboah from Eintracht Frankfurt for £3.4 million. Yeboah quickly justifies his price tag with 12 goals in 18 matches to end as United's top scorer. Leeds again finish fifth.

Best wins 4-0 over QPR and Ipswich; worst defeats 3-0 at Everton and Nottingham Forest. Top scorer: Tony Yeboah (12).

1995-96

PRE-SEASON: While other clubs are investing heavily in new players, Wilkinson prefers to stick with his tried and tested squad.

THE SEASON: Leeds make an impressive start to the season, winning 2-1 at West Ham then beating Liverpool 1-0. Tony Yeboah thrills the supporters with 'Goal-of-the-Season' contenders every week. Their worst-ever defeat in Europe – 8-3 on aggregate by PSV Eindhoven – is offset by their progress to the Coca-Cola Cup Final but they lose that 3-0 to Aston Villa.

The signing of Swedish striker Tomas Brolin from Parma for £4.5 million fails to prevent their free-fall down the table. Chairman Leslie Silver steps down and Wilkinson becomes the target of increasing hostility from the Elland Road fans. United finish 13th with 43 points.

Best win 4-2 at Wimbledon in September; worst defeat 5-0 away at Liverpool. Top scorer: Tony Yeboah (12).

LEEDS
Supporters' Club Best XI Since 1993 (4-4-2)

Supporter/Manager: Eric Caraile

NIGEL MARTYN – England 'keeper who left Crystal Palace for Elland Road in July 1996 for £2.25 million.

GARY KELLY – Tireless Republic of Ireland full-back who began his career with Home Farm, signing for Leeds in September 1991.

CHRIS FAIRCLOUGH – Strong-tackling central defender who left Leeds in July 1995 for Bolton in a £500,000 deal.

LUCAS RADEBE – South African international who signed from Kaizer Chiefs in September 1994 for £250,000.

TONY DORIGO – Forceful left back who arrived at Elland Road from Chelsea in June 1991 for £1.3 million.

GARY McALLISTER – Scotland captain who led Leeds to the First Division title in 1991-92 but has since moved to Coventry.

GORDON STRACHAN – Wily Scottish midfielder who joined Leeds for £300,000 in March 1989 and played over 200 matches for the club.

DAVID BATTY – Combative England midfielder who began his professional career at Elland Road.

GARY SPEED – Pacy Welsh winger who played over 300 games for Leeds before joining Everton for £3.5 million in June 1996.

LEE CHAPMAN – Journeyman striker who scored 80 goals for Leeds before joining Portsmouth for £250,000 in August 1993.

TONY YEBOAH – Explosive Ghanaian striker who arrived at Leeds from Eintracht Frankfurt for £3.4 million in January 1995.

LEICESTER CITY – The Premiership History

Emile Heskey

Steve Claridge

1996-97

PRE-SEASON: With the emergence of England Under-21 striker Emile Heskey, Martin O'Neill is prepared to allow Iwan Roberts to leave Filbert Street for Wolves in a £1 million deal. He strengthens his team by purchasing Kasey Keller from Millwall for £900,000, Spencer Prior from Norwich for £600,000 and Ian Marshall from Ipswich for £800,000.

THE SEASON: Leicester exceed their wildest dreams by lifting the Coca-Cola Cup and comfortably avoiding relegation. O'Neill's team mirror his combative nature by scrapping for every point.

The Foxes win just one of their opening six matches but successive victories over Tottenham and Leeds establish a place in mid-table.

O'Neill pulls off one of the deals of the season in January when he signs Oxford's highly-rated defender Matt Elliott for £1.6 million. Robert Ullathorne and Steve Guppy also arrive.

City always seem to come up with a win when it is most needed. A 1-0 success over Aston Villa on March 5 means they can approach the Coca-Cola Cup Final knowing that their Premiership future is almost secured.

They need a late equaliser from Emile Heskey to take Middlesbrough to a replay, in which Steve Claridge's goal clinches a European place for City.

A 4-2 victory at Blackburn on the final day completes a happy season for the Foxes. They finish ninth with 47 points.

Best wins 4-2 v Derby and Blackburn; worst defeat 3-0 at Leeds in January. Top scorer: Steve Claridge (12).

Leicester facts and figures

CLUB ADDRESS: City Stadium, Filbert St, Leicester LE2 7FL.

TELEPHONE: 0116-291 5000

FAX: 01162-247 0585

CLUBCALL: 0891 121185

The club was formed in 1884 and turned professional in 1888.

PREVIOUS GROUNDS: Victoria Park, Belgrave Road.

The club was previously called Leicester Fosse.

RECORD ATTENDANCE: 47,298 v Tottenham, FA Cup 5th rnd, February 1928.

BIGGEST WIN: 10-0 v Portsmouth, Division 1, October 1928.

BIGGEST DEFEAT: 0-12 (as Leicester Fosse) v Nottingham Forest, Division 1, 1909.

TOP LEAGUE SCORER IN A SEASON: Arthur Rowley (44), 1956-57.

HIGHEST AGGREGATE SCORER: Arthur Chandler (273), 1923-34.

MOST CAPPED PLAYER: John O'Neill (39) for Northern Ireland.

STARS OF YESTERYEAR: Arthur Chandler (1923-34), Don Revie (1946-49), Arthur Rowley (1950-57), Gordon Banks (1959-66), Peter Shilton (1965-74), David Nish (1966-72), Keith Weller (1971-78), Gary Lineker (1978-85).

GREAT MANAGERS: Willie Orr (1926-32), Matt Gillies (1959-68), Jimmy Bloomfield (1971-77), Jock Wallace (1978-82), Martin O'Neill (1995-).

HONOURS: 1924-25, 1936-37, 1953-54, 1956-57 – Division 2 champions, 1963-64 – League Cup winners, 1970-71, 1979-80 – Division 2 champions, 1996-97 – Coca-Cola Cup winners.

PREMIER MANAGERS: Brian Little 1991-94, Mark McGhee 1994-95, Martin O'Neill 1995-

1992-93

PRE-SEASON: Brian Little signs David Lowe from Ipswich for £250,000 and Colin Hill comes in from Sheffield United for £200,000. Kevin Russell, Ally Mauchlen, Tommy Wright and Paul Reid all leave.

THE SEASON: The Foxes suffer a Wembley play-off heartache after battling back from 3-0 down to Swindon. They level the scores before losing to a late penalty.

Inconsistency denies them automatic promotion, 14 defeats undermining their 22 victories. The arrival of Steve Agnew from Blackburn sparks a run of seven successive wins, in which they score 20 goals, in March. But then they can manage just two draws in their final five away games and finish sixth with 76 points.

Best win 5-2 v Watford in January; worst defeat 7-1 at champions Newcastle in May. Top scorer: Steve Walsh (16).

1993-94

PRE-SEASON: Goalkeeper Gavin Ward and defender Brian Carey both join for transfer fees decided by tribunals. David Speedie signs on a free transfer from Southampton.

THE SEASON: Leicester, in the top six all season, finally make it to the promised land of the Premiership. They briefly top the First Division table in November following a 3-0 victory over Southend.

Too many matches are drawn, including a 4-4 Christmas thriller at Watford. Successive wins over Middlesbrough and Birmingham set them up for a promotion push that does not materialise. They register only two more wins in their remaining 12 games to finish fourth and reach the play-offs with 73 points. They beat Tranmere in the semi-final before two Steve Walsh goals give them a memorable Wembley victory over Derby.

Best win 4-0 at home to Millwall in August; worst defeat 4-0 at Nottingham Forest in February. Top scorer: Iwan Roberts (13).

1994-95

PRE-SEASON: Leicester prepare for the Premiership by signing midfielder Mark Draper from Notts County for £1.25 million but most experts are tipping them for relegation.

THE SEASON: The Foxes lose four of their first five games before beating Tottenham 3-1. By that stage, however, they are set for a struggle. It gets worse as Brian Little resigns in November to take over at Aston Villa. Mark McGhee is prised away from Reading as his replacement.

City remain in the bottom two for the rest of the season and are relegated without playing on April 13 when West Ham beat Wimbledon. They manage only 29 points from 42 games to end in 21st position.

Best win 3-1 v Tottenham in September; worst defeats 4-0 at Chelsea and Manchester United. Top scorer: Iwan Roberts (9).

1995-96

PRE-SEASON: Mark McGhee sells Gavin Ward, Nicky Mohan and Ian Ormondroyd to Bradford and Mark Draper leaves to rejoin former City boss Brian Little at Aston Villa for £3.25 million.

THE SEASON: After a 1-0 win at Derby in September, Leicester top the table and remain in the hunt despite a five-game run entering December when they fail to win. McGhee then becomes the second manager to leave the struggling club in as many seasons. Martin O'Neill is appointed four days before Christmas.

City slip to ninth at the end of March but win their last four games to make the play-offs. They finish fifth with 71 points and come from behind to defeat Crystal Palace at Wembley, with Steve Claridge scoring the vital winner in the last minute of extra time.

Best win 3-0 v Birmingham in their final home match; worst defeat 4-2 at Ipswich in February. Top scorer: Iwan Roberts (19).

LEICESTER Supporters' Club Best XI Since 1993 (4-3-3)

Supporter/Manager: Mike Cosgrove

KASEY KELLER – American international 'keeper signed from Millwall for £900,000 in August 1996.

STEVE WALSH – Loyal left-sided defender who joined the Foxes from Wigan in June 1986 for £100,000.

MATT ELLIOTT – Dynamic centre back who signed for Leicester in January 1997 for £1.6 million.

PONTUS KAAMARK – Swedish international midfielder who left IFK Gothenberg for Leicester for £840,000 in November 1995.

SIMON GRAYSON – Versatile full back or right-sided midfielder who began his career as a trainee at Leeds United. Sold to Aston Villa in July 1997 for £1.2 million.

NEIL LENNON – Creative Northern Ireland midfielder signed from Crewe in March 1996 for £750,000.

GARRY PARKER – Experienced and influential midfielder who arrived at Filbert Street from Aston Villa for £300,000 in February 1995.

MARK DRAPER – Flamboyant former England Under-21 player who moved on to Aston Villa in July 1995 for £3.25 million.

STEVE CLARIDGE – Well-travelled striker who arrived at Leicester from Birmingham City in a £1 million deal in March 1996.

DAVID SPEEDIE – Determined Scottish international who was forced to quit the game at Premiership level with a knee injury.

EMILE HESKEY – Powerful England Under-21 striker who started out as a Leicester trainee, turning professional on October 1995.

LIVERPOOL – The Premiership History

Jason McAteer

1996-97 PRE-SEASON: The greatest Liverpool goalscorer of all time, Ian Rush, leaves Anfield for Leeds on a free transfer. The only arrival is Czech Republic star Patrick Berger for £3.5 million from Borussia Dortmund.

THE SEASON: Berger brings his blistering Euro 96 form to the Liverpool team, who lead the Premiership with six wins in their opening eight games. With Robbie Fowler in top form, they are still leading in December.

Fowler scores four in the 5-1 demolition of Middlesbrough and hits another three days later as Liverpool beat Nottingham Forest 4-2.

But the New Year brings a stutter and Liverpool are one point behind Manchester United in late February. Then it all goes wrong in a big way as they pick up just 15 points in their final 11 matches to miss out on the runners-up spot and Champions League football in 1997-98. They slip to fourth place with 68 points.

During that period the European adventure also turns sour. A disastrous 3-0 defeat in the first leg of the European Cup Winners' Cup semi-final against Paris St Germain puts paid to their hopes of salvaging some silverware from a campaign that for a long time promised much.

After the dust has settled on the season, Liverpool sell Stan Collymore to Aston Villa for £7 million.

Best wins 5-1 over Chelsea and Middlesbrough; worst defeat 3-0 at Blackburn in November. Top scorer: Robbie Fowler (18).

Liverpool facts and figures

CLUB ADDRESS: Anfield Road, Liverpool L4 0TH.

TELEPHONE: 0151-263 2361

FAX: 0151-260 8813

CLUBCALL: 0891 121184

The club was formed in 1892, turning professional the same year.

PREVIOUS GROUNDS: None.

RECORD ATTENDANCE: 61,905 v Wolves, FA Cup 4th rnd, February 1952.

BIGGEST WIN: 11-0 v Stromsgodset Drammen, European Cup-Winners' Cup 1st rnd, September 1974.

BIGGEST DEFEAT: 1-9 v Birmingham City, Div 2, December 1954.

TOP LEAGUE SCORER IN A SEASON: Roger Hunt (41), 1961-62.

HIGHEST AGGREGATE SCORER: Ian Rush (344), 1980-96.

MOST CAPPED PLAYER: Ian Rush 67 (73) for Wales.

STARS OF YESTERYEAR: Elisha Scott (1915-35), Billy Liddell (1946-61), Roger Hunt (1959-69), Ian St. John (1961-71), Ron Yeats (1961-71), Tommy Smith (1962-78), Emlyn Hughes (1966-78), Ray Clemence (1967-81), Kevin Keegan (1971-77), Ray Kennedy (1974-82), Kenny Dalglish (1977-85), Alan Hansen (1977-90), Graeme Souness (1978-84), Ronnie Whelan (1979-94), Ian Rush (1980-96). Peter Beardsley (1987-91),

GREAT MANAGERS: Bill Shankly (1959-74) Bob Paisley (1974-83), Kenny Dalglish (1985-91).

HONOURS: 1893-94, 1895-96 – Second Division champions, 1900-01 – First Division champions, 1904-05 – Second Division champions, 1905-06, 1921-22, 1922-23, 1946-47 – First Division champions, 1961-62 – Second Division champions, 1963-64 – First Division champions, 1964-65 – FA Cup winners, 1965-66 – First Division champions, 1972-73 – First Division champions, Uefa Cup winners, 1973-74 – FA Cup winners, 1975-76 – First Division champions, Uefa Cup winners, 1976-77 – First Division champions, European Cup winners, 1977-78 – European Cup winners, 1978-79, 1979-80 – First Division champions, 1980-81 – League Cup winners, European Cup winners, 1981-82, 1982-83 – First Division champions, League Cup winners, 1983-84 – First Division champions, League Cup winners, European Cup winners, 1985-86 – First Division champions, FA Cup winners, 1987-88 – First Division champions, 1988-89 – FA Cup winners, 1989-90 – First Division champions, 1991-92 – FA Cup winners, 1994-95 – Coca-Cola Cup winners.

PREMIER MANAGERS: Graeme Souness 1991-94, Roy Evans 1994-

1992-93

PRE-SEASON: Graeme Souness sells experienced Barry Venison and Ray Houghton, then pays £1 million to Watford for David James and £2.3 million to Tottenham for Paul Stewart.

THE SEASON: A season of transition for the FA Cup holders. Jamie Redknapp, Rob Jones and Steve McManaman break through to the first team. Dean Saunders is sold to Villa in September. Liverpool finish only sixth with 59 points because of their away form – they win three matches and concede 37 goals.

Best win 5-0 v Crystal Palace in November; worst defeat 5-1 at Coventry. Top scorer: Ian Rush (14).

1993-94

PRE-SEASON: Souness spends £2.5 million on Tottenham's Neil Ruddock and £2.275 million on Forest's Nigel Clough.

THE SEASON: Liverpool win four of their first five games, Clough scoring four, then lose four successive games without scoring. Julian Dicks arrives from West Ham for £1.5 million and Robbie Fowler makes his debut alongside Ian Rush. Souness resigns in January, then new manager Roy Evans brings back Ronnie Whelan and Liverpool finish eighth with 60 points.

Best win 5-0 v Swindon in August; worst defeat 3-0 at Newcastle. Top scorer: Ian Rush (14).

Robbie Fowler

1994-95

PRE-SEASON: Trouble before a ball is kicked when Mark Wright and Julian Dicks miss the Germany tour for disciplinary reasons.

THE SEASON: Liverpool begin with a 6-1 victory at Crystal Palace. Robbie Fowler scores six goals in the first three games as the Reds remain in the top five all season. In the end, erratic home form – they lose to struggling Ipswich and Coventry – costs them a real title shot. Consolation comes in the Coca-Cola Cup Final when they beat Bolton 2-1.

Best win 6-1 v Crystal Palace; worst defeat 3-0 at West Ham. Top scorer: Robbie Fowler (25).

1995-96

PRE-SEASON: Liverpool break the British transfer record to sign Collymore for £8.5 million from Nottingham Forest in mid-June.

THE SEASON: A stunning opening-day goal from Collymore against Sheffield Wednesday raises hopes at Anfield but they lose three games in November, including a home derby defeat by arch-rivals Everton, and draw two. Despite a strong finish, Newcastle and Manchester United have pulled away. Liverpool finish third with 71 points and they lose the FA Cup Final 1-0 to Manchester United.

Best win 6-0 at home to Manchester City in October; worst defeats 2-1 at home to Everton, and away to Newcastle and Middlesbrough. Top scorer: Robbie Fowler (28).

LIVERPOOL
Supporters' Club Best XI Since 1993 (5-3-2)

Supporter/Manager: Andrew Williams

BRUCE GROBBELAAR – Eccentric Zimbabwean 'keeper who enjoyed 12 seasons at Anfield before joining Southampton on a free transfer.

ROB JONES – Composed former England full back who signed for Liverpool from Crewe in October 1991 for £300,000.

MARK WRIGHT – Cultured central defender who arrived at Anfield from Derby in July 1991 for £2.2 million.

JOHN SCALES – Classy central defender who left Liverpool for Tottenham in December 1996 for £2.6 million.

NEIL RUDDOCK – Abrasive defender who joined from Tottenham for £2.5 million in July 1993.

STIG INGE BJORNEBYE – Attacking left-sided Norwegian international who was signed from Rosenborg in December 1992 for £600,000.

JOHN BARNES – Silky former England midfielder who left Watford for Liverpool in June 1987 in a £900,000 deal.

RONNIE WHELAN – Long-serving Eire midfielder who left Anfield after 15 years on a free transfer to Southend in September 1994.

STEVE McMANAMAN – Elusive England winger who began his career as a Liverpool trainee, turning professional in February 1990.

ROBBIE FOWLER – Phenomenal young striker who signed professional forms at Liverpool in April 1992.

IAN RUSH – Prolific Welsh striker who scored 229 League goals for Liverpool during his two magnificent spells at Anfield.

MANCHESTER UNITED
– The Premiership History

1996-97

PRE-SEASON: Alex Ferguson catches Euro 96 fever by signing two of the tournament's foreign stars. Jordi Cruyff arrives from Barcelona for a knockdown price of £800,000, while Karel Poborsky joins from Slavia Prague for £3.5 million, but it is unknown Norwegian striker Ole-Gunnar Solskjaer who makes the biggest impact.

THE SEASON: Action starts a week early for United who, as holders of the double, open up at Wembley in the Charity Shield where they demolish Newcastle United 4-0.

United then prove themselves masters of the Premiership class once again. David Beckham makes the jump from promising youngster to England regular. His sensational lob from his own half over Wimbledon 'keeper Neil Sullivan on the opening day sets the tone.

Beckham's winner over Liverpool on October 12 puts United within a point of leaders Newcastle, but a nightmare 5-0 defeat at St James' Park is followed by a 6-3 thrashing at Southampton and for a moment United are rocking.

They then lose for the first time ever at home in European club football when Fenerbahce win 1-0 at Old Trafford and that is followed by another home defeat – this time Chelsea triumph 2-1.

Eight wins in nine matches around the turn of the year re-establish United's title credentials. They turn their attention to the Champions League with a 4-0 defeat of Portuguese side FC Porto at Old Trafford. Missed chances, however, cost them the match in the semi-final against Borussia Dortmund.

A 3-1 victory at Liverpool on April 19 effectively clinches United's fourth Premier Championship in five seasons. They finish seven points clear with 75 points. The season ends in sensational fashion when Eric Cantona announces his retirement from football at the age of 30.

Best win 5-0 v Sunderland in December; worst defeat 5-0 at Newcastle in October. Top scorer: Ole-Gunnar Solskjaer (18).

Above left: Ole-Gunnar Solskjaer
Left: Nicky Butt

Manchester United facts and figures

CLUB ADDRESS: Old Trafford, Manchester M16 0RA.
TELEPHONE: 0161-872 1661
FAX: 0161-876 5502
CLUBCALL: 0891 121161
The club was formed in 1878, turning professional in 1902.
PREVIOUS GROUNDS: North Road and Monsall Road, Bank Street, Old Trafford, Maine Road.
The club was previously called Newton Heath.
RECORD ATTENDANCE: 70,504 v Aston Villa, Div 1, December 1920.
BIGGEST WIN: 10-0 v RS Anderlecht, European Cup, Prelim round, September 1956.
BIGGEST DEFEAT: 0-7 v Blackburn, Div 1, April 1926.
TOP LEAGUE SCORER IN A SEASON: Dennis Viollet (32), 1959-60.
HIGHEST AGGREGATE SCORER: Bobby Charlton (198), 1956-73.
MOST CAPPED PLAYER: Bobby Charlton (106) for England.
STARS OF YESTERYEAR: Johnny Carey (1936-53), Jack Rowley (1946-54), Roger Byrne (1949-58), Tommy Taylor (1953-58), Bill Foulkes (1952-69), Duncan Edwards (1953-58), Bobby Charlton (1956-72), Nobby Stiles (1959-71), Denis Law (1962-72), Pat Crerand (1963-70), George Best (1963-73), Brian Kidd (1966-74), Bryan Robson (1981-94), Eric Cantona (1992-97).

1992-93

PRE-SEASON: Alex Ferguson aims to make amends for the disappointing previous season when United faded to lose the title to Leeds.

THE SEASON: United make an appalling start, losing their first two matches, but are then beaten only four more times. The signing of Eric Cantona in November, for £1.2 million from Leeds, proves to be the deal of the decade. The Frenchman's flair and self-confidence make all the difference as United lift the Championship, for the first time since 1967, by ten clear points.

Best win 5-0 v Coventry; worst defeat 3-0 at home to Everton in August. Top scorer: Mark Hughes (15).

1993-94

PRE-SEASON: Alex Ferguson, hoping for an assault on the European Cup, breaks the English transfer record to sign Roy Keane from Nottingham Forest for £3.75 million.

THE SEASON: Ferguson's team become only the fourth in modern times to secure the 'double' after a disastrous Champions' Cup exit to Turkish side Galatasaray. They lead the Premiership from start to finish to end on 92 points, eight clear of Blackburn. Two Cantona penalties help to crush Chelsea 4-0 in the FA Cup Final.

Best win 5-0 v Sheffield Wednesday; worst defeat 2-0 by Blackburn. Top scorer: Eric Cantona (18).

1994-95

PRE-SEASON: United pull out of the chase for Norwich's Chris Sutton – eventually bought by Blackburn. It is a decision which they were to regret.

THE SEASON: A frustrating season as United target the Champions League but fail to pass the group stage. Then, in the most sensational episode in the history of the Premier League, Eric Cantona assaults a spectator at Crystal Palace moments after being sent off and is banned for nine months. Ferguson breaks the British transfer record with £7 million for Andy Cole of Newcastle. Despite a late charge, United finish with 88 points, one behind Blackburn and also lose the FA Cup Final 1-0 to Everton.

Best win a Premiership record 9-0 hammering of Ipswich in March; worst defeat 2-0 at Liverpool. Top scorer: Andrei Kanchelskis (14).

1995-96

PRE-SEASON: Alex Ferguson surprisingly sells Paul Ince, Andrei Kanchelskis and Mark Hughes in big-money transfers.

THE SEASON: Ferguson turns to his youngsters – the Nevilles, Butt, Scholes and Beckham – and the dividend is a second 'double' in three seasons. They struggle early on, however, until Eric Cantona provides their salvation. Back from lengthy suspension, he scores a critical winner at Newcastle in early March. United complete an amazing title success on the final day with a 3-0 victory at Middlesbrough. Seven days later, another Cantona goal defeats Liverpool in the FA Cup Final.

Best win 5-0 at home over Nottingham Forest in April; worst defeat 4-1 at Tottenham in January. Top scorer: Eric Cantona (14).

GREAT MANAGERS: Ernest Magnall (1900-12), Herbert Bamlett (1927-31), Jimmy Porter (1938-44), Matt Busby (1945-69), Tommy Docherty (1972-77), Ron Atkinson (1981-86), Alex Ferguson (1986-).

HONOURS: 1907-08 – First Division champions, 1909 – FA Cup winners, 1910-11 First Division champions, 1935-36 – Second Division champions, 1948 – FA Cup winners, 1951-52, 1955-56, 1956-57 – First Division champions, 1963 – FA Cup winners, 1964-65, 1966-67 – First Division champions, 1967-68 – European Cup winners, 1974-75 – Second Division champions, 1976-77, 1982-83, 1984-85, 1989-90 – FA Cup winners, 1991 – European Cup Winners' Cup winners, 1992 – League Cup winners, 1992-93 – FA Premier League champions, 1993-94, 1995-96 – FA Premiership champions, FA Cup winners, 1996-97 – FA Premiership champions.

PREMIER MANAGER: Alex Ferguson 1986-

MAN. UNITED
Supporters' Club Best XI Since 1993 (4-4-2)

Supporter/Manager: Eddie Mansell

PETER SCHMEICHEL – Dominating Danish international 'keeper who signed from Brondby for £550,000 in August 1991.

PAUL PARKER – Versatile former England defender who signed for United from QPR in August 1991 for £2 million.

STEVE BRUCE – Fiercely competitive central defender who left Old Trafford in 1996 to join Birmingham.

GARY PALLISTER – Massive England centre back signed from Middlesbrough in August 1989 in a £2.3 million deal.

DENIS IRWIN – Consistent Republic of Ireland full back transferred from Oldham to United for £625,000 in June 1990.

ANDREI KANCHELSKIS – Gifted Ukranian winger who signed for United from Shakhtyor Donetsk in March 1991 for £650,000.

BRYAN ROBSON – Legendary midfielder who left United to become Middlesbrough player-manager on a free transfer in May 1994.

ROY KEANE – Dynamic and temperamental Eire midfielder signed from Nottingham Forest in July 1993 for £3.75 million.

RYAN GIGGS – Mercurial Welsh left winger who graduated through the United youth ranks, turning pro in December 1990.

ERIC CANTONA – Enigmatic French striker who arrived at Old Trafford from Leeds United in November 1992 for £1.2 million.

MARK HUGHES – Physical Wales forward who left United after 13 glorious seasons to join Chelsea for £1.5 million in July 1995.

NEWCASTLE UNITED – The Premiership History

1996-97 PRE-SEASON: Newcastle break the bank to bring local lad Alan Shearer to St James' Park for a record fee of £15 million. The signing still does not satisfy Kevin Keegan's doubters, though. They wonder why he has bought another striker when it is the defence which seems to need most attention.

THE SEASON: United make a shaky start, losing two of their first three matches after a 4-0 mauling in the Charity Shield by Manchester United.

Then seven successive victories take the Magpies top by October. The highlight is a super five-goal revenge show over Alex Ferguson's team.

Shearer forms a potent partnership with Les Ferdinand. Between them they score 41 Premiership goals, but they can do little as Newcastle slip out of the title picture in December, failing to win during a disastrous seven-match run.

A 7-1 drubbing of Tottenham appears to have put them back on track until Keegan stuns the football world in January by announcing his resignation. His successor is Kenny Dalglish, who offers a more pragmatic approach.

Defeat by Monaco in the Uefa Cup quarter-final is compensated for by a late charge in the league where a 5-0 victory over Nottingham Forest on the final day gives Newcastle a Champions' League place for the 1997-98 season. They finish second with 68 points, seven points behind Manchester United.

Best win 7-1 over Tottenham in December; worst defeats 2-0 by Everton and Leicester. Top scorer: Alan Shearer (25).

Above left: Alan Shearer

Left: Philippe Albert

Newcastle facts and figures

CLUB ADDRESS: St James' Park, Newcastle-upon-Tyne NE1 4ST.

TELEPHONE: 0191-201 8400

FAX: 0191-232 9875

CLUBCALL: 0891 121190

The club was formed in 1881 and turned professional in 1889.

PREVIOUS GROUNDS: South Byker, Chillingham Road.

The club was previously called Stanley and Newcastle East End.

RECORD ATTENDANCE: 68,386 v Chelsea, Div 1, September 1930.

BIGGEST WIN: 13-0 v Newport County, Div 2, October 1946.

BIGGEST DEFEAT: 0-9 v Burton Wanderers, Div 2, April 1895.

TOP LEAGUE SCORER IN A SEASON: Hughie Gallacher (36), 1926-27.

HIGHEST AGGREGATE SCORER: Jackie Milburn (200), 1946-57.

MOST CAPPED PLAYER: Alf McMichael (40) for Northern Ireland.

STARS OF YESTERYEAR: Hughie Gallacher (1925-30), Jackie Milburn (1946-57), Len Shackleton (1946-48), Joe Harvey (1946-52), Bobby Mitchell (1949-60), Vic Keeble (1952-57), Bryan 'Pop' Robson (1962-71), Malcolm Macdonald (1971-76), Tommy Craig (1974-78), Chris Waddle (1980-85), Paul Gascoigne (1983-88), Mirandinha (1987-90), Andy Cole (1993-95).

GREAT MANAGERS: Stan Seymour (1939-47, 1950-54 & 1956-58), Joe Harvey (1962-75), Arthur Cox (1980-84), Jim Smith (1988-91), Kevin Keegan (1992-97).

HONOURS: 1904-05 – First Division champions, 1906-07 – First Division champions, 1908-09 – First Division champions, 1910 – FA Cup winners, 1924 – FA Cup winners, 1926-27 – First Division champions, 1932 – FA Cup winners, 1951 – FA Cup winners, 1952 – FA Cup winners, 1955 – FA Cup winners, 1964-65 – Second Division champions, 1968-69 – Inter Cities Fairs Cup winners, 1992-93 – First Division champions.

PREMIER MANAGERS: Kevin Keegan 1992-97, Kenny Dalglish 1997-

1992-93

PRE-SEASON: Having saved Newcastle from dropping into the Second Division, Kevin Keegan starts the new season with a clean slate. He soon adds future England star Robert Lee to his squad. The fee is £700,000 from Charlton Athletic.

THE SEASON: United make a blistering start to the season. They win their first 11 games, a run that is halted by a 1-0 home defeat by Grimsby on October 24.

It is their only home reverse of the season. Indeed, they storm through the First Division, winning 29 of their 46 matches. Just to make sure of their promotion, Keegan buys Andy Cole from Bristol City for £1.75 million. Keegan is hailed on Tyneside as the club's saviour. He leads Newcastle to the title with 96 points – eight more than second-placed West Ham.

Best wins 7-1 v Leicester and 6-0 v Barnsley; worst defeat 3-0 at Tranmere. Top scorer: David Kelly (24).

1993-94

PRE-SEASON: Former St James' Park favourite Peter Beardsley returns for £1.5 million from Everton. However, he suffers a triple fracture of the cheekbone in Ronnie Whelan's testimonial at Liverpool.

THE SEASON: The philosophy is simple, attack being the best form of defence, but Newcastle have to overcome their Premiership naivety. They lose their opening two matches before a 1-1 draw at Manchester United steadies the nerves.

A string of good away results at the turn of the year – including wins at Aston Villa, Tottenham, Everton and Norwich – help to propel Newcastle to third in the table. Darren Peacock arrives for £2.7 million from QPR. United finish third with 77 points, having scored 82 goals.

Best win 7-1 v Swindon in March; worst defeat 4-2 at Wimbledon in February. Top scorer: Andy Cole (34).

1994-95

PRE-SEASON: Marc Hottiger, the Swiss full-back, is signed for £600,000 and Belgian defender Philippe Albert for £2.65 million.

THE SEASON: Sparkling early form is highlighted by wins at Leicester, West Ham and Arsenal and Newcastle go top after scoring 22 goals in their first six matches. The first defeat is on October 29, 2-0 at Manchester United, but by Christmas they have slipped to third.

Keegan decides to sell star striker Andy Cole to Manchester United for £6 million plus £1 million-rated winger Keith Gillespie. His side finishes sixth with 72 points.

Best win 5-1 v Southampton in August; worst defeat 3-0 at QPR in February. Top scorer: Peter Beardsley (12).

1995-96

PRE-SEASON: Keegan buys Les Ferdinand from QPR for £6 million, Warren Barton from Wimbledon for £4 million and Frenchman David Ginola from Paris St Germain for £2.5 million. Reading goalkeeper Shaka Hislop is also signed.

THE SEASON: The Toon Army is left with nothing but broken dreams as Newcastle start like champions only to watch a 12-point Premiership lead disappear.

Keegan promises his side will attack come what may but defensive lapses creep into their game, especially away from home where they lose four matches out of five in the run-in. The signings of Colombian striker Faustino Asprilla for £6.7 million from Parma and David Batty, £3.75 from Blackburn, fail to halt their slide. The pivotal match is a 1-0 home defeat by Manchester United in March. They finish with two successive 1-1 draws and 78 points, four behind Manchester United.

Best win 6-1 at home to Wimbledon in October; worst defeats 2-0 at Manchester United and West Ham. Top scorer: Les Ferdinand (25).

NEWCASTLE
Supporters' Club Best XI Since 1993 (4-3-3)

Supporter/Manager: David Craggs

PAVEL SRNICEK – Agile Czech international 'keeper who arrived at St James' Park from Banik Ostrava in February 1991 for a bargain £350,000.

STEVE WATSON – Versatile former England Under-21 defender who signed professional forms with Newcastle in April 1991.

ROBBIE ELLIOTT – Strong-tackling defender who graduated through the Newcastle junior ranks, turning pro in April 1991.

DARREN PEACOCK – Long-striding centre back who signed from QPR in a £2.7 million deal in March 1994.

STEVE HOWEY – Combative England defender who turned professional with the Magpies in December 1989.

DAVID BATTY – Aggressive England midfielder signed from Blackburn Rovers in March 1996 for £3.75 million.

PETER BEARDSLEY – Skilful striker or midfielder who returned to St James' Park in July 1993 after successful spells with Liverpool and Everton.

ROBERT LEE – All-action midfielder who started his career with Charlton, signing for Newcastle in September 1992.

FAUSTINO ASPRILLA – Entertaining Colombian striker signed from Parma in February 1996 for £6.7 million.

LES FERDINAND – Athletic former QPR marksman who joined Newcastle in June 1995 for £6 million.

ALAN SHEARER – Deadly England captain who left Blackburn in a world record £15 million deal in the summer of 1996.

SHEFFIELD WEDNESDAY
– The Premiership History

Benito Carbone

1996-97 PRE-SEASON: Astute buying by David Pleat brings in four youngsters – Andy Booth (£2.7 million from Huddersfield), Scott Oakes (Luton Town), Wayne Collins (Crewe) and goal-keeper Matt Clarke (Rotherham).

THE SEASON: Wednesday come out of the blocks like a train – four wins out of four, including an impressive 2-1 success at Newcastle. As August turns to September, they peer down on the rest of the Premiership.

They then run out of steam, particularly away from home where they are to win one Premiership match between mid-September and February, although significantly that was 1-0 at Anfield.

Home form is better but sprinkled with too many draws, and only one Premiership side is to visit Hillsborough and come away with maximum points – Chelsea, 2-0 victors in September.

A month later and Pleat buys from abroad, signing Benito Carbone for £2.6 million from Internazionale. He makes his debut in a 1-1 home draw with Blackburn.

Andy Booth

The season winds down with a dreadful away run, four successive defeats, 12 goals conceded and two scored. They finish seventh. A creditable performance but also one that left them wondering what might have been.

Best wins, both at home, 3-1 over Middlesbrough and Wimbledon; worst defeat 5-1 at West Ham. Top scorer: Andy Booth (10).

Sheffield Wednesday facts and figures

CLUB ADDRESS: Hillsborough, Sheffield, S6 1SW.

TELEPHONE: 0114-221 2121

FAX: 0114-233 7145

CLUBCALL: 0891 121186

The club was formed in 1867 and turned professional in 1887, becoming Sheffield Wednesday in 1929. Previous name: The Wednesday.

PREVIOUS GROUNDS: Highfield, Myrtle Road, Sheaf House, Olive Grove and Owlerton (known as Hillsborough since 1912).

RECORD ATTENDANCE: 72,841 v Manchester City, FA Cup 5th rnd, February 1934.

BIGGEST WIN: 12-0 v Halliwell, FA Cup 1st rnd, January 1891.

BIGGEST DEFEAT: 0-10 v Aston Villa, Div 1, October 1912.

TOP LEAGUE SCORER IN A SEASON: Derek Dooley (46), 1951-52.

HIGHEST AGGREGATE SCORER: Andy Wilson (216), 1900-20.

MOST CAPPED PLAYER: Nigel Worthington (63) for Northern Ireland.

STARS OF YESTERYEAR: Ernie Blenkinsop (1923-34), Alf Strange (1927-35), Derek Dooley (1947-52), Albert Quixall (1950-58), Jackie Sewell (1951-55), John Fantham (1956-69), Ron Springett (1958-67).

GREAT MANAGERS: Robert Brown (1920-33) Billy Walker (1933-37), Harry Catterick (1958-61), Howard Wilkinson (1983-88).

HONOURS: 1895-96 – FA Cup winners, 1899-1900 – Second Division champions, 1902-03, 1903-04 – First Division champions, 1906-07 – FA Cup winners, 1925-26 – Second Division champions, 1928-29, 1929-30 – First Division champions, 1934-35 – FA Cup winners, 1951-52, 1955-56, 1958-59 - Second Division champions, 1990-91 – League Cup winners.

PREMIER MANAGERS: Trevor Francis 1991-95, David Pleat 1995-

1992-93

PRE-SEASON: Manager Trevor Francis keeps faith with the team which finished third the year before.

THE SEASON: An opening day 1-1 draw at Everton leads to a run without a win that lasts until mid-September when they beat Nottingham Forest 2-1.

Mark Bright signs from Crystal Palace in September but cannot immediately halt the slide to 17th. Seven wins in a row at the turn of the year changes the outlook and converted striker Paul Warhurst scores four goals in four successive games. After a patchy end to the season, they finish seventh with 59 points.

Best win 5-2 at home to Southampton in April; worst defeat a 3-0 defeat by Manchester City in September. Top scorer: Mark Bright (11).

1993-94

PRE-SEASON: Wednesday make two major buys – Des Walker from Sampdoria for £2.7 million and Andy Sinton £2.75 million from QPR.

THE SEASON: Another dreadful start for Wednesday, beaten 2-0 at Liverpool and without a win until their eighth game, against Southampton. Paul Warhurst is sold to Blackburn for £2.7 million.

By October they are 20th and in big trouble but Mark Bright scores eight goals in eight games, the results come together and by February they have scaled the heights to sixth place. A run without a win turns into a good finish of nine matches undefeated as they end the season seventh with 64 points.

Best wins 5-0 at home to West Ham and Ipswich; worst defeat 5-0 at Old Trafford against Manchester United. Top scorer: Mark Bright (19).

1994-95

PRE-SEASON: Trevor Francis sells Carlton Palmer to Leeds for £2.6 million and buys Peter Atherton and Ian Taylor to strengthen a squad missing an injured Chris Waddle.

THE SEASON: A poor start with one win from eight and a crisis in attack, where Mark Bright and David Hirst manage only one goal each. Hirst is injured in October and Wednesday react by buying Guy Whittingham in December for £700,000.

Waddle returns and immediately improves the Owls' fortunes. Whittingham scores four goals in his opening two games and ends the season with nine. Wednesday go eight games without defeat and reach eighth in the table before sliding again to finish 13th with 51 points.

Best win 5-1 at home to Coventry; worst defeat 7-1 at home to Nottingham Forest. Top scorer: Mark Bright (11).

1995-96

PRE-SEASON: New manager David Pleat succeeds Trevor Francis and quickly makes his mark, selling Chris Bart-Williams to Nottingham Forest for £2.5 million and buying Marc Degryse and Mark Pembridge from Anderlecht and Derby for £1.5 million and £900,000 respectively.

THE SEASON: Another bad start, 1-0 defeat at Anfield, but they then beat champions Blackburn 2-1. Dan Petrescu goes to Chelsea for £2.3 million.

Their form is patchy, although a 6-2 victory at home to Leeds is a tonic, and the club spend £4 million on Darko Kovacevic and Dejan Stefanovic. They lose three games in March, including a disastrous defeat against Bolton, and only a draw on the last day of the season at West Ham guarantees safety.

Best win 6-2 at home to Leeds in December; worst defeat 5-2 by Everton. Top scorer: David Hirst (13).

SHEFFIELD WED.
Supporters' Club
Best XI Since 1993
(4-4-2)

Supporter/Manager: Rita Nettleship

KEVIN PRESSMAN – Imposing 'keeper who made it through the Sheffield Wednesday youth ranks, turning professional in November 1985.

ROLAND NILSSON – Elegant Swedish international full back signed from IFK Gothenburg.

NIGEL PEARSON – Experienced central defender who left Hillsborough to join Middlesbrough in July 1994 for £500,000.

DES WALKER – Pacy former England centre back signed from Sampdoria in July 1993 for £2.7 million.

NIGEL WORTHINGTON – Gritty Northern Ireland international who moved to Leeds in July 1994 for £325,000.

DANNY WILSON – Tireless Northern Ireland midfielder who left the Owls for Barnsley in July 1993 for £200,000.

MARK PEMBRIDGE – Compact Welsh midfielder signed from Derby County for £900,000 in July 1995.

PAUL WARHURST – Versatile former England Under-21 player signed by Blackburn in August 1993 for £2.7 million.

CARLTON PALMER – Long-striding ex-England midfielder who moved to Leeds for £2.6 million in June 1994.

TREVOR FRANCIS – Cultured England striker who joined the Owls from QPR after spells with Sampdoria, Atlanta and Rangers.

DAVID HIRST – Consistent striker who signed for Wednesday from Barnsley in August 1986 for a bargain £200,000.

SOUTHAMPTON – The Premiership History

1996-97

PRE-SEASON: Two days after Richard Hall leaves for West Ham in a £1.5 million deal in July, Graeme Souness is appointed manager on a three-year contract as successor to Dave Merrington. He brings in only one player, Bristol City defender Richard Dryden, for £150,000.

THE SEASON: Souness is soon wheeler-dealing as Saints take only two points from their first seven Premiership matches. With barely a month of the season gone, in come Robbie Slater from West Ham (£250,000), Claus Lundekvam from SK Brann (£400,000) and striker Egil Ostenstad from Viking Stavanger (£900,000).

League results improve slightly before hitting a surreal peak with a 6-3 win over Manchester United. Ostenstad and Eyal Berkovitch, a £1 million buy from Maccabi Haifa, each score twice. But two weeks later, Souness has an unhappy return to Merseyside, where Saints are humbled 7-1 by Everton despite including Ulrich van Gobbel, a £1.3million defender from Galatasaray.

Souness collects £1 million from Crystal Palace for Neil Shipperley, £500,000 from Manchester City for Neil Heaney and £550,000 from Bradford for Gordon Watson. Then he makes two bargain buys; goalkeeper Maik Taylor (£500,000 from Barnet) in January and striker Mick Evans (£500,000 from Plymouth) in March.

Evans scores four times in the last seven games of the season, four of which are won as Saints narrowly survive, finishing 16th and just one point above relegated Sunderland.

Best win 4-0 v Middlesbrough; worst defeat 7-1 v Everton. Top scorer: Matthew Le Tissier (13).

Above left: Egil Ostenstadt
Left: Neil Shipperley

Southampton facts and figures

CLUB ADDRESS: The Dell, Milton Road, Southampton SO15 2XH.
TELEPHONE: 01703 220505
FAX: 01703 330360
CLUBCALL: 0891 121178
The club was formed in 1885, turning professional in 1894.
Previously called Southampton St Mary's.
PREVIOUS GROUNDS: Antelope Ground, County Cricket Ground.
RECORD ATTENDANCE: 31,044 v Manchester Utd, Div 1, October 1969.
BIGGEST WIN: 8-0 v Northampton, Div 3 South, December 1921, 9-3 v Wolves, Div 2, September 1968.
BIGGEST DEFEATS: 0-8 v Tottenham Hotspur, Div 2, March 1936, and 0-8 v Everton, Div 1, November 1971.
TOP LEAGUE SCORER IN A SEASON: Derek Reeves (39), 1959-60.
HIGHEST AGGREGATE SCORER: Mike Channon (185), 1966-77 and 1979-82.
MOST CAPPED PLAYER: Peter Shilton 49 (125) for England.
STARS OF YESTERYEAR: Alf Ramsey (1946-48), Terry Paine (1956-74), Martin Chivers (1962-67), Ron Davies (1966-72), Mike Channon (1966-77 and 1979-82), Bobby Stokes (1968-76), Peter Osgood (1974-77), Alan Ball (1976-80), Kevin Keegan (1980-82), Peter Shilton (1982-87), Tim Flowers (1986-93), Alan Shearer (1988-92).
GREAT MANAGERS: Jimmy McIntyre (1919-24), Ted Bates (1955-73), Lawrie McMenemy (1973-85).
HONOURS: 1921-22 – Third Division (South) champions, 1959-60 – Third Division champions, 1975-76 – FA Cup winners.
PREMIER MANAGERS: Ian Branfoot 1991-94, Alan Ball 1994-95, Dave Merrington 1995-96, Graeme Souness 1996-97, David Jones 1997-

1992-93

PRE-SEASON: Saints' manager Ian Branfoot sells Neil Ruddock to Tottenham, Barry Horne to Everton and Alan Shearer to Blackburn for a British record £3.3 million. Ken Monkou, Perry Groves, Kerry Dixon and David Speedie arrive at The Dell.

THE SEASON: Southampton score just 12 goals in the first three months of the season and appear certainties for relegation before a spring scoring spree guarantees survival.

They finish in 18th position with 50 points, only one more than relegated Crystal Palace, having won a mere three away games.

Best win 3-0 against Norwich; worst defeat 5-2 at Sheffield Wednesday. Top scorer: Matthew Le Tissier (18).

1993-94

PRE-SEASON: Branfoot signs Tottenham midfielder Paul Allen for £550,000.

THE SEASON: Another desperate fight against the drop. The highest position Saints achieve all season is 17th and they ensure survival on the final day with a nerve-jangling 3-3 draw at West Ham.

The club's plight forces Branfoot to resign in January to be replaced by former Saints player Alan Ball, who signs Jim Magilton from Oxford for £600,000. An amazing 5-4 victory at Norwich in April turns the tide for Southampton, ending a seven-match run without a win. Again they finish just a point clear of relegation, in 18th place with 43 points.

Best win a 5-1 thrashing of Swindon; worst defeat 4-0 at home to Arsenal. Top scorer: Matthew Le Tissier (25).

1994-95

PRE-SEASON: Danish forward Ronnie Ekelund joins on loan from Barcelona and goalkeeper Bruce Grobbelaar on a free transfer from Liverpool.

THE SEASON: By Saints' standards, a glorious season spent in the comfort zone of mid-table. Manager Alan Ball breaks the club transfer record when he buys Chelsea striker Neil Shipperley for £1.2 million, matching it in March when he adds Gordon Watson from Sheffield Wednesday to his squad.

The season's only black spot is the arrest of Bruce Grobbelaar on match-rigging charges. Southampton finish in a comfortable 10th position with 54 points, their highest placing for six years.

Best wins 3-1 against Coventry, Ipswich, Newcastle and Crystal Palace; worst defeat 5-1 at Newcastle. Top scorer: Matthew Le Tissier (29).

1995-96

PRE-SEASON: Alan Ball leaves to take charge at Manchester City and his assistant Dave Merrington takes over at The Dell.

THE SEASON: Saints re-assume the role of Premiership strugglers. Merrington brings former England international Barry Venison back from an unhappy spell with Galatasaray in Turkey for £850,000 in October. Victories over Manchester United and struggling Bolton provide Southampton with an escape route.

Saints finish 17th with 38 points, the same as relegated Manchester City, but a better goal difference proves crucial. They win just two games away from The Dell.

Best win 3-1 over Manchester United in April; worst defeat 4-1 by United at Old Trafford in November. Top scorer: Neil Shipperley (13).

SOUTHAMPTON Supporters' Club Best XI Since 1993 (3-5-2)

Supporter/Manager: Karl Hopgood

TIM FLOWERS – Fiercely competitive England 'keeper who joined Blackburn for £2 million in November 1993.

FRANCIS BENALI – Stalwart defender who began his career as a Southampton apprentice, turning pro in January 1987.

RICHARD HALL – Strong former England Under-21 defender transferred from Scunthorpe in February 1991 for £200,000.

ULRICH VAN GOBBEL – Powerful Dutch international signed from Galatasaray for £1.3 million in October 1996.

KEN MONKOU – Imposing central defender who left Chelsea for the Saints in a £750,000 deal in August 1992.

JEFF KENNA – Composed Republic of Ireland defender who joined Blackburn in March 1995 for £1.5 million.

JIM MAGILTON – Northern Ireland midfielder signed from Oxford United for £600,000 in February 1994.

EYAL BERKOVIC – Israeli international winger signed from Maccabi Haifa in October 1996 for £1 million.

RONNIE EKELUND – Danish international who arrived at The Dell on loan from Barcelona in September 1994.

MATT LE TISSIER – Mercurial England midfield star who started out as a Southampton apprentice, turning pro in October 1986.

EGIL OSTENSTAD – Norwegian international striker signed from Viking Stavanger for £900,000 in September 1996.

TOTTENHAM HOTSPUR
– The Premiership History

Steffen Iversen

Ian Walker

1996-97 PRE-SEASON: Manager Gerry Francis keeps the club wallet closed fairly tight amid the summer spending sprees in the Premiership. His only indulgence is the Danish midfielder Allan Nielsen, bought from Brondby for £1.65 million.

THE SEASON: A season of frustration at White Hart Lane, where a catalogue of injuries wreck their hopes of making an impact. The tone is set on the opening day when captain Gary Mabbutt suffers a broken leg in a 2-0 victory at Blackburn.

Striker Chris Armstrong is another early casualty, while England international Darren Anderton plays only 15 matches all season after suffering a series of niggling injury problems.

With an ever-changing line-up, Spurs fail to build any rhythm to their game, as is proven by the fact that they cannot win more than two successive matches while their worst losing streak is only three games.

A humiliating 6-1 defeat at First Division Bolton in the Coca-Cola Cup causes the club to have a hard think about the direction they are taking and Francis is forced to spend as the list of casualties lengthens by the day.

He brings in reinforcements in the shape of Steffen Iversen (£2.7 million from Rosenborg), John Scales (£2.6 million from Liverpool) and Ramon Vega (£3.75 million from Cagliari), but is forced to accept it is a learning season for his team. They finish 10th with 46 points.

Best win 4-0 at Sunderland in March; worst defeat a 7-1 hammering at the hands of Newcastle in December. Top scorer: Teddy Sheringham (7).

Tottenham facts and figures

CLUB ADDRESS: White Hart Lane, 748 High Road, Tottenham, London N17 OAP.
TELEPHONE: 0181-365 5000
FAX: 0181-365 5005
CLUBCALL: 0891 335555
The club was formed in 1882, turning professional in 1895.
PREVIOUS GROUNDS: Tottenham Marshes and Northumberland Park.
The club was previously called Hotspur Football Club between 1882-85.
RECORD ATTENDANCE: 75,038 v Sunderland, FA Cup 6th round, March 1938.
BIGGEST WIN: 13-2 v Crewe, FA Cup 4th round replay, February 1960.
BIGGEST DEFEAT: 0-7 v Liverpool, Div 1, Sept 1978.
TOP LEAGUE SCORER IN A SEASON: Jimmy Greaves (37), 1962-63.
HIGHEST AGGREGATE SCORER: Jimmy Greaves (266), 1961-70.
MOST CAPPED PLAYER: Pat Jennings (74) for Northern Ireland.
STARS OF YESTERYEAR: Vivian Woodward (1901-09), Jimmy Dimmock (1918-31), Bill Nicholnson (1936-54), Ted Ditchburn (1939-59), Ted Duquemin (1946-59), Alf Ramsey (1949-55), Danny Blanchflower (1954-64), Dave Mackay (1958-68), Jimmy Greaves (1961-70), Alan Mullery (1964-72), Pat Jennings (1964-77), Glenn Hoddle (1975-87), Ossie Ardiles (1978-88), Chris Waddle (1985-89), Paul Gascoigne (1988-92), Gary Lineker (1989-92).
GREAT MANAGERS: Arthur Rowe (1949-55), Bill Nicholson (1958-74), Keith Burkinshaw (1976-84).
HONOURS: 1900-01 – FA Cup winners, 1919-20 – Second Division champions, 1920-21 - FA Cup winners, 1949-50 – Second Division champions, 1950-51 – First Division champions, 1960-61 – First Division champions, FA Cup win ners, 1961-62 – FA Cup winners, 1962-63 – European Cup-Winners' Cup winners, 1966-67 – FA Cup winners, 1970-71 – League Cup winners, 1971-72 – Uefa Cup winners, 1972-73 – League Cup winners, 1980-81, 1981-82 – FA Cup winners, 1983-84 – Uefa Cup winners, 1990-91 – FA Cup winners.
PREMIER MANAGERS: Peter Shreeves 1991-92, Terry Venables 1992-93, Ossie Ardiles 1993-94, Gerry Francis 1994-

1992-93

PRE-SEASON: Tottenham spend £2.1 million on Nottingham Forest striker Teddy Sheringham. He does not disappoint, scoring 21 goals to become the Premier League's first leading scorer.

THE SEASON: Tottenham spend too much of the first half of the season in the bottom half of the table but find their scoring touch in the New Year. Five wins on the trot, in which they score 16 goals, take them briefly to sixth, but they fall away to finish eighth with 59 points. The season ends in turmoil when Tottenham chairman Alan Sugar fires Terry Venables, the club's manager and chief executive.

Best win 5-1 v Norwich in April; worst defeat a 6-0 hammering at Sheffield United in March. Top scorer: Teddy Sheringham (21).

1993-94

PRE-SEASON: Alan Sugar appoints Ossie Ardiles as the man to return the glory days to White Hart Lane. Another former Tottenham favourite Steve Perryman becomes his assistant. Meanwhile, Ardiles' predecessor Terry Venables begins legal action, claiming "wrongful dismissal".

THE SEASON: Colin Calderwood and Jason Dozzell join Spurs but awful home form leaves the club 15th as only four matches are won at White Hart Lane, the best a 5-0 victory over Oldham. Better results away from home save the club from a worse fate. Ten matches without a win from New Year's Day, the first seven of which are lost, make for a nervous spring, but then Nicky Barmby emerges to help Tottenham reach safety and 45 points.

Best win 5-0 v Oldham; worst defeat 4-1 by West Ham at White Hart Lane. Top scorer: Teddy Sheringham (14).

1994-95

PRE-SEASON: Tottenham are stunned when the FA docks them 12 Premiership points and throws them out of the FA Cup for financial irregularities before the season has even begun. Ossie Ardiles lifts the gloom by signing German striker Jurgen Klinsmann for £2 million. Romanians Ilie Dumitrescu and Gica Popescu also arrive.

THE SEASON: A 4-3 opening-day victory at Sheffield Wednesday sets the tone for the Ardiles style. Spurs score plenty of goals but concede just as many.

Three successive home defeats mean the end for Ardiles in November. Gerry Francis takes over. His arrival leads to a tightening-up of the Tottenham defence and a string of good results. The club wins an appeal against both the points deduction and the FA Cup ban. They then reach the FA Cup semi-final where they lose to Everton. Despite the Sheringham-Klinsmann partnership producing 38 Premiership goals, Tottenham finish only seventh with 62 points.

Best win 4-0 at Coventry in December; worst defeat 5-2 at Manchester City in October. Top scorer: Jurgen Klinsmann (20).

1995-96

PRE-SEASON: Jurgen Klinsmann leaves for Bayern Munich. Gerry Francis pays Crystal Palace £4.5 million to replace him with Chris Armstrong, while Nick Barmby moves to Middlesbrough.

THE SEASON: Spurs make a slow start before the Teddy Sheringham-Armstrong partnership gels. It is helped considerably by the £4.2 million signing of Newcastle winger Ruel Fox in October.

Inconsistency at home costs Spurs a place in Europe, although it comes right on New Year's Day when Manchester United are hammered 4-1. A 1-1 draw at Newcastle on the final day of the season leaves Tottenham in eighth place with 61 points.

Best win 4-1 at home to Manchester United; worst defeat 3-1 at home to Liverpool. Top scorer: Teddy Sheringham (16).

TOTTENHAM
Supporters' Club Best XI Since 1993 (4-4-2)

Supporter/Manager: Tim Davidson

IAN WALKER – Spectacular England 'keeper who graduated through the Spurs ranks, turning professional in December 1989.

CLIVE WILSON – Reliable full-back or midfielder who arrived at White Hart Lane from QPR on a free transfer in July 1995.

GARY MABBUTT – Stalwart former England centre back who has played over 450 League games for Spurs since August 1982.

SOL CAMPBELL – Powerful England defender who has had a meteoric rise since signing professional forms in September 1992.

STEVE CARR – Pacy young right-sided defender who turned professional in August 1983.

PAUL ALLEN – Industrious Spurs winger for eight years before joining Southampton in 1993.

NICK BARMBY – Inventive England striker who graduated through the Spurs ranks before signing for Middlesbrough for £5.25 million in August 1995.

DARREN ANDERTON – Skilful England winger who left Portsmouth for Tottenham in June 1992 for £1.75 million.

ANDY SINTON – Dependable England midfielder signed from Sheffield Wednesday for £1.5 million in January 1996.

TEDDY SHERINGHAM – Intelligent England regular who arrived at White Hart Lane from Nottingham Forest in a £2.1 million deal in August 1992.

JURGEN KLINSMANN – Explosive German striker who scored 29 goals in his one season with Spurs after leaving Bayern Munich in June 1995.

WEST HAM UNITED
– The Premiership History

Iain Dowie

Eyal Berkovic

1996-97

PRE-SEASON: Harry Redknapp sets a new West Ham record when he spends £2.4 million on Florin Raducioiu of Espanol. At the same time he is nurturing his younger players, including Frank Lampard jnr and Rio Ferdinand, both of whom appear in the opening game of the season.

THE SEASON: A rocky start to the season as the Hammers lose 2-0 at Arsenal on the opening day, draw at home with Coventry and beat Southampton before losing 4-1 at Middlesbrough.

Successive defeats by Merseyside opposition highlight the club's goal-scoring problem. Iain Dowie, in 18 Premiership matches, fails to find the net once.

Even so, West Ham manage to squeeze out a win here and there, including 2-0 at Nottingham Forest and 2-1 at home to Blackburn.

But as the Hammers head towards 1997, the results grow steadily worse. They go seven matches without a win and are knocked out of the Coca-Cola Cup by lowly Stockport County.

The New Year marks an even worse turn of events and it is to be late February before the Hammers win again. During this spell they are knocked out of the FA Cup by York City.

Redknapp, staring the real prospect of relegation in the face, makes a desperate bid to save the club with a double-signing. John Hartson moves from Arsenal for a new West Ham record of £3.3 million and Paul Kitson signs from Newcastle for £2.3 million.

It is an inspired move. The results pick up, West Ham score four goals then five in a match, and reach safety with 42 points and 14th place in the Premiership.

Best win 5-1 over Sheffield Wednesday in May; worst defeat 4-1 at Middlesbrough in September. Top scorer Paul Kitson (8).

West Ham facts and figures

CLUB ADDRESS: Boleyn Ground, Green Street, Upton Park, London E13 9AZ.

TELEPHONE: 0181-548 2748

FAX: 0181-548 2758

CLUBCALL: 0891 121165

The club was formed in 1895, turning professional in 1900.

PREVIOUS GROUNDS: Memorial Recreation Ground, Canning Town.

RECORD ATTENDANCE: 42,322 v Tottenham, Div 1, October 1970.

BIGGEST WIN: 10-0 v Bury, League Cup 2nd round, 2nd leg, October 1984.

BIGGEST DEFEAT: 8-2 v Blackburn Rovers, Div 1, December 1963.

TOP LEAGUE SCORER IN A SEASON: Vic Watson (42), 1929-30.

HIGHEST AGGREGATE SCORER: Vic Watson (298), 1920-35.

MOST CAPPED PLAYER: Bobby Moore (108) for England.

STARS OF YESTERYEAR: Vic Watson (1920-35), Bobby Moore (1958-73), Geoff Hurst (1959-71), Martin Peters (1961-69), Johnny Byrne (1962-67), Trevor Brooking (1965-82), Billy Bonds (1967-86).

GREAT MANAGERS: Syd King (1902-32), Charlie Paynter (1932-50), Ted Fenton (1950-61), Ron Greenwood (1961-74), John Lyall (1974-89), Billy Bonds (1990-94), Harry Redknapp (1994-).

HONOURS: 1957-58 – Second Division champions, 1963-64 – FA Cup winners, 1964-65 – European Cup Winners' Cup winners, 1974-75, 1979-80 – FA Cup winners.

PREMIER MANAGERS: Billy Bonds 1990-94, Harry Redknapp 1994 –

1992-93

PRE-SEASON: Relegated in the last year of the old First Division, West Ham sell Stuart Slater to Celtic for £1.5 million.

THE SEASON: An away win at Barnsley proves to be a false dawn, but the Hammers hit form in December and embark on a 15-match unbeaten run to put them in the thick of the promotion battle.

Victory in their last four games of the season proves enough to take them automatically back to the top flight. West Ham finish, like Portsmouth, on 88 points – eight behind champions Newcastle. Yet the Hammers pip Portsmouth by virtue of one goal.

Best win 6-0 v Sunderland in October; worst defeat 5-2 v Tranmere in December. Top scorer: Trevor Morley (20).

1993-94

PRE-SEASON: Dale Gordon joins from Glasgow Rangers for £750,000.

THE SEASON: Wimbledon win 2-0 at Upton Park on the opening day and then the Hammers lose at Leeds United. Relief comes with a win over Sheffield Wednesday.

Home form is to be a problem all season and they win just six games at Upton Park, compared with seven away from home including successive triumphs at Tottenham, Oldham and Arsenal. That is enough to leave the club safe in 13th place on 52 points.

Best win 4-1 at Tottenham in April; worst defeat 5-0 at Sheffield Wednesday in December. Top scorer: Trevor Morley (13).

1994-95

PRE-SEASON: An era ends after 27 years as Billy Bonds, player then manager, leaves and is replaced by his assistant, Harry Redknapp.

THE SEASON: A record of nine home wins points to an improvement for the Hammers, who open with a 0-0 draw at Upton Park against Leeds.

Away form, however, is another matter and the struggles on the road leave the club with a battle to keep clear of the relegation dog-fight. Don Hutchison arrives from Liverpool and old favourite Tony Cottee returns from Everton. West Ham finish 14th with 50 points.

Best wins 3-0 v Manchester City, Wimbledon and Liverpool – all home games; worst defeat 3-0 at Manchester City. Top scorer: Tony Cottee (13).

1995-96

PRE-SEASON: The club spend £1 million on Marco Boogers from Sparta Rotterdam and allow Matthew Holmes to leave for Blackburn in exchange for Robbie Slater and £600,000.

THE SEASON: A slow start and a first win in September is followed by the re-signing of Iain Dowie from Crystal Palace. He has an immediate effect as the results come together and they score away wins at Sheffield Wednesday and Wimbledon.

In the New Year, Redknapp spends and spends – £1.5 million for Ilie Dumitrescu from Tottenham, Michael Hughes for £200,000 from Strasbourg and Slaven Bilic for £1.65 million from Karlsruhe – while Don Hutchison is sold to Sheffield United for £1.2 million. A good finish to the season sees the club end their programme in a respectable 10th place.

Best win 3-0 at Bolton; worst defeat 4-1 at home to Aston Villa in November. Top scorer: Julian Dicks and Tony Cottee (10).

WEST HAM Supporters' Club Best XI Since 1993 (5-3-2)

Supporter/Manager: Larry Little

LUDEK MIKLOSKO – Czech international 'keeper who has enjoyed life with the Hammers since his £300,000 move from Banik Ostrava in February 1990.

STEVE POTTS – Versatile stalwart defender who has been at Upton Park since 1993.

ALVIN MARTIN – Long-serving former England defender who played over 550 games for the Hammers before joining Leyton Orient in 1996.

SLAVEN BILIC – Abrasive Croat defender who signed for £1.65 million from German club Karlsruhe in February 1996.

JULIAN DICKS – Crunching left back who returned to West Ham from Liverpool in October 1994 for £1 million.

RIO FERDINAND – Highly promising young midfielder or defender who graduated through the West Ham youth system, turning pro in November 1995.

HUGO PORFIRIO – Exciting Portuguese midfielder who arrived at West Ham in September 1996 on loan from Sporting Lisbon.

IAN BISHOP – Veteran Hammers midfielder signed from Manchester City in December 1989 for £500,000.

MICHAEL HUGHES – Northern Ireland midfielder who began his career at Manchester City.

JOHN HARTSON – Powerful Welsh striker who injected pace and muscle into the West Ham attack after his £3.3 million move from Arsenal in February 1997.

PAUL KITSON – Effective former England Under-21 striker signed from Newcastle in February 1997 for £2.3 million.

Efan Ekoku

WIMBLEDON – The Premiership History

1996-97

PRE-SEASON: Suddenly Wimbledon are a buying club, splashing a record £2 million on Millwall defender Ben Thatcher and £125,000 on Fulham full-back Duncan Jupp.

THE SEASON: The surprise package Dons remain in contention for the three major domestic prizes until March. Kinnear's 'Crazy Gang' show magnificent consistency with a run of 19 matches unbeaten from September 4 to December 22. It ends in spectacular fashion when they are thrashed 5-0 at Aston Villa.

An opening-day fixture sees Wimbledon lose 3-0 at home to champions Manchester United and they lose their next two matches before embarking on a club record seven-match winning run.

In total they lose just twice in 28 matches, reaching the semi-finals of both cups. But the sparkle fades as they topple from the Coca-Cola Cup against Leicester on away goals and then can find no answer to a Gianfranco Zola special for Chelsea in the FA Cup.

A season promising so much ends with six defeats in the last 12 games, a dive from third to eighth (with 56 points), and no place in Europe.

Speculation about a club headquarters move to Dublin continues. Despite scepticism from critics and opposition from supporters, club officials keep insisting it is a genuine option.

Best win 4-0 at home to Everton in September; worst defeat 5-0 at Aston Villa in December. Top scorer: Efan Ekoku (11).

Far left: Neil Sullivan
Left: Chris Perry

Wimbledon facts and figures

CLUB ADDRESS: Selhurst Park, South Norwood, London SE25 6PY.
TELEPHONE: 0181-771 2233
FAX: 0181-768 0640
CLUBCALL: 0891 121175
The club was formed in 1889, turning professional in 1964.
PREVIOUS GROUNDS: Plough Lane.
The club was previously called Wimbledon Old Centrals.
RECORD ATTENDANCE: 30,115 v Manchester United, FA Premier League, May 1993.
BIGGEST WIN: 6-0 v Newport County, Div 3, Sept 1983.
BIGGEST DEFEAT: 0-8 v Everton, League Cup 2nd rnd, August 1978.
TOP LEAGUE SCORER IN A SEASON: Alan Cork (29), 1983-84.
HIGHEST AGGREGATE SCORER: Alan Cork (167), 1977-92.
MOST CAPPED PLAYER: Terry Phelan (8) for the Republic of Ireland.
STARS OF YESTERYEAR: Dickie Guy (1968-78), Alan Cork (1977-92), Dave Beasant (1979-88), Dennis Wise (1984-90), Lawrie Sanchez (1984-94), John Fashanu (1986-94), Keith Curle (1988-91).
GREAT MANAGERS: Dave Bassett (1981-87), Bobby Gould (1987-90).
HONOURS: 1962-63 – Amateur Cup winners, 1982-83 – Fourth Division champions, 1987-88 – FA Cup winners.
PREMIER MANAGER: Joe Kinnear 1991-

1992-93

PRE-SEASON: Wimbledon buy Brentford striker Dean Holdsworth for £750,000 nine days before the season starts. Holdsworth's goals ensure Wimbledon's survival.

THE SEASON: Their first Premier League game is at Leeds where they lose 2-1. It is four games before they gain their first point in a 2-2 draw at Sheffield United. The Dons stay in the bottom three until January.

Terry Phelan is sold to Manchester City for a then club record-equalling fee of £2.5 million.

Former 'Crazy Gang' member Vinnie Jones is welcomed back from Chelsea for £700,000. A 2-0 win at Coventry in January begins a run of seven wins in nine games which lift Wimbledon to 12th with 54 points.

Best win 4-0 v Crystal Palace; worst defeat 6-2 at Oldham. Top scorer: Dean Holdsworth (19).

1993-94

PRE-SEASON: Wimbledon set their sights on Europe, as Alan Kimble comes in from Cambridge and Gary Blissett from Brentford.

THE SEASON: The Dons have their best-ever season in league football to finish sixth – a position which, a year later, would have qualified them for Europe.

Scoring goals is a problem early in the season. with 13 in the first 13 games, but tight defence keeps Joe Kinnear's men in comfortable mid-table. Wimbledon break loose in the springtime, picking up 17 points out of 21 in April. They are involved in a dramatic finale to the season when their 3-2 defeat at Goodison on the final Saturday keeps Everton in the top flight.

Best win 4-1 v Blackburn; worst defeats 4-0 at Leeds and Newcastle. Top scorer: Dean Holdsworth (17).

1994-95

PRE-SEASON: Cult hero John Fashanu leaves Wimbledon for Aston Villa in a £1.35 million deal. In nine seasons with the club, the striker notched up 107 goals in 276 matches.

THE SEASON: Wimbledon win just two of their first 11 games and defender John Scales is sold to Liverpool for what was then a club record £3.5 million. Goalkeeper Hans Segers is named in the Grobbelaar alleged bribes case.

Wheeler-dealing by Joe Kinnear helps the club to a respectable mid-table position. He confirms his reputation for unearthing lower-division players by signing defender Alan Reeves from Rochdale for £300,000. Striker Efan Ekoku arrives from Norwich for £1 million; the same fee is paid to Millwall for Kenny Cunningham and Jon Goodman. The Dons finish in the top half again with 56 points, but with a negative goal difference.

Best wins 2-0 successes over Coventry, Crystal Palace and Manchester City; worst defeat 7-1 at Aston Villa. Top scorer: Efan Ekoku (9).

1995-96

PRE-SEASON: A typical summer at Wimbledon. Warren Barton moves to Newcastle for £4 million, while bargain-basement goalkeeper Paul Heald joins from Leyton Orient for £125,000.

THE SEASON: Wimbledon's famed tenacity is much in evidence as they beat Liverpool 1-0 in their third home match of the season to go third. It proves to be a false dawn as the Dons slump to seven successive defeats. Christmas is the turning point as they win away at Chelsea and Arsenal, while at home they claim another London victim in QPR. The Dons eventually finish 14th with 41 points.

Best wins 3-0 at home to Manchester City in April and away at QPR in August; worst defeat 6-1 at Newcastle. Top scorer: Robbie Earle (11).

WIMBLEDON Supporters' Club Best XI Since 1993 (4-3-3)

Supporter/Manager: David Norton

NEIL SULLIVAN – Scotland international 'keeper who began his career as a Wimbledon trainee, turning pro in July 1988.

KENNY CUNNINGHAM – Consistent right back who joined the Dons from London neighbours Millwall in November 1994.

KEITH CURLE – Fast central defender who moved to Manchester City in August 1991 in a £2.5 million deal.

JOHN SCALES – Classy and composed centre back who left the Dons for Liverpool for £3.5 million in August 1994.

ALAN KIMBLE – Competitive left back who arrived at Wimbledon from Cambridge United in July 1993 for £175,000.

VINNIE JONES – Famously aggressive Wales international midfielder in his second spell with the "Crazy Gang".

ROBBIE EARLE – Athletic midfielder signed by Wimbledon in July 1991 from Port Vale for a mere £775,000.

OYVIND LEONHARDSEN – Influential Norwegian international who left the Dons in a £3.75 million move to Liverpool in June 1997

DEAN HOLDSWORTH – Bustling striker who joined Wimbledon from Brentford in July 1992 for £750,000.

EFAN EKOKU – Hard-running Nigerian striker who spent one season at Norwich before signing for Wimbledon in October 1994.

MARCUS GAYLE – All-action midfielder or striker signed from Brentford in March 1994 for £250,000.

The 1997 Awards and Premiership Facts and Figures

CARLING PLAYER OF THE YEAR:
Juninho (Middlesbrough)

CARLING MANAGER OF THE YEAR:
Alex Ferguson (Manchester United)

CARLING PLAYER OF THE MONTH AND MANAGER OF THE MONTH AWARDS FOR 1996-97

MONTH	PLAYER	TEAM	MANAGER	TEAM
August	**David Beckham**	Manchester United	**David Pleat**	Sheffield Wednesday
September	**Patrik Berger**	Liverpool	**Joe Kinnear**	Wimbledon
October	**Matt Le Tissier**	Southampton	**Graeme Souness**	Southampton
November	**Ian Wright**	Arsenal	**Jim Smith**	Derby County
December	**Gianfranco Zola**	Chelsea	**Gordon Strachan**	Coventry City
January	**Tim Flowers**	Blackburn Rovers	**Stuart Pearce**	Nottingham Forest
February	**Robbie Earle**	Wimbledon	**Alex Ferguson**	Manchester United
March	**Juninho**	Middlesbrough	**Bryan Robson**	Middlesbrough
April	**Mickey Evans**	Southampton	**Graeme Souness**	Southampton

PFA PLAYER OF THE YEAR:
Alan Shearer
(Newcastle)

PFA YOUNG PLAYER OF THE YEAR:
David Beckham
(Manchester United)

FOOTBALLER OF THE YEAR:
(Awarded by Football Writers' Association)
Gianfranco Zola (Chelsea)

PREMIERSHIP TOP SCORERS 1996-97

Alan Shearer Newcastle United	25
Ian Wright Arsenal	23
Ole-Gunnar Solskjaer Manchester United	18
Robbie Fowler Liverpool	18
Dwight Yorke Aston Villa	17
Fabrizio Ravanelli Middlesbrough	16
Les Ferdinand Newcastle United	16
Dion Dublin Coventry City	14
Matt Le Tissier Southampton	13
Stan Collymore Liverpool	12
Steve Claridge Leicester City	12
Juninho Middlesbrough	12
Dennis Bergkamp Arsenal	12
Dean Sturridge Derby County	11
Eric Cantona Manchester United	11
Efan Ekoku Wimbledon	11
Chris Sutton Blackburn Rovers	11

PREMIERSHIP ALL-TIME TOP GOALSCORERS (to end of 1996-97)

Alan Shearer Blackburn Rovers and Newcastle United	137
Les Ferdinand Queens Park Rangers and Newcastle United	101
Ian Wright Arsenal	94
Robbie Fowler Liverpool	83
Matt Le Tissier Southampton	80
Teddy Sheringham Nottingham Forest and Tottenham Hotspur	76
Andy Cole Newcastle United and Manchester United	72
Eric Cantona Leeds United and Manchester United	72
Dwight Yorke Aston Villa	63

THE 1996-97 PREMERSHIP EVER-PRESENTS

There were 12 players who appeared in all their club's Premiership matches during the season:

GOALKEEPERS:
Tim Flowers (Blackburn), **Steve Ogrizovic** (Coventry City), **David James** (Liverpool), **Kevin Pressman** (Sheffield Wednesday),

OUTFIELD PLAYERS:
Nigel Winterburn (Arsenal), **Ugo Ehiogu** (Aston Villa), **Alan Wright** (Aston Villa), **Gary McAllister** (Coventry City), **Stig Bjornebye** (Liverpool), **Colin Cooper** (Nottingham Forest), **Ian Nolan** (Sheffield Wednesday), **Sol Campbell** (Tottenham Hotspur).

THE GOOD BEHAVIOUR LEAGUE 1996-97
(One point for a yellow card, three for a red)

	YELLOW	RED	POINTS
Wimbledon	38	1	**41**
Liverpool	45	1	**48**
Leicester City	51	1	**54**
Manchester United	54	1	**57**
Aston Villa	51	2	**57**
Sheffield Wednesday	49	3	**58**
Newcastle United	55	2	**61**
Blackburn Rovers	61	1	**64**
Coventry City	49	5	**64**
Sunderland	53	4	**65**
Nottingham Forest	67	0	**67**
Tottenham Hotspur	64	1	**67**
Everton	61	2	**67**
Derby County	63	2	**69**
West Ham United	67	2	**73**
Southampton	66	4	**78**
Middlesbrough	73	3	**82**
Chelsea	79	2	**85**
Leeds United	85	1	**88**
Arsenal	83	5	**98**

PREMIERSHIP ATTENDANCES 1996-97

	TOTAL	96-97 (avg)	95-96 (avg)	DIFF%
Arsenal	718,604	37,821	37,568	**+0.7**
Aston Villa	684,520	36,027	32,614	**+10.5**
Blackburn Rovers	473,999	24,947	27,714	**-10.0**
Chelsea	524,722	27,617	25,466	**+8.4**
Coventry City	372,884	19,625	18,507	**+6.0**
Derby County	339,882	17,889	14,327	**+24.9**
Everton	687,572	36,188	35,435	**+2.1**
Leeds United	610,235	32,117	32,578	**-1.4**
Leicester City	404,083	21,268	16,530	**+28.7**
Liverpool	755,307	39,753	39,553	**+0.5**
Manchester United	1,046,567	55,082	41,700	**+32.0**
Middlesbrough	567,191	29,852	29,283	**+1.9**
Newcastle United	692,866	36,467	36,507	**-0.1**
Nottingham Forest	497,039	25,160	25,916	**-2.9**
Sheffield Wednesday	488,155	25,692	24,877	**+3.3**
Southampton	286,989	15,105	14,820	**+1.9**
Sunderland	396,594	20,873	17,482	**+19.4**
Tottenham Hotspur	590,277	31,067	30,510	**+1.8**
West Ham United	441,601	23,242	22,340	**+4.0**
Wimbledon	303,376	15,967	13,246	**+20.5**

TOTAL PREMIERSHIP ATTENDANCES 1992-97

SEASON	TOTAL	GAMES	AVERAGE	DIFF%
1996-97	10,882,453	380	28,638	**+3.9**
1995-96	10,469,107	380	27,550	**+11.9**
1994-95	11,213,168	462	24,271	**+5.3**
1993-94	10,644,551	462	23,040	**+9.1**
1992-93	9,759,809	462	21,125	**-2.3**

PAST WINNERS OF PREMIERSHIP AWARDS

PFA PLAYER OF THE YEAR

1993: Paul McGrath
(Aston Villa)
1994: Eric Cantona
(Manchester United)
1995: Alan Shearer
(Blackburn Rovers)
1996: Les Ferdinand
(Newcastle United)

MANAGER OF THE YEAR

1993: Alex Ferguson
(Manchester United)
1994: Alex Ferguson
(Manchester United)
1995: Kenny Dalglish
(Blackburn Rovers)
1996: Alex Ferguson
(Manchester United)

FOOTBALLER OF THE YEAR
(Awarded by Football Writers' Association)

1993: Chris Waddle
(Sheffield Wednesday)
1994: Alan Shearer
(Blackburn Rovers)
1995: Jurgen Klinsmann
(Tottenham Hotspur)
1996: Eric Cantona
(Manchester United)

PFA YOUNG PLAYER OF THE YEAR

1993: Ryan Giggs
(Manchester United)
1994: Andy Cole
(Newcastle United)
1995: Robbie Fowler
(Liverpool)
1996: Robbie Fowler
(Liverpool)

MANAGER OF THE MONTH AWARDS 1992-96

1992-93:

August:	**Mike Walker**	Norwich
September:	**Bobby Gould**	Coventry
October:	**Ron Atkinson**	Aston Villa
November:	**Mike Walker**	Norwich
December:	**Steve Coppell**	Crystal Palace
January:	**Trevor Francis**	Sheff Wed
February:	**Doug Livermore**	Tottenham
March:	**George Graham**	Arsenal
April:	**Alex Ferguson**	Man Utd

Above: Joe Kinnear. Below: Brian Little

1993-94:

August:	**Alex Ferguson**	Man Utd
September:	**Joe Kinnear**	Wimbledon
October:	**Mike Walker**	Norwich
November:	**Kevin Keegan**	Newcastle
December:	**Trevor Francis**	Sheff Wed
January:	**Kenny Dalglish**	Blackburn
February:	**Joe Royle**	Oldham
March:	**Joe Kinnear**	Wimbledon
April:	**Joe Kinnear**	Wimbledon

1994-95:

August:	**Kevin Keegan**	Newcastle
September:	**Frank Clark**	Nott'm Forest
October:	**Alex Ferguson**	Man Utd
November:	**Kenny Dalglish**	Blackburn
December:	**Gerry Francis**	Tottenham
January:	**Brian Little**	Aston Villa
February:	**Kevin Keegan**	Newcastle
March:	**Ron Atkinson**	Coventry
April:	**Howard Wilkinson**	Leeds

1995-96:

August:	**Kevin Keegan**	Newcastle
September:	**Kevin Keegan**	Newcastle
October:	**Frank Clark**	Nott'm Forest
November:	**Alan Ball**	Man City
December:	**Roy Evans**	Liverpool
January:	**Roy Evans**	Liverpool
February:	**Alex Ferguson**	Man Utd
March:	**Alex Ferguson**	Man Utd
April:	**Dave Merrington**	Southampton

CLUB PLAYER OF THE YEAR AWARDS 1992-97

1992-93:

Arsenal:	**Ian Wright**
Aston Villa:	**Paul McGrath**
Blackburn Rovers:	**Colin Hendry**
Chelsea:	**Frank Sinclair**
Coventry City:	**Peter Atherton**
Crystal Palace:	**Andy Thorn**
Everton:	**Tony Cottee**
Ipswich Town:	**Mick Stockwell**
Leeds United:	**Gordon Strachan**
Liverpool:	**Jamie Redknapp**
Manchester City:	**Garry Flitcroft**
Manchester United:	**Paul Ince**
Middlesbrough:	**John Hendrie**
Norwich City:	**Bryan Gunn**

1992-93 (continued):

Nottingham Forest:	**Nigel Clough**
Oldham Athletic:	**Mike Milligan**
Queens Park Rangers:	**Les Ferdinand**
Sheffield United:	**Alan Kelly & Paul Beesley**
Sheffield Wednesday:	**Chris Waddle**
Southampton:	**Tim Flowers**
Tottenham Hotspur:	**Paul Allen**
Wimbledon:	**John Scales**

1993-94:

Arsenal:	**Ian Wright**
Aston Villa:	**Mark Bosnich**
Blackburn Rovers:	**David Batty**
Chelsea:	**Steve Clarke**

CLUB PLAYER OF THE YEAR AWARDS 1992-97 (continued)

1993-94 (continued):

Coventry City:	**Phil Babb**
Everton:	**Graham Stuart**
Ipswich Town:	**John Wark**
Leeds United:	**Gary McAllister**
Liverpool:	**Ian Rush**
Manchester City:	**Tony Coton**
Manchester United:	**Eric Cantona**
Newcastle United:	**Peter Beardsley**
Norwich City:	**Chris Sutton**
Oldham Athletic:	**Richard Jobson**
Queens Park Rangers:	**David Bardsley**
Sheffield United:	**Carl Bradshaw**
Sheffield Wednesday:	**Des Walker**
Southampton:	**Matthew Le Tissier**
Swindon Town:	**John Moncur**
Tottenham Hotspur:	**Darren Anderton**
West Ham United:	**Trevor Morley**
Wimbledon:	**Dean Holdsworth**

1994-95:

Arsenal:	**Tony Adams**
Aston Villa:	**Dean Saunders**
Blackburn Rovers:	**Alan Shearer**
Chelsea:	**Erland Johnsen**
Coventry City:	**Brian Borrows**
Crystal Palace:	**Richard Shaw**
Everton:	**David Unsworth**
Ipswich Town:	**Craig Forrest**
Leeds United:	**Brian Deane**
Leicester City:	**Kevin Poole**
Liverpool:	**Steve McManaman**
Manchester City:	**Uwe Rosler**
Manchester United:	**Andrei Kanchelskis**
Newcastle United:	**Barry Venison**
Norwich City:	**Jon Newsome**
Nottingham Forest:	**Steve Stone**
Queens Park Rangers:	**Andy Impey**
Sheffield Wednesday:	**Peter Atherton**
Southampton:	**Matthew Le Tissier**
Tottenham Hotspur:	**Jurgen Klinsmann**
West Ham United:	**Steve Potts**
Wimbledon:	**Warren Barton**

1995-96:

Arsenal:	**David Seaman**
Aston Villa:	**Dwight Yorke**
Blackburn Rovers:	**Colin Hendry**
Bolton Wanderers:	**Keith Branagan**
Chelsea:	**Ruud Gullit**
Coventry City:	**Paul Williams**

Ruud Gullit

Andrei Kanchelskis

1995-96 (continued):

Everton:	**Andrei Kanchelskis**
Leeds United:	**Tony Yeboah**
Liverpool:	**Robbie Fowler**
Manchester City:	**Georgi Kinkladze**
Manchester United:	**Eric Cantona**
Middlesbrough:	**Steve Vickers**
Newcastle United:	**Les Ferdinand**
Nottingham Forest:	**Stuart Pearce**
Queens Park Rangers:	**Trevor Sinclair**
Sheffield Wednesday:	**Marc Degryse**
Southampton:	**Dave Beasant**
Tottenham Hotspur:	**Teddy Sheringham**
West Ham United:	**Julian Dicks**
Wimbledon:	**Oyvind Leonhardsen**

1996-97:

Arsenal:	**Martin Keown**
Aston Villa:	**Dwight Yorke**
Blackburn Rovers:	**Tim Sherwood**
Chelsea:	**Gianfranco Zola**
Coventry City:	**Steve Ogrizovic**
Derby County:	**Chris Powell**
Everton:	**Gary Speed**
Leeds United:	**Nigel Martyn**
Leicester City:	**Simon Grayson**
Liverpool:	**Robbie Fowler**
Manchester United:	**Roy Keane**
Middlesbrough:	**Juninho**
Newcastle United:	**Darren Peacock**
Nottingham Forest:	**Colin Cooper**
Sheffield Wednesday:	**Mark Pembridge**
Southampton:	**Egil Ostenstadt**
Sunderland:	**Lionel Perez**
Tottenham Hotspur:	**Sol Campbell**
West Ham United:	**Julian Dicks**
Wimbledon:	**Chris Perry**

The Conquest of Europe

by Eric Brown

Nottingham Forest triumphed in the European Cup in 1979 and 1980

Two major Manchester United anniversaries will herald the relentless search for the Holy Grail at Old Trafford. February 6, 1998, is the unhappy one – 40 years since Matt Busby's Babes were tragically wiped out among the slush on a Munich runway. And May 29, 1998, marks better days – 30 years to the day since Busby's Braves were crowned the first English club Champions of Europe. So what could be more fitting than for Alex Ferguson to achieve his ultimate goal by capturing the European Cup for United and England at the end of the 1997-98 season?

United were England's European pathfinders in the late 1950s when they defied misguided advice from Alan Hardaker, the Football League chief, not to compete in the fledgling tournament. Impressed by Busby's stand, other clubs followed the United example, sweeping aside official opposition. By the time 100 European club trophies had been lost and won, England were clearly top dogs with 23 tournament triumphs, four more than the second-placed nation, Spain.

And United, almost inevitably, brought up that success number 23 when two Mark Hughes goals beat Barcelona in the 1991 Cup-Winners' Cup Final in Rotterdam. Fittingly the bustling Dutch port had provided the backdrop for England's first European glory in the same competition. It was there in 1963 that Bill Nicholson's all-conquering Tottenham team thrashed Atletico Madrid 5-1.

Two years on from a League and FA Cup double in 1961, Tottenham realised their full potential with a daunting demonstration of attacking power which overwhelmed the pride of Spain. Jimmy Greaves and Terry Dyson scored a couple each, John White was also on the scoresheet – and suddenly English clubs had thrown down a gauntlet to the rest of Europe.

Matt Busby's magic moment is shared by Bobby Charlton after the European Cup triumph of 1968

Next on to the European honours board came West Ham – in their very first season of continental competition. Ron Greenwood's side enjoyed the advantage of meeting Munich 1860 at Wembley Stadium in the 1965 Cup-Winners' Cup Final and perhaps that success was an omen because it came 12 months before England's World Cup triumph on the same stage, with Bobby Moore and Geoff Hurst contributing to a 2-0 win over the German club side. Reserve Alan Sealey made sure of glory with both goals.

Three years later, England captured two of the three European crowns, with Manchester United whipping Benfica 4-1 for the glittering prize of European football and Leeds beating Ferencvaros 1-0 to claim the Fairs Cup.

Bobby Charlton, a survivor of the horrors of Munich, scored twice on a May night of raw Wembley emotion which spilled into extra time before Busby's European Cup dream was realised.

Three months later, Bobby's brother Jack scored to win the Fairs Cup for Leeds. The Yorkshire club's success began a six-year English stranglehold on this competition. Newcastle in 1969, Arsenal a year later and Leeds again in 1971 had their names engraved on the trophy. Newcastle captain Bobby Moncur scored three times as his side beat Ujpest Dozsa 6-2 on aggregate after being roared to a 3-0 first-leg victory by 60,000 fanatical Geordies.

Bobby the Busby Babe . . .

. . . and big brother Jack at Leeds. Both scored in the 1968 European victories

For Arsenal it was a very different story. They flew home from Brussels trailing

Anderlecht 3-1, but a 51,612 Highbury crowd saw scorers Eddie Kelly, John Radford and Jon Sammels complete a dramatic recovery in the second leg.

In 1972 England supplied both clubs in the inaugural final of the renamed Uefa Cup, with Tottenham beating Wolves 3-2 on aggregate. English domination ended after Liverpool's Kevin Keegan-inspired 1973 victory over Borussia Moenchengladbach – but only temporarily.

In 1976 Liverpool brought the trophy back home when they recorded their second win, Keegan scoring in both legs of a 4-3 aggregate triumph over Bruges. Ipswich Town (1981) and Tottenham (1984) also captured Uefa honours for England.

It's another wonderful Wembley night as Liverpool celebrate their single goal victory over Bruges in 1978

Bobby Robson constructed a magnificently-talented Ipswich side around the silky skills of Dutchmen Frans Thijssen and Arnold Muhren. For most of the season they hunted a treble but their top-class resources were too thin. Aston Villa sneaked the title, Manchester City dumped them out of the FA Cup semi-finals and eventually one of the most attractive club sides ever assembled in England had to be content with the Uefa spoils, ironically beating Dutch club AZ Alkmaar 5-4 on aggregate.

Tottenham succeeded by an even narrower margin. They pipped Anderlecht on penalties during a night of high drama which ended with goalkeeper Tony Parks a White Hart Lane hero. The North London giants thus added a second Uefa Cup to their 1963 Cup-Winners' Cup.

Capital neighbours Chelsea carried off the Cup-Winners prize in 1971, a year after Manchester City recorded their solitary European success in the same competition. Chelsea, who needed a replay to deprive Leeds of the FA Cup, also required two matches to see off the once invincible Real Madrid in Athens, with Peter Osgood and John Dempsey scoring in a 2-1 replay win. There had been only 10,000 spectators to watch Manchester City's 2-1 win over the Poles of Gornik Zabrze in Vienna, where goals from Neil Young and Francis Lee (penalty) captured the trophy.

Leeds, West Ham and Arsenal all lost Cup-Winners' Cup Finals before Everton recaptured the prize for England in 1985. Everton, newly crowned Football League champions, crushed Rapid Vienna 3-1 in Rotterdam with Andy Gray among the scorers.

The awful events at Heysel in 1985 cast a giant shadow over the game and Everton were denied a crack at the European Cup after a ban on English clubs. Norwich City and Manchester United were among the others to be denied a chance to strut in the other European competitions.

Before that ban English clubs had established a reputation as the most feared in Europe and for all the right reasons. It started with Liverpool's 1977 European Cup defeat of Borussia Moenchengladbach in Rome and marked an era when that trophy returned to England seven times in eight years, an unrivalled spread of success by a single nation in the premier European tournament.

Tommy Smith, the tough Liverpool defender, took a Roman road to retire-

European success for Nottingham Forest and skipper John McGovern

ment with one of the goals in Liverpool's 3-1 victory – his only goal of that season – and a year later Liverpool retained the trophy. A new hero emerged that night as Kenny Dalglish poached the only goal in a Wembley final against Bruges.

As the 1970's drew to a close, Brian Clough nudged Bob Paisley off the European managerial pedestal. Clough, renowned for his unique style of man-management, persuaded his Nottingham Forest players they could be the best in Europe. They proved it when £1 million signing Trevor Francis headed the goal which defeated Malmo in a Munich final and the club then showed it was no fluke when they successfully defended their prize. John Robertson's goal defeated Hamburg in a Madrid climax.

Peter Taylor and Brian Clough, Forest's touchline duo on two great European occasions

Paisley completed a hat-trick for Liverpool in 1981 when full-back Alan Kennedy's goal sank Real Madrid in Paris. Next it was Aston Villa's turn. They ended five years of domination by Liverpool and Forest but kept the English flag flying after Tony Barton succeeded Ron Saunders as the manager at Villa Park. Peter Withe's goal was enough to conquer Bayern Munich in the 1982 Rotterdam final.

Arsenal's Nigel Winterburn hurdles the challenging Asprilla of Parma in the 1994 Cup-Winners' Cup Final. Below, Paul Davis and the trophy

English clubs drew a blank in 1983 but Liverpool were back in the final a year later. Joe Fagan was in charge and the Reds did not let him down as they returned to Rome and came away with a 4-2 win on penalties after being held 1-1 by Roma after extra time.

Liverpool reached the final again in 1985 but lost what was a meaningless match against Juventus. Sport came a poor second that night, after officials decided to go ahead with the match despite the deaths of 39 spectators when a wall collapsed following a stampede of Liverpool fans across the crumbling Heysel terraces.

The inquiry and outrage that followed led to English clubs being barred from European competition for five years. When the ban was lifted, Manchester United restored England to the European honours list with that Cup-winners' Cup triumph over Barcelona in 1991, and an Alan Smith goal made Arsenal the fourth London club to capture it, with a 1-0 win over Parma in Copenhagen three years later.

That made Arsenal unique, as they are the only club to have collected a European prize as a Premiership club. Manchester United fell one hurdle short in the 1996-97 Champions' Cup and Ferguson will be desperate to go one step beyond.

And now that the Champions' Cup is no longer confined to champions, Newcastle expect the enormous experience of Kenny Dalglish to underpin their own challenge. Expectancy levels are also high among Uefa candidates Arsenal, Liverpool, Leicester and Aston Villa, while Chelsea nurse their own Cup-Winners' Cup ambitions.

Success at home is but a step in the push for the final frontier in Europe.

FA PREMIER LEAGUE RESULTS 1992-93

Read across for home results, down for away

	ARSENAL	ASTON VILLA	BLACKBURN ROVERS	CHELSEA	COVENTRY CITY	CRYSTAL PALACE	EVERTON	IPSWICH TOWN	LEEDS UNITED	LIVERPOOL	MANCHESTER CITY	MANCHESTER UNITED	MIDDLESBROUGH	NORWICH CITY
ARSENAL	–	0-1	0-1	2-1	3-0	3-0	2-0	0-0	0-0	0-1	1-0	0-1	1-1	2-4
ASTON VILLA	1-0	–	0-0	1-3	0-0	3-0	2-1	2-0	1-1	4-2	3-1	1-0	5-1	2-3
BLACKBURN ROVERS	1-0	3-0	–	2-0	2-5	1-2	2-3	2-1	3-1	4-1	1-0	0-0	1-1	7-1
CHELSEA	1-0	0-1	0-0	–	2-1	3-1	2-1	2-1	1-0	0-0	2-4	1-1	4-0	2-3
COVENTRY CITY	0-2	3-0	0-2	1-2	–	2-2	0-1	2-2	3-3	5-1	2-3	0-1	2-1	1-1
CRYSTAL PALACE	1-2	1-0	3-3	1-1	0-0	–	0-2	3-1	1-0	1-1	0-0	0-2	4-1	1-2
EVERTON	0-0	1-0	2-1	0-1	1-1	0-2	–	3-0	2-0	2-1	1-3	0-2	2-2	0-1
IPSWICH TOWN	1-2	1-1	2-1	1-1	0-0	2-2	1-0	–	4-2	2-2	3-1	2-1	0-1	3-1
LEEDS UNITED	3-0	1-1	5-2	1-1	2-2	0-0	2-0	1-0	–	2-2	1-0	0-0	3-0	0-0
LIVERPOOL	0-2	1-2	2-1	2-1	4-0	5-0	1-0	0-0	2-0	–	1-1	1-2	4-1	4-1
MANCHESTER CITY	0-1	1-1	3-2	0-1	1-0	0-0	2-5	3-1	4-0	1-1	–	1-1	0-1	3-1
MANCHESTER UNITED	0-0	1-1	3-1	3-0	5-0	1-0	0-3	1-1	2-0	2-2	2-1	–	3-0	1-0
MIDDLESBROUGH	1-0	2-3	3-2	0-0	0-2	0-1	1-2	2-2	4-1	1-2	2-0	1-1	–	3-3
NORWICH CITY	1-1	1-0	0-0	2-1	1-1	4-2	1-1	0-2	4-2	1-0	2-1	1-3	1-1	–
NOTTINGHAM FOREST	0-1	0-1	1-3	3-0	1-1	1-1	0-1	0-1	1-1	1-0	0-2	0-2	1-0	0-3
OLDHAM ATHLETIC	0-1	1-1	0-1	3-1	0-1	1-1	1-0	4-2	2-2	3-2	0-1	1-0	4-1	2-3
QUEENS PARK RANGERS	0-0	2-1	0-3	1-1	2-0	1-3	4-2	0-0	2-1	0-1	1-1	1-3	3-3	3-1
SHEFFIELD UNITED	1-1	0-2	1-3	4-2	1-1	0-1	1-0	3-0	2-1	1-0	1-1	2-1	2-0	0-1
SHEFFIELD WEDNESDAY	1-0	1-2	0-0	3-3	1-2	2-1	3-1	1-1	1-1	1-1	0-3	3-3	2-3	1-0
SOUTHAMPTON	2-0	2-0	1-1	1-0	2-2	1-0	0-0	4-3	1-1	2-1	0-1	0-1	2-1	3-0
TOTTENHAM HOTSPUR	1-0	0-0	1-2	1-2	0-2	2-2	2-1	0-2	4-0	2-0	3-1	1-1	2-2	5-1
WIMBLEDON	3-2	2-3	1-1	0-0	1-2	4-0	1-3	0-1	1-0	2-0	0-1	1-2	2-0	3-0

NOTTINGHAM FOREST	OLDHAM ATHLETIC	QUEENS PARK RANGERS	SHEFFIELD UNITED	SHEFFIELD WEDNESDAY	SOUTHAMPTON	TOTTENHAM HOTSPUR	WIMBLEDON
1-1	2-0	0-0	1-1	2-1	4-3	1-3	0-1
2-1	0-1	2-0	3-1	2-0	1-1	0-0	1-0
4-1	2-0	1-0	1-0	1-0	0-0	0-2	0-0
0-0	1-1	1-0	1-2	0-2	1-1	1-1	4-2
0-1	3-0	0-1	1-3	1-0	2-0	1-0	0-2
1-1	2-2	1-1	2-0	1-1	1-2	1-3	2-0
3-0	2-2	3-5	0-2	1-1	2-1	1-2	0-0
2-1	1-2	1-1	0-0	0-1	0-0	1-1	2-1
1-4	2-0	1-1	3-1	3-1	2-1	5-0	2-1
0-0	1-0	1-0	2-1	1-0	1-1	6-2	2-3
2-2	3-3	1-1	2-0	1-2	1-0	0-1	1-1
2-0	3-0	0-0	2-1	2-1	2-1	4-1	0-1
1-2	2-3	0-1	2-0	1-1	2-1	3-0	2-0
3-1	1-0	2-1	2-1	1-0	1-0	0-0	2-1
–	2-0	1-0	0-2	1-2	1-2	2-1	1-1
5-3	–	2-2	1-1	1-1	4-3	2-1	6-2
4-3	3-2	–	3-2	3-1	3-1	4-1	1-2
0-0	2-0	1-2	–	1-1	2-0	6-0	2-2
2-0	2-1	1-0	1-1	–	5-2	2-0	1-1
1-2	1-0	1-2	3-2	1-2	–	0-0	2-2
2-1	4-1	3-2	2-0	0-2	4-2	–	1-1
1-0	5-2	0-2	2-0	1-1	1-2	1-1	–

FA PREMIER LEAGUE – 1992-93

		HOME					AWAY					
	P	W	D	L	F	A	W	D	L	F	A	Pts
Manchester United	42	14	5	2	39	14	10	7	4	28	17	84
Aston Villa	42	13	5	3	36	16	8	6	7	21	24	74
Norwich City	42	13	6	2	31	19	8	3	10	30	46	72
Blackburn Rovers	42	13	4	4	38	18	7	7	7	30	28	71
Queens Park Rangers	42	11	5	5	41	32	6	7	8	22	23	63
Liverpool	42	13	4	4	41	18	3	7	11	21	37	59
Sheffield Wednesday	42	9	8	4	34	26	6	6	9	21	25	59
Tottenham Hotspur	42	11	5	5	40	25	5	6	10	20	41	59
Manchester City	42	7	8	6	30	25	8	4	9	26	26	57
Arsenal	42	8	6	7	25	20	7	5	9	15	18	56
Chelsea	42	9	7	5	29	22	5	7	9	22	32	56
Wimbledon	42	9	4	8	32	23	5	8	8	24	32	54
Everton	42	7	6	8	26	27	8	2	11	27	28	53
Sheffield United	42	10	6	5	33	19	4	4	13	21	34	52
Coventry City	42	7	4	10	29	28	6	9	6	23	29	52
Ipswich Town	42	8	9	4	29	22	4	7	10	21	33	52
Leeds United	42	12	8	1	40	17	0	7	14	17	45	51
Southampton	42	10	6	5	30	21	3	5	13	24	40	50
Oldham Athletic	42	10	6	5	43	30	3	4	14	20	44	49
Crystal Palace	42	6	9	6	27	25	5	7	9	21	36	49
Middlesbrough	42	8	5	8	33	27	3	6	12	21	48	44
Nottingham Forest	42	6	4	11	17	25	4	6	11	24	37	40

FA CARLING PREMIERSHIP RESULTS 1993-94

Read across for home results, down for away

	ARSENAL	ASTON VILLA	BLACKBURN ROVERS	CHELSEA	COVENTRY CITY	EVERTON	IPSWICH TOWN	LEEDS UNITED	LIVERPOOL	MANCHESTER CITY	MANCHESTER UNITED	NEWCASTLE UNITED	NORWICH CITY	OLDHAM ATHLETIC
ARSENAL	–	1-2	1-0	1-0	0-3	2-0	4-0	2-1	1-0	0-0	2-2	2-1	0-0	1-1
ASTON VILLA	1-2	–	0-1	1-0	0-0	0-0	0-1	1-0	2-1	0-0	1-2	0-2	0-0	1-2
BLACKBURN ROVERS	1-1	1-0	–	2-0	2-1	2-0	0-0	2-1	2-0	2-0	2-0	1-0	2-3	1-0
CHELSEA	0-2	1-1	1-2	–	1-2	4-2	1-1	1-1	1-0	0-0	1-0	1-0	1-2	0-1
COVENTRY CITY	1-0	0-1	2-1	1-1	–	2-1	1-0	0-2	1-0	4-0	0-1	2-1	2-1	1-1
EVERTON	1-1	0-1	0-3	4-2	0-0	–	0-0	1-1	2-0	1-0	0-1	0-2	1-5	2-1
IPSWICH TOWN	1-5	1-2	1-0	1-0	0-2	0-2	–	0-0	1-2	2-2	1-2	1-1	2-1	0-0
LEEDS UNITED	2-1	2-0	3-3	4-1	1-0	3-0	0-0	–	2-0	3-2	0-2	1-1	0-4	1-0
LIVERPOOL	0-0	2-1	0-1	2-1	1-0	2-1	1-0	2-0	–	2-1	3-3	0-2	0-1	2-1
MANCHESTER CITY	0-0	3-0	0-2	2-2	1-1	1-0	2-1	1-1	1-1	–	2-3	2-1	1-1	1-1
MANCHESTER UNITED	1-0	3-1	1-1	0-1	0-0	1-0	0-0	0-0	1-0	2-0	–	1-1	2-2	3-2
NEWCASTLE UNITED	2-0	5-1	1-1	0-0	4-0	1-0	2-0	1-1	3-0	2-0	1-1	–	3-0	3-2
NORWICH CITY	1-1	1-2	2-2	1-1	1-0	3-0	1-0	2-1	2-2	1-1	0-2	1-2	–	1-1
OLDHAM ATHLETIC	0-0	1-1	1-2	2-1	3-3	0-1	0-3	1-1	0-3	0-0	2-5	1-3	2-1	–
QUEENS PARK RANGERS	1-1	2-2	1-0	1-1	5-1	2-1	3-0	0-4	1-3	1-1	2-3	1-2	2-2	2-0
SHEFFIELD UNITED	1-1	1-2	1-2	1-0	0-0	0-0	1-1	2-2	0-0	0-1	0-3	2-0	1-2	2-1
SHEFFIELD WEDNESDAY	0-1	0-0	1-2	3-1	0-0	5-1	5-0	3-3	3-1	1-1	2-3	0-1	3-3	3-0
SOUTHAMPTON	0-4	4-1	3-1	3-1	1-0	0-2	0-1	0-2	4-2	0-1	1-3	2-1	0-1	1-3
SWINDON TOWN	0-4	1-2	1-3	1-3	3-1	1-1	2-2	0-5	0-5	1-3	2-2	2-2	3-3	0-1
TOTTENHAM HOTSPUR	0-1	1-1	0-2	1-1	1-2	3-2	1-1	1-1	3-3	1-0	0-1	1-2	1-3	5-0
WEST HAM UNITED	0-0	0-0	1-2	1-0	3-2	0-1	2-1	0-1	1-2	3-1	2-2	2-4	3-3	2-0
WIMBLEDON	0-3	2-2	4-1	1-1	1-2	1-1	0-2	1-0	1-1	1-0	1-0	4-2	3-1	3-0

QUEENS PARK RANGERS	SHEFFIELD UNITED	SHEFFIELD WEDNESDAY	SOUTHAMPTON	SWINDON TOWN	TOTTENHAM HOTSPUR	WEST HAM UNITED	WIMBLEDON
0-0	3-0	1-0	1-0	1-1	1-1	0-2	1-1
4-1	1-0	2-2	0-2	5-0	1-0	3-1	0-1
1-1	0-0	1-1	2-0	3-1	1-0	0-2	3-0
2-0	3-2	1-1	2-0	2-0	4-3	2-0	2-0
0-1	0-0	1-1	1-1	1-1	1-0	1-1	1-2
0-3	4-2	0-2	1-0	6-2	0-1	0-1	3-2
1-3	3-2	1-4	1-0	1-1	2-2	1-1	0-0
1-1	2-1	2-2	0-0	3-0	2-0	1-0	4-0
3-2	1-2	2-0	4-2	2-2	1-2	2-0	1-1
3-0	0-0	1-3	1-1	2-1	0-2	0-0	0-1
2-1	3-0	5-0	2-0	4-2	2-1	3-0	3-1
1-2	4-0	4-2	1-2	7-1	0-1	2-0	4-0
3-4	0-1	1-1	4-5	0-0	1-2	0-0	0-1
4-1	1-1	0-0	2-1	2-1	0-2	1-2	1-1
–	2-1	1-2	2-1	1-3	1-1	0-0	1-0
1-1	–	1-1	0-0	3-1	2-2	3-2	2-1
3-1	3-1	–	2-0	3-3	1-0	5-0	2-2
0-1	3-3	3-1	–	5-1	1-0	0-2	1-0
1-0	0-0	4-4	2-1	–	2-1	1-1	2-4
1-2	2-2	1-3	3-0	1-1	–	1-4	1-1
0-4	0-0	2-0	3-3	0-0	1-3	–	0-2
1-1	2-0	2-1	1-0	3-0	2-1	1-2	–

FA CARLING PREMIERSHIP – 1993-94

		HOME					AWAY					
	P	W	D	L	F	A	W	D	L	F	A	Pts
Manchester United	42	14	6	1	39	13	13	5	3	41	25	92
Blackburn Rovers	42	14	5	2	31	11	11	4	6	32	25	84
Newcastle United	42	14	4	3	51	14	9	4	8	31	27	77
Arsenal	42	10	8	3	25	15	8	9	4	28	13	71
Leeds United	42	13	6	2	37	18	5	10	6	28	21	70
Wimbledon	42	12	5	4	35	21	6	6	9	21	32	65
Sheffield Wednesday	42	10	7	4	48	24	6	9	6	28	30	64
Liverpool	42	12	4	5	33	23	5	5	11	26	32	60
Queens Park Rangers	42	8	7	6	32	29	8	5	8	30	32	60
Aston Villa	42	8	5	8	23	18	7	7	7	23	32	57
Coventry City	42	9	7	5	23	17	5	7	9	20	28	56
Norwich City	42	4	9	8	26	29	8	8	5	39	32	53
West Ham United	42	6	7	8	26	31	7	6	8	21	27	52
Chelsea	42	11	5	5	31	20	2	7	12	18	33	51
Tottenham Hotspur	42	4	8	9	29	33	7	4	10	25	26	45
Manchester City	42	6	10	5	24	22	3	8	10	14	27	45
Everton	42	8	4	9	26	30	4	4	13	16	33	44
Southampton	42	9	2	10	30	31	3	5	13	19	35	43
Ipswich Town	42	5	8	8	21	32	4	8	9	14	26	43
Sheffield United	42	6	10	5	24	23	2	8	11	18	37	42
Oldham Athletic	42	5	8	8	24	33	4	5	12	18	35	40
Swindon Town	42	4	7	10	25	45	1	8	12	22	55	30

FA CARLING PREMIERSHIP RESULTS 1994-95

Read across for home results, down for away

	ARSENAL	ASTON VILLA	BLACKBURN ROVERS	CHELSEA	COVENTRY CITY	CRYSTAL PALACE	EVERTON	IPSWICH TOWN	LEEDS UNITED	LEICESTER CITY	LIVERPOOL	MANCHESTER CITY	MANCHESTER UNITED	NEWCASTLE UNITED
ARSENAL	–	0-0	0-0	3-1	2-1	1-2	1-1	4-1	1-3	1-1	0-1	3-0	0-0	2-3
ASTON VILLA	0-4	–	0-1	3-0	0-0	1-1	0-0	2-0	0-0	4-4	2-0	1-1	1-2	0-2
BLACKBURN ROVERS	3-1	3-1	–	2-1	4-0	2-1	3-0	4-1	1-1	3-0	3-2	2-3	2-4	1-0
CHELSEA	2-1	1-0	1-2	–	2-2	0-0	0-1	2-0	0-3	4-0	0-0	3-0	2-3	1-1
COVENTRY CITY	0-1	0-1	1-1	2-2	–	1-4	0-0	2-0	2-1	4-2	1-1	1-0	2-3	0-0
CRYSTAL PALACE	0-3	0-0	0-1	0-1	0-2	–	1-0	3-0	1-2	2-0	1-6	2-1	1-1	0-1
EVERTON	1-1	2-2	1-2	3-3	0-2	3-1	–	4-1	3-0	1-1	2-0	1-1	1-0	2-0
IPSWICH TOWN	0-2	0-1	1-3	2-2	2-0	0-2	0-1	–	2-0	4-1	1-3	1-2	3-2	0-2
LEEDS UNITED	1-0	1-0	1-1	2-3	3-0	3-1	1-0	4-0	–	2-1	0-2	2-0	2-1	0-0
LEICESTER CITY	2-1	1-1	0-0	1-1	2-2	0-1	2-2	2-0	1-3	–	1-2	0-1	0-4	1-3
LIVERPOOL	3-0	3-2	2-1	3-1	2-3	0-0	0-0	0-1	0-1	2-0	–	2-0	2-0	2-0
MANCHESTER CITY	1-2	2-2	1-3	1-2	0-0	1-1	4-0	2-0	0-0	0-1	2-1	–	0-3	0-0
MANCHESTER UNITED	3-0	1-0	1-0	0-0	2-0	3-0	2-0	9-0	0-0	1-1	2-0	5-0	–	2-0
NEWCASTLE UNITED	1-0	3-1	1-1	4-2	4-0	3-2	2-0	1-1	1-2	3-1	1-1	0-0	1-1	–
NORWICH CITY	0-0	1-1	2-1	3-0	2-2	0-0	0-0	3-0	2-1	2-1	1-2	1-1	0-2	2-1
NOTTINGHAM FOREST	2-2	1-2	0-2	0-1	2-0	1-0	2-1	4-1	3-0	1-0	1-1	1-0	1-1	0-0
QUEENS PARK RANGERS	3-1	2-0	0-1	1-0	2-2	0-1	2-3	1-2	3-2	2-0	2-1	1-2	2-3	3-0
SHEFFIELD WEDNESDAY	3-1	1-2	0-1	1-1	5-1	1-0	0-0	4-1	1-1	1-0	1-2	1-1	1-0	0-0
SOUTHAMPTON	1-0	2-1	1-1	0-1	0-0	3-1	2-0	3-1	1-3	2-2	0-2	2-2	2-2	3-1
TOTTENHAM HOTSPUR	1-0	3-4	3-1	0-0	1-3	0-0	2-1	3-0	1-1	1-0	0-0	2-1	0-1	4-2
WEST HAM UNITED	0-2	1-0	2-0	1-2	0-1	1-0	2-2	1-1	0-0	1-0	3-0	3-0	1-1	1-3
WIMBLEDON	1-3	4-3	0-3	1-1	2-0	2-0	2-1	1-1	0-0	2-1	0-0	2-0	0-1	3-2

	NORWICH CITY	NOTTINGHAM FOREST	QUEENS PARK RANGERS	SHEFFIELD WEDNESDAY	SOUTHAMPTON	TOTTENHAM HOTSPUR	WEST HAM UNITED	WIMBLEDON
	5-1	1-0	1-3	0-0	1-1	1-1	0-1	0-0
	1-1	0-2	2-1	1-1	1-1	1-0	0-2	7-1
	0-0	3-0	4-0	3-1	3-2	2-0	4-2	2-1
	2-0	0-2	1-0	1-1	0-2	1-1	1-2	1-1
	1-0	0-0	0-1	2-0	1-3	0-4	2-0	1-1
	0-1	1-2	0-0	2-1	0-0	1-1	1-0	0-0
	2-1	1-2	2-2	1-4	0-0	0-0	1-0	0-0
	1-2	0-1	0-1	1-2	2-1	1-3	1-1	2-2
	2-1	1-0	4-0	0-1	0-0	1-1	2-2	3-1
	1-0	2-4	1-1	0-1	4-3	3-1	1-2	3-4
	4-0	1-0	1-1	4-1	3-1	1-1	0-0	3-0
	2-0	3-3	2-3	3-2	3-3	5-2	3-0	2-0
	1-0	1-2	2-0	1-0	2-1	0-0	1-0	3-0
	3-0	2-1	2-1	2-1	5-1	3-3	2-0	2-1
	–	0-1	4-2	0-0	2-2	0-2	1-0	1-2
	1-0	–	3-2	4-1	3-0	2-2	1-1	3-1
	2-0	1-1	–	3-2	2-2	2-1	2-1	0-1
	0-0	1-7	0-2	–	1-1	3-4	1-1	0-1
	1-1	1-1	2-1	0-0	–	4-3	1-1	2-3
	1-0	1-4	1-1	3-1	1-2	–	3-1	1-2
	2-2	3-1	0-0	0-2	2-0	1-2	–	3-0
	1-0	2-2	1-3	0-1	0-2	1-2	1-0	–

FA CARLING PREMIERSHIP – 1994-95

		HOME					AWAY					
	P	W	D	L	F	A	W	D	L	F	A	Pts
Blackburn Rovers	42	17	2	2	54	21	10	6	5	26	18	89
Manchester United	42	16	4	1	42	4	10	6	5	35	24	88
Nottingham Forest	42	12	6	3	36	18	10	5	6	36	25	77
Liverpool	42	13	5	3	38	13	8	6	7	27	24	74
Leeds United	42	13	5	3	35	15	7	8	6	24	23	73
Newcastle United	42	14	6	1	46	20	6	6	9	21	27	72
Tottenham Hotspur	42	10	5	6	32	25	6	9	6	34	33	62
Queens Park Rangers	42	11	3	7	36	26	6	6	9	25	33	60
Wimbledon	42	9	5	7	26	26	6	6	9	22	39	56
Southampton	42	8	9	4	33	27	4	9	8	28	36	54
Chelsea	42	7	7	7	25	22	6	8	7	25	33	54
Arsenal	42	6	9	6	27	21	7	3	11	25	28	51
Sheffield Wednesday	42	7	7	7	26	26	6	5	10	23	31	51
West Ham United	42	9	6	6	28	19	4	5	12	16	29	50
Everton	42	8	9	4	31	23	3	8	10	13	28	50
Coventry City	42	7	7	7	23	25	5	7	9	21	37	50
Manchester City	42	8	7	6	37	28	4	6	11	16	36	49
Aston Villa	42	6	9	6	27	24	5	6	10	24	32	48
Crystal Palace	42	6	6	9	16	23	5	6	10	18	26	45
Norwich City	42	8	8	5	27	21	2	5	14	10	33	43
Leicester City	42	5	6	10	28	37	1	5	15	17	43	29
Ipswich Town	42	5	3	13	24	34	2	3	16	12	59	27

FA CARLING PREMIERSHIP RESULTS 1995-96

Read across for home results, down for away

	ARSENAL	ASTON VILLA	BLACKBURN ROVERS	BOLTON WANDERERS	CHELSEA	COVENTRY CITY	EVERTON	ILEEDS UNITED	LIVERPOOL	MANCHESTER CITY	MANCHESTER UNITED	MIDDLESBROUGH	NEWCASTLE UNITED	NOTTINGHAM FOREST
ARSENAL	–	2-0	0-0	2-1	1-1	1-1	1-2	2-1	0-0	3-1	1-0	1-1	2-0	1-1
ASTON VILLA	1-1	–	2-0	1-0	0-1	4-1	1-0	3-0	0-2	0-1	3-1	0-0	1-1	1-1
BLACKBURN ROVERS	1-1	1-1	–	3-1	3-0	5-1	0-3	1-0	2-3	2-0	1-2	1-0	2-1	7-0
BOLTON WANDERERS	1-0	0-2	2-1	–	2-1	1-2	1-1	0-2	0-1	1-1	0-6	1-1	1-3	1-1
CHELSEA	1-0	1-2	2-3	3-2	–	2-2	0-0	4-1	2-2	1-1	1-4	5-0	1-0	1-0
COVENTRY CITY	0-0	0-3	5-0	0-2	1-0	–	2-1	0-0	1-0	2-1	0-4	0-0	0-1	1-1
EVERTON	0-2	1-0	1-0	3-0	1-1	2-2	–	2-0	1-1	2-0	2-3	4-0	1-3	3-0
LEEDS UNITED	0-3	2-0	0-0	0-1	1-0	3-1	2-2	–	1-0	0-1	3-1	0-1	0-1	1-3
LIVERPOOL	3-1	3-0	3-0	5-2	2-0	0-0	1-2	5-0	–	6-0	2-0	1-0	4-3	4-2
MANCHESTER CITY	0-1	1-0	1-1	1-0	0-1	1-1	0-2	0-0	2-2	–	2-3	0-1	3-3	1-1
MANCHESTER UNITED	1-0	0-0	1-0	3-0	1-1	1-0	2-0	1-0	2-2	1-0	–	2-0	2-0	5-0
MIDDLESBROUGH	2-3	0-2	2-0	1-4	2-0	2-1	0-2	1-1	2-1	4-1	0-3	–	1-2	1-1
NEWCASTLE UNITED	2-0	1-0	1-0	2-1	2-0	3-0	1-0	2-1	2-1	3-1	0-1	1-0	–	3-1
NOTTINGHAM FOREST	0-1	1-1	1-5	3-2	0-0	0-0	3-2	2-1	1-0	3-0	1-1	1-0	1-1	–
QUEENS PARK RANGERS	1-1	1-0	0-1	2-1	1-2	1-1	3-1	1-2	1-2	1-0	1-1	1-1	2-3	1-1
SHEFFIELD WEDNESDAY	1-0	2-0	2-1	4-2	0-0	4-3	2-5	6-2	1-1	1-1	0-0	0-1	0-2	1-3
SOUTHAMPTON	0-0	0-1	1-0	1-0	2-3	1-0	2-2	1-1	1-3	1-1	3-1	2-1	1-0	3-4
TOTTENHAM HOTSPUR	2-1	0-1	2-3	2-2	1-1	3-1	0-0	2-1	1-3	1-0	4-1	1-1	1-1	0-1
WEST HAM UNITED	0-1	1-4	1-1	1-0	1-3	3-2	2-1	1-2	0-0	4-2	0-1	2-0	2-0	1-0
WIMBLEDON	0-3	3-3	1-1	3-2	1-1	0-2	2-3	2-4	1-0	3-0	2-4	0-0	3-3	1-0

QUEENS PARK RANGERS	SHEFFIELD WEDNESDAY	SOUTHAMPTON	TOTTENHAM HOTSPUR	WEST HAM UNITED	WIMBLEDON
3-0	4-2	4-2	0-0	1-0	1-3
4-2	3-2	3-0	2-1	1-1	2-0
1-0	3-0	2-1	2-1	4-2	3-2
0-1	2-1	0-1	2-3	0-3	1-0
1-1	0-0	3-0	0-0	1-2	1-2
1-0	0-1	1-1	2-3	2-2	3-3
2-0	2-2	2-0	1-1	3-0	2-4
1-3	2-0	1-0	1-3	2-0	1-1
1-0	1-0	1-1	0-0	2-0	2-2
2-0	1-0	2-1	1-1	2-1	1-0
2-1	2-2	4-1	1-0	2-1	3-1
1-0	3-1	0-0	0-1	4-2	1-2
2-1	2-0	1-0	1-1	3-0	6-1
3-0	1-0	1-0	2-1	1-1	4-1
–	0-3	3-0	2-3	3-0	0-3
1-3	–	2-2	1-3	0-1	2-1
2-0	0-1	–	0-0	0-0	0-0
1-0	1-0	1-0	–	0-1	3-1
1-0	1-1	2-1	1-1	–	1-1
2-1	2-2	1-2	0-1	0-1	–

FA CARLING PREMIERSHIP – 1995-96

		HOME					AWAY					
	P	W	D	L	F	A	W	D	L	F	A	Pts
Manchester United	38	15	4	0	36	9	10	3	6	37	26	82
Newcastle United	38	17	1	1	38	9	7	5	7	28	28	78
Liverpool	38	14	4	1	46	13	6	7	6	24	21	71
Aston Villa	38	11	5	3	32	15	7	4	8	20	20	63
Arsenal	38	10	7	2	30	16	7	5	7	19	16	63
Everton	38	10	5	4	35	19	7	5	7	29	25	61
Blackburn Rovers	38	14	2	3	44	19	4	5	10	17	28	61
Tottenham Hotspur	38	9	5	5	26	19	7	8	4	24	19	61
Nottingham Forest	38	11	6	2	29	17	4	7	8	21	37	58
West Ham United	38	9	5	5	25	21	5	4	10	18	31	51
Chelsea	38	7	7	5	30	22	5	7	7	16	22	50
Middlesbrough	38	8	3	8	27	27	3	7	9	8	23	43
Leeds United	38	8	3	8	21	21	4	4	11	19	36	43
Wimbledon	38	5	6	8	27	33	5	5	9	28	37	41
Sheffield Wednesday	38	7	5	7	30	31	3	5	11	18	30	40
Coventry City	38	6	7	6	21	23	2	7	10	21	37	38
Southampton	38	7	7	5	21	18	2	4	13	13	34	38
Manchester City	38	7	7	5	21	19	2	4	13	12	39	38
Queens Park Rangers	38	6	5	8	25	26	3	1	15	13	31	33
Bolton Wanderers	38	5	4	10	16	31	3	1	15	23	40	29

FA CARLING PREMIERSHIP RESULTS 1996-97

Read across for home results, down for away

	ARSENAL	ASTON VILLA	BLACKBURN ROVERS	CHELSEA	COVENTRY CITY	DERBY COUNTY	EVERTON	LEEDS UNITED	LEICESTER CITY	LIVERPOOL	MANCHESTER UNITED	MIDDLESBROUGH	NEWCASTLE UNITED	NOTTINGHAM FOREST
ARSENAL	–	2-2	1-1	3-3	0-0	2-2	3-1	3-0	2-0	1-2	1-2	2-0	0-1	2-0
ASTON VILLA	2-2	–	1-0	0-2	2-1	2-0	3-1	2-0	1-3	1-0	0-0	1-0	2-2	2-0
BLACKBURN ROVERS	0-2	0-2	–	1-1	4-0	1-2	1-1	0-1	2-4	3-0	2-3	0-0	1-0	1-1
CHELSEA	0-3	1-1	1-1	–	2-0	3-1	2-2	0-0	2-1	1-0	1-1	1-0	1-1	1-1
COVENTRY CITY	1-1	1-2	0-0	3-1	–	1-2	0-0	2-1	0-0	0-1	0-2	3-0	2-1	0-3
DERBY COUNTY	1-3	2-1	0-0	3-2	2-1	–	0-1	3-3	2-0	0-1	1-1	2-1	0-1	0-0
EVERTON	0-2	0-1	0-2	1-2	1-1	1-0	–	0-0	1-1	1-1	0-2	1-2	2-0	2-0
LEEDS UNITED	0-0	0-0	0-0	2-0	1-3	0-0	1-0	–	3-0	0-2	0-4	1-1	0-1	2-0
LEICESTER CITY	0-2	1-0	1-1	1-3	0-2	4-2	1-2	1-0	–	0-3	2-2	1-3	2-0	2-2
LIVERPOOL	2-0	3-0	0-0	5-1	1-2	2-1	1-1	4-0	1-1	–	1-3	5-1	4-3	4-2
MANCHESTER UNITED	1-0	0-0	2-2	1-2	3-1	2-3	2-2	1-0	3-1	1-0	–	0-0	0-0	4-1
MIDDLESBROUGH	0-2	3-2	2-1	1-0	4-0	6-1	4-2	0-0	0-2	3-3	2-2	–	0-1	1-1
NEWCASTLE UNITED	1-2	4-3	2-1	3-1	4-0	3-1	4-1	3-0	4-3	1-1	5-0	3-1	–	5-0
NOTTINGHAM FOREST	2-1	0-0	2-2	2-0	0-1	1-1	0-1	1-1	0-0	1-1	0-4	1-1	0-0	–
SHEFFIELD WEDNESDAY	0-0	2-1	1-1	0-2	0-0	0-0	2-1	2-2	2-1	1-1	1-1	3-1	1-1	2-0
SOUTHAMPTON	0-2	0-1	2-0	0-0	2-2	3-1	2-2	0-2	2-2	0-1	6-3	4-0	2-2	2-2
SUNDERLAND	1-0	1-0	0-0	3-0	1-0	2-0	3-0	0-1	0-0	1-2	2-1	2-2	1-2	1-1
TOTTENHAM HOTSPUR	0-0	1-0	2-1	1-2	1-2	1-1	0-0	1-0	1-2	0-2	1-2	1-0	1-2	0-1
WEST HAM UNITED	1-2	0-2	2-1	3-2	1-1	1-1	2-2	0-2	1-0	1-2	2-2	0-0	0-0	0-1
WIMBLEDON	2-2	0-2	1-0	0-1	2-2	1-1	4-0	2-0	1-3	2-1	0-3	1-1	1-1	1-0

SHEFFIELD WEDNESDAY	SOUTHAMPTON	SUNDERLAND	TOTTENHAM HOTSPUR	WEST HAM UNITED	WIMBLEDON
4-1	3-1	2-0	3-1	2-0	0-1
0-1	1-0	1-0	1-1	0-0	5-0
4-1	2-1	1-0	0-2	2-1	3-1
2-2	1-0	6-2	3-1	3-1	2-4
0-0	1-1	2-2	1-2	1-3	1-1
2-2	1-1	1-0	4-2	1-0	0-2
2-0	7-1	1-3	1-0	2-1	1-3
0-2	0-0	3-0	0-0	1-0	1-0
1-0	2-1	1-1	1-1	0-1	1-0
0-1	2-1	0-0	2-1	0-0	1-1
2-0	2-1	5-0	2-0	2-0	2-1
4-2	0-1	0-1	0-3	4-1	0-0
1-2	0-1	1-1	7-1	1-1	2-0
0-3	1-3	1-4	2-1	0-2	1-1
–	1-1	2-1	2-1	0-0	3-1
2-3	–	3-0	0-1	2-0	0-0
1-1	0-1	–	0-4	0-0	1-3
1-1	3-1	2-0	–	1-0	1-0
5-1	2-1	2-0	4-3	–	0-2
4-2	3-1	1-0	1-0	1-1	–

FA CARLING PREMIERSHIP – 1996-97

		HOME					AWAY					
	P	W	D	L	F	A	W	D	L	F	A	Pts
Manchester United	38	12	5	2	38	17	9	7	3	38	27	75
Newcastle United	38	13	3	3	54	20	6	8	5	19	20	68
Arsenal	38	10	5	4	36	18	9	6	4	26	14	68
Liverpool	38	10	6	3	38	19	9	5	5	24	18	68
Aston Villa	38	11	5	3	27	13	6	5	8	20	21	61
Chelsea	38	9	8	2	33	22	7	3	9	25	33	59
Sheffield Wednesday	38	8	10	1	25	16	6	5	8	25	35	57
Wimbledon	38	9	6	4	28	21	6	5	8	21	25	56
Leicester City	38	7	5	7	22	26	5	6	8	24	28	47
Tottenham Hotspur	38	8	4	7	19	17	5	3	11	25	34	46
Leeds United	38	7	7	5	15	13	4	6	9	13	25	46
Derby County	38	8	6	5	25	22	3	7	9	20	36	46
Blackburn Rovers	38	8	4	7	28	23	1	11	7	14	20	42
West Ham United	38	7	6	6	27	25	3	6	10	12	23	42
Everton	38	7	4	8	24	22	3	8	8	20	35	42
Southampton	38	6	7	6	32	24	4	4	11	18	32	41
Coventry City	38	4	8	7	19	23	5	6	8	19	31	41
Sunderland	38	7	6	6	20	18	3	4	12	15	35	40
Middlesbrough*	38	8	5	6	34	25	2	7	10	17	35	39
Nottingham Forest	38	3	9	7	15	27	3	7	9	16	32	34

* Middlesbrough deducted 3 points

Carling Premiership Fixtures 1997-98

Compiled in association with the SEMA GROUP

Saturday 9 August
Barnsley v West Ham
Blackburn v Derby
Coventry v Chelsea
Everton v Crystal Palace
Leeds v Arsenal
Leicester v Aston Villa
Newcastle v Sheff Wed
Southampton v Bolton
Wimbledon v Liverpool

Sunday 10 August
Tottenham v Man Utd

Monday 11 August
Arsenal v Coventry

Tuesday 12 August
Crystal Palace v Barnsley

Wednesday 13 August
Aston Villa v Blackburn
Derby v Wimbledon
Liverpool v Leicester
Man Utd v Southampton
Sheff Wed v Leeds
West Ham v Tottenham

Saturday 23 August
Blackburn v Liverpool
Coventry v Bolton
Everton v West Ham
Leeds v Crystal Palace
Leicester v Man Utd
Newcastle v Aston Villa
Southampton v Arsenal
Tottenham v Derby
Wimbledon v Sheff Wed

Sunday 24 August
Barnsley v Chelsea

Monday 25 August
Blackburn v Sheff Wed

Tuesday 26 August
Barnsley v Bolton
Leeds v Liverpool
Wimbledon v Chelsea

Wednesday 27 August
Coventry v West Ham
Everton v Man Utd
Leicester v Arsenal
Southampton v Crystal Palace
Tottenham v Aston Villa

Saturday 30 August
Arsenal v Tottenham
Aston Villa v Leeds
Chelsea v Southampton
Crystal Palace v Blackburn
Derby v Barnsley
Man Utd v Coventry
Sheff Wed v Leicester
West Ham v Wimbledon

Sunday 31 August
Liverpool v Newcastle

Monday 1 September
Bolton v Everton

Saturday 13 September
Arsenal v Bolton
Barnsley v Aston Villa
Coventry v Southampton
Crystal Palace v Chelsea
Derby v Everton
Leicester v Tottenham
Liverpool v Sheff Wed
Man Utd v West Ham
Newcastle v Wimbledon

Sunday 14 September
Blackburn v Leeds

Saturday 20 September
Aston Villa v Derby
Bolton v Man Utd
Everton v Barnsley
Leeds v Leicester
Sheff Wed v Coventry
Southampton v Liverpool
Tottenham v Blackburn
West Ham v Newcastle
Wimbledon v Crystal Palace

Sunday 21 September
Chelsea v Arsenal

Monday 22 September
Liverpool v Aston Villa

Tuesday 23 September
Arsenal v West Ham
Bolton v Tottenham
Wimbledon v Barnsley

Wednesday 24 September
Coventry v Crystal Palace
Leicester v Blackburn
Man Utd v Chelsea
Newcastle v Everton
Sheff Wed v Derby
Southampton v Leeds

Saturday 27 September
Aston Villa v Sheff Wed
Barnsley v Leicester
Chelsea v Newcastle
Crystal Palace v Bolton
Derby v Southampton
Everton v Arsenal
Leeds v Man Utd
Tottenham v Wimbledon
West Ham v Liverpool

Sunday 28 September
Blackburn v Coventry

Saturday 4 October
Arsenal v Barnsley
Bolton v Aston Villa
Coventry v Leeds
Man Utd v Crystal Palace
Newcastle v Tottenham
Sheff Wed v Everton
Southampton v West Ham
Wimbledon v Blackburn

Sunday 5 October
Liverpool v Chelsea

Monday 6 October
Leicester v Derby

Saturday 18 October
Aston Villa v Wimbledon
Blackburn v Southampton
Chelsea v Leicester
Crystal Palace v Arsenal
Derby v Man Utd
Everton v Liverpool
Leeds v Newcastle
West Ham v Bolton

Sunday 19 October
Tottenham v Sheff Wed

Monday 20 October
Barnsley v Coventry

Saturday 25 October
Bolton v Chelsea
Coventry v Everton
Leicester v West Ham
Liverpool v Derby
Man Utd v Barnsley
Newcastle v Blackburn
Sheff Wed v Crystal Palace
Southampton v Tottenham
Wimbledon v Leeds

Sunday 26 October
Arsenal v Aston Villa

Monday 27 October
Leicester v West Ham

Saturday 1 November
Aston Villa v Chelsea
Barnsley v Blackburn
Bolton v Liverpool
Derby v Arsenal
Man Utd v Sheff Wed
Newcastle v Leicester
Tottenham v Leeds
Wimbledon v Coventry

Sunday 2 November
Everton v Southampton

Monday 3 November
West Ham v Crystal Palace

Saturday 8 November
Blackburn v Everton
Chelsea v West Ham
Coventry v Newcastle
Crystal Palace v Aston Villa
Leeds v Derby
Liverpool v Tottenham
Sheff Wed v Bolton
Southampton v Barnsley

Sunday 9 November
Arsenal v Man Utd

Monday 10 November
Leicester v Wimbledon

Saturday 22 November
Aston Villa v Everton
Blackburn v Chelsea
Derby v Coventry
Leicester v Bolton
Liverpool v Barnsley
Newcastle v Southampton
Sheff Wed v Arsenal
Wimbledon v Man Utd

Sunday 23 November
Leeds v West Ham

Monday 24 November
Tottenham v Crystal Palace

Wednesday 26 November
Chelsea v Everton

Saturday 29 November
Barnsley v Leeds
Bolton v Wimbledon
Chelsea v Derby
Coventry v Leicester
Crystal Palace v Newcastle
Everton v Tottenham
Man Utd v Blackburn
Southampton v Sheff Wed
West Ham v Aston Villa

Sunday 30 November
Arsenal v Liverpool

Monday 1 December
Bolton v Newcastle

Saturday 6 December
Aston Villa v Coventry
Blackburn v Bolton
Derby v West Ham
Leeds v Everton
Leicester v Crystal Palace
Liverpool v Man Utd
Newcastle v Arsenal
Tottenham v Chelsea

Sunday 7 December
Wimbledon v Southampton

Monday 8 December
Sheff Wed v Barnsley

Saturday 13 December
Arsenal v Blackburn
Barnsley v Newcastle
Chelsea v Leeds
Coventry v Tottenham
Crystal Palace v Liverpool
Everton v Wimbledon
Southampton v Leicester
West Ham v Sheff Wed

Sunday 14 December
Bolton v Derby

Monday 15 December
Man Utd v Aston Villa

Wednesday 17 December
Newcastle v Derby

Saturday 20 December
Aston Villa v Southampton
Blackburn v West Ham
Derby v Crystal Palace
Leeds v Bolton
Leicester v Everton
Liverpool v Coventry
Sheff Wed v Chelsea
Tottenham v Barnsley

Sunday 21 December
Newcastle v Man Utd

Monday 22 December
Wimbledon v Arsenal

Friday 26 December
Arsenal v Leicester
Aston Villa v Tottenham
Bolton v Barnsley
Chelsea v Wimbledon
Crystal Palace v Southampton
Derby v Newcastle
Liverpool v Leeds
Man Utd v Everton
Sheff Wed v Blackburn
West Ham v Coventry

Sunday 28 December
Barnsley v Derby
Blackburn v Crystal Palace
Coventry v Man Utd
Everton v Bolton
Leeds v Aston Villa
Leicester v Sheff Wed
Newcastle v Liverpool
Tottenham v Arsenal
Wimbledon v West Ham

Monday 29 December
Southampton v Chelsea

Saturday 10 January
Arsenal v Leeds
Aston Villa v Leicester
Bolton v Southampton
Chelsea v Coventry
Crystal Palace v Everton
Derby v Blackburn
Liverpool v Wimbledon
Man Utd v Tottenham
Sheff Wed v Newcastle
West Ham v Barnsley

Saturday 17 January
Barnsley v Crystal Palace
Blackburn v Aston Villa
Coventry v Arsenal
Everton v Chelsea
Leeds v Sheff Wed
Leicester v Liverpool
Newcastle v Bolton
Southampton v Man Utd
Tottenham v West Ham
Wimbledon v Derby

Saturday 31 January
Arsenal v Southampton
Aston Villa v Newcastle
Bolton v Coventry
Chelsea v Barnsley
Crystal Palace v Leeds
Derby v Tottenham
Liverpool v Blackburn
Man Utd v Leicester
Sheff Wed v Wimbledon
West Ham v Everton

Saturday 7 February
Arsenal v Chelsea
Barnsley v Everton
Blackburn v Tottenham
Coventry v Sheff Wed
Crystal Palace v Wimbledon
Derby v Aston Villa
Leicester v Leeds
Liverpool v Southampton
Man Utd v Bolton
Newcastle v West Ham

Saturday 14 February
Aston Villa v Barnsley
Bolton v Arsenal
Chelsea v Crystal Palace
Everton v Derby
Leeds v Blackburn
Sheff Wed v Liverpool
Southampton v Coventry

Tottenham v Leicester
West Ham v Man Utd
Wimbledon v Newcastle

Saturday 21 February
Arsenal v Crystal Palace
Bolton v West Ham
Coventry v Barnsley
Leicester v Chelsea
Liverpool v Everton
Man Utd v Derby
Newcastle v Leeds
Sheff Wed v Tottenham
Southampton v Blackburn
Wimbledon v Aston Villa

Saturday 28 February
Aston Villa v Liverpool
Barnsley v Wimbledon
Blackburn v Leicester
Chelsea v Man Utd
Crystal Palace v Coventry
Derby v Sheff Wed
Everton v Newcastle
Leeds v Southampton
Tottenham v Bolton
West Ham v Arsenal

Saturday 7 March
Arsenal v Derby
Blackburn v Barnsley
Chelsea v Aston Villa
Coventry v Wimbledon
Crystal Palace v West Ham
Leeds v Tottenham
Leicester v Newcastle
Liverpool v Bolton
Sheff Wed v Man Utd
Southampton v Everton

Saturday 14 March
Aston Villa v Crystal Palace
Barnsley v Southampton
Bolton v Sheff Wed
Derby v Leeds
Everton v Blackburn
Man Utd v Arsenal
Newcastle v Coventry
Tottenham v Liverpool
West Ham v Chelsea
Wimbledon v Leicester

Saturday 28 March
Arsenal v Sheff Wed
Barnsley v Liverpool
Bolton v Leicester
Chelsea v Blackburn
Coventry v Derby
Crystal Palace v Tottenham
Everton v Aston Villa
Man Utd v Wimbledon
Southampton v Newcastle
West Ham v Leeds

Saturday 4 April
Aston Villa v West Ham
Blackburn v Man Utd
Derby v Chelsea
Leeds v Barnsley
Leicester v Coventry
Liverpool v Arsenal
Newcastle v Crystal Palace
Sheff Wed v Southampton
Tottenham v Everton
Wimbledon v Bolton

Saturday 11 April
Arsenal v Newcastle
Barnsley v Sheff Wed
Bolton v Blackburn
Chelsea v Tottenham
Coventry v Aston Villa
Crystal Palace v Leicester
Everton v Leeds
Man Utd v Liverpool
Southampton v Wimbledon
West Ham v Derby

Monday 13 April
Aston Villa v Man Utd
Blackburn v Arsenal
Derby v Bolton
Leeds v Chelsea
Leicester v Southampton
Liverpool v Crystal Palace
Newcastle v Barnsley
Sheff Wed v West Ham
Tottenham v Coventry
Wimbledon v Everton

Saturday 18 April
Arsenal v Wimbledon
Barnsley v Tottenham
Bolton v Leeds
Chelsea v Sheff Wed
Coventry v Liverpool
Crystal Palace v Derby
Everton v Leicester
Man Utd v Newcastle
Southampton v Aston Villa
West Ham v Blackburn

Saturday 25 April
Aston Villa v Bolton
Barnsley v Arsenal
Blackburn v Wimbledon
Chelsea v Liverpool
Crystal Palace v Man Utd
Derby v Leicester
Everton v Sheff Wed
Leeds v Coventry
Tottenham v Newcastle
West Ham v Southampton

Saturday 2 May
Arsenal v Everton
Bolton v Crystal Palace
Coventry v Blackburn
Leicester v Barnsley
Liverpool v West Ham
Man Utd v Leeds
Newcastle v Chelsea
Sheff Wed v Aston Villa
Southampton v Derby
Wimbledon v Tottenham

Sunday 10 May
Aston Villa v Arsenal
Barnsley v Man Utd
Blackburn v Newcastle
Chelsea v Bolton
Crystal Palace v Sheff Wed
Derby v Liverpool
Everton v Coventry
Leeds v Wimbledon
Tottenham v Southampton
West Ham v Leicester

Published by Stopwatch Publishing Limited
for Bookmart Limited
Registered number 2372865
Trading as Bookmart Limited
Desford Road
Enderby
Leicester LE9 5AD

ISBN 1 900032 07 4

This edition published 1997

The views and opinions of the writers in this book are not necessarily those of Bass Brewers Limited

Printed and bound in Great Britain by Butler & Tanner Ltd, Frome and London

Designed by Peter Ward

443 Oxford Street, London W1R 1DA
Production Director: David Brown
House Editor: Christopher Haughton
Sports Editor: Barrie Gill